THE WORLD LEADERS
IN EDUCATION

This book is part of the Peter Lang Education list.
Every volume is peer reviewed and meets
the highest quality standards for content and production.

PETER LANG
New York • Bern • Frankfurt • Berlin
Brussels • Vienna • Oxford • Warsaw

THE WORLD LEADERS IN EDUCATION

LESSONS FROM THE SUCCESSES AND DRAWBACKS OF THEIR METHODS

EDITED BY HANI MORGAN
AND CHRISTOPHER BARRY

PETER LANG
New York • Bern • Frankfurt • Berlin
Brussels • Vienna • Oxford • Warsaw

Library of Congress Cataloging-in-Publication Data

The world leaders in education: lessons from the successes and drawbacks
of their methods / edited by Hani Morgan, Christopher Barry.
pages cm
Includes bibliographical references and index.
1. Comparative education. 2. Education—Cross-cultural studies.
3. Education and state—Cross-cultural studies. 4. Academic achievement—
Cross-cultural studies. 5. Educational evaluation—Cross-cultural studies.
I. Morgan, Hani, editor. II. Barry, Christopher T., editor.
LB43.W69   370.9—dc23   2015023823
ISBN 978-1-4331-2957-5 (hardcover)
ISBN 978-1-4331-2956-8 (paperback)
ISBN 978-1-4539-1592-9 (e-book)

Bibliographic information published by **Die Deutsche Nationalbibliothek**.
Die Deutsche Nationalbibliothek lists this publication in the "Deutsche
Nationalbibliografie"; detailed bibliographic data are available
on the Internet at http://dnb.d-nb.de/.

Cover design by Malak Morgan

© 2016 Peter Lang Publishing, Inc., New York
29 Broadway, 18th floor, New York, NY 10006
www.peterlang.com

All rights reserved.
Reprint or reproduction, even partially, in all forms such as microfilm,
xerography, microfiche, microcard, and offset strictly prohibited.

Table of Contents

Chapter One: Introduction—What World-Class Nations in Education
  Do That Makes Them So Good. 1
  Hani Morgan

Chapter Two: Finland—Ethos of Equality:
  Finnish Educational Policy and Practice 15
  Riitta Jyrhämä and Katriina Maaranen

Chapter Three: The United States—Schooling in the United States: What We
  Learn from International Assessments of Reading and Math Literacy 37
  William G. Brozo and Sarah Crain

Chapter Four: Japan—The High-Achieving Educational System of Japan 61
  Lawrence Baines and Mano Yasuda

Chapter Five: Canada—Education in Canada: Separate but Similar Systems
  in the Pursuit of Excellence and Equity. 79
  Jason D. Edgerton, Lance W. Roberts, and Veronika Eliasova

Chapter Six: South Korea—South Korea's Education: A National Obsession 107
  Michael J. Seth

Chapter Seven: Singapore—Success in Singapore: A Model for
  Excellence in Education 127
  Vivien Geneser and Hsiao-ping Wu

Chapter Eight: New Zealand—Education in New Zealand:
  Maintaining Quality in an Era of Change 145
  Michael Forret and Logan Moss
Chapter Nine: China—Reconciling Fairness with Efficiency: Reforming the
  Chinese Examination System 169
  Andreas Schleicher and Yan Wang
Chapter Ten: Conclusion—What We Can Learn from High-Ranking
  Nations in Education 181
  Hani Morgan

About the Contributors 195

Index 199

CHAPTER ONE

Introduction

What World-Class Nations in Education Do That Makes Them So Good

HANI MORGAN

Imagine a country with a utopian school system. In every classroom you enter, you see outstanding teachers with expertise in the subject they teach and in the methods they use to teach it. This country recruits its teachers only from the top-performing students in its secondary schools, requiring them to have high scores on college entrance exams, a strong grade point average, and a high level of participation in extracurricular activities. Candidates hoping to enroll in a university program to become teachers must score well on a written exam on teaching, demonstrate effective communication skills, and perform satisfactorily in an interview in which they explain why they wish to become teachers.

You do not have to worry if your child underachieves in a particular subject, because in the early years of schooling, teachers intervene promptly and provide strong support for pupils with learning problems—support that continues as students get older. Teachers adhere to national standards, but enjoy autonomy to teach the way they feel students will learn best. They do not worry about being held accountable through frequent external standardized tests that put pupils and teachers under pressure and promote lower-level thinking skills, because everyone in the nation knows that these teachers are experts in their field. As a result of the respect they receive and the freedom they have to use different methods of teaching, teachers enjoy their profession. Students from this country score higher on international tests than those from almost all other countries, because all pupils, regardless of their socioeconomic circumstances, get outstanding teachers, receive the help they need when they struggle, and learn in a manner that emphasizes thinking critically, rather than recalling information.

The only problem with the preceding description is that it is not about a utopian country, but a real one: Finland. This book is about the countries with the highest-performing school systems in the world and includes chapters on Finland, Japan, South Korea, Singapore, China, New Zealand, Canada, and the United States. Why include a chapter on the United States in a book about outstanding education systems considering all the negative attention this nation gets on its issues in education? Two reasons are its large number of strong performers on international tests and its notable history in education.

REASONS FOR INCLUDING THE UNITED STATES

Contrary to what we hear in the news, some students in the United States have achieved the highest scores in international testing in the world in the twenty-first century, but they often receive little attention. Unfortunately, the United States also has too many poor-scoring students who lower the overall test score averages the mass media emphasize when they report these scores. In 2009, for example, the PISA test score averages indicated lackluster achievement: the United States ranked 25th in mathematics, 14th in reading, and 17th in science among the 34 member nations of the Organisation for Economic Cooperation and Development (Duke, 2013).

Many U.S. schools located in disadvantaged districts fail to provide students with optimal learning environments. Severe socioeconomic inequality at these schools—a condition that does not exist in world-class nations in education—lead privileged students to score much higher on international assessments than the less fortunate students who are more likely to attend these inferior institutions (Darling-Hammond, 2010). Such schools suffer from overcrowded classes, lack of curricular materials, unskilled teachers, and limited course offerings that hinder students' chances to be eligible for college (Darling-Hammond, 2011/12). Although out-of-school factors often have a stronger impact on student achievement levels than the school and its teachers, inequalities in U.S. schools contribute to mediocre scores.

When international test scores are announced, the media typically do not mention America's high-achieving students because they normally report only average test scores. However, the United States has a significant number of high performers. In their analysis of international test scores, Salzman and Lowell (2008) showed that in 2006 the United States had more top-performing students in math and science than any of the highest-ranking nations in international testing, but news reports generally ignored this accomplishment because the United States also had the highest number of low-performing students, a circumstance that lowers its national averages dramatically. Data on the 2006 PISA test indicated that the United States had about 67,000 students achieving level 6, the highest category, and Japan had about 34,000, the second-highest number (Bracey, 2009).

Additionally, Salzman and Lowell (2008) suggest that average test scores are a less important measure of economic potential than the number of top-performing students. They suggest that since the United States has a sizeable number of strong performers, Americans sometimes overreact to international test score averages. Although Americans may at times worry too much, Salzman and Lowell regard the inequalities in American schools as a severe problem that needs attention. Although they make a good point, analyzing international test scores through a different perspective reveals that the United States has far fewer than an adequate number of high-scoring students in math and science.

When Tucker (2011) discussed the 2009 PISA results, he mentioned that even top performers were not doing well in the United States, because he compared the percentages of these students in the United States to those from the highest-ranking countries and found significant differences. Tucker explained that the PISA categorizes performance into six bands. According to him, the 2009 PISA results showed that the proportion of U.S. students scoring in the top band in reading was 1.5%, or higher than the OECD average of 0.8%. Japan, Australia, New Zealand, Canada, Singapore, Finland, and Shanghai all had higher percentages ranging from 1.8 to 2.9%.

In math, however, students in the United States fared much worse. Only 2% reached the top level, lower than the OECD average of 3%, and there were greater differences between the proportion of U.S. students reaching the top and the proportion of those achieving this level abroad. For example, 27% of students in Shanghai scored in the top band, considerably higher than the percentage of U.S. students. In science, the percentage of American students achieving the top band was 1%, near the OECD average, but Singapore, Shanghai, New Zealand, Finland, and Australia all had a greater percentage of pupils scoring at this level (Tucker, 2011).

Unfortunately, the United States is having difficulty correcting problems in its educational system and has made little progress in recent years. This lack of improvement results from short-term reform efforts that are often politically motivated rather than research based. These haphazard approaches are antithetical to the clear goals of the leading nations in education, because outstanding educational systems use a systematic ideology and implement a decades-long plan with the guidance of ministries of education (Darling-Hammond, 2011).

A NOTABLE HISTORY IN EDUCATION

The United States has an impressive history in education. Although in 2006 high school graduation rates in the United States fell to 18th out of 24 industrialized countries, over 40 years ago the country was first in the world in this category (Jerald, 2008). Furthermore, when the GI bill made it possible for many veterans returning from World War II to get a college education, the United States was the world leader in the number of people with university degrees (Paine & Schleicher, 2011).

The United States was also the first country to create universal secondary education and to achieve mass higher education (Stewart, 2012). The implementation of universal secondary education at the start of the twentieth century led the United States to have the most educated workforce in the world in the 1940s (Paine & Schleicher, 2011). Finally, the United States is the home of some of the most influential figures in education, including John Dewey. Some of the countries now experiencing success in international testing have implemented practices based on theories of teaching that originated in the United States. For example, when Finland reformed, it created a new system based on the democratic idea that *all* students are capable of learning, a philosophy of education that John Dewey promoted generations earlier (Sahlberg, 2012).

Since some policymakers in the United States are increasingly interested in borrowing educational practices from other countries to improve the U.S. system, the editors of this book included the United States in order to explore what it can learn from other countries. Some researchers believe the United States can regain its high status by implementing the methods other countries have used to achieve their success. In *Surpassing Shanghai: An Agenda for American Education Built on the World's Leading Systems*, Marc Tucker (2011) not only mentioned that Americans have a growing interest in learning from the world leaders in education; he also discussed that in 2010, for the first time, a U.S. secretary of education (Arne Duncan) expressed interest in the methods these nations use when he consulted OECD to request a report on the strategies they implemented to attain their status.

Some countries reached their high ranking only recently, having experienced mediocrity for many years. For example, before reforming its educational system, Finland faced many of the challenges that plague the United States today. However, after implementing systematic efforts beginning in the early 1970s, Finland now enjoys recognition as one of the world leaders in education.

HOW ARE THE TOP-PERFORMING SCHOOL SYSTEMS DETERMINED?

Every 3 years, the Organisation for Economic Co-operation and Development (OECD) administers the Program for International Student Assessment (PISA). OECD was founded in 1961, but its history dates back to 1948 when it emerged as the Organisation for European Economic Cooperation (OEEC). Its purpose at that time was to implement the Marshall Plan for the reconstruction of Europe after World War II. In 1961, the OEEC was reformed and became the OECD, extending membership to non-European states.

The PISA is an assessment test that 15-year-olds take to evaluate their skills in mathematics, science, and reading. The OECD currently administers this test every 3 years to approximately 70 countries and economies, but the number of countries participating in a given year can vary and has increased considerably since this test was first implemented in 2000. One reason the PISA is so important is that it compares student achievement internationally using countries that make up close to 90% of the world economy (Schleicher, 2011). In addition, the PISA evaluates skills connected to workforce knowledge, whereas some other international tests, such as the Trends in International Mathematics and Science Study (TIMSS), lack this link (Rutkowski, Rutkowski, & Plucker, 2014).

When the PISA was developed, it was designed for economically developed countries, but in order to make comparisons, economically developing countries also participate with the wealthy OECD countries. Of the 67 educational systems participating in the PISA in 2012, 34 were members of the OECD, and the rest were partner countries. Since students take the test in countries that differ linguistically, culturally, and geographically, it is adjusted to be appropriate for each group and to provide valid comparisons (Rutkowski, Rutkowski, & Plucker, 2014).

The PISA attracts the attention of many educators and policymakers. If a country performs poorly on the PISA, or continuously falls further behind other countries, it is not unusual for that country's educational leaders to worry and to consider a plan for improvement. In December 2010, for example, when the OECD announced PISA scores showing China to be in first place for the first time in math, reading, and science, some educators in the United States compared this outcome to the launching of Sputnik and the crisis it created in the late 1950s.

In addition to the PISA, students throughout the world take other international tests, but the PISA tends to receive more media coverage. Some other tests used to assess students throughout the world include the Trends in International Mathematics and Science Study (TIMSS) and the Progress in International Reading Literacy Study (PIRLS). The International Association for the Evaluation of Educational Achievement (IEA) administers these tests to younger students. The IEA offers the TIMSS every 4 years to evaluate fourth- and eighth-grade students on their mathematics and science skills and the PIRLS every 5 years to measure fourth-grade students on their reading skills.

The PISA and these other tests determine how countries rank in education. The PISA test assesses students on their higher-order thinking ability and demands more skill than typical standardized tests that merely measure what students can recall, because it requires students to apply information and defend their answers. Organizers designed the PISA to evaluate how well students used their knowledge to solve new problems. It is possible for students to get full credit for a math problem even if they provide a numerically inaccurate answer, as long as they identify the correct procedure for finding the answer (Bracey, 2002). The recent success that some countries have experienced, while others have declined or remained stagnant, has led policymakers to consider borrowing the practices of the leaders.

BORROWING THE EDUCATIONAL PRACTICES OF THE LEADERS

In the twenty-first century, new technologies have accelerated globalization and transformed the way in which corporations do business by allowing the exchange of information in seconds on a 24-hour basis through the Internet. Technological and economic trends have created new demands for high skills and lowered the need for low skills. An expanding middle class overseas, where an increasing number of highly skilled workers live, enhances the chances that American businesses will relocate if it is cost effective, or that they will hire those from abroad rather than from their own nation. Additionally, corporations can do business electronically with those overseas rather than employ personnel in their own country. Any work that can be automated, digitized, or outsourced can be done anywhere in the world where there are qualified people to do it (Schleicher, 2011).

One consequence of the increase in global interdependency is that American students, more than ever before, are competing with students in other countries for positions requiring advanced skills. Thus, the increase in globalization has ramifications for educational systems throughout the world. As economies expand and the need for high-skills jobs increases, countries lacking a workforce with the expertise needed to compete for these positions will likely encounter problems. Educators concerned about large numbers of students scoring poorly on international tests that measure higher-level skills linked to workforce knowledge, such as the PISA, worry for good reason. The strong-performing educational systems developing this talent are inextricably linked to a nation's economy. The OECD, in collaboration with Stanford University, conducted a study, the results of which have enormous implications: they suggest that if the United States could increase its average PISA scores by 25 points per year over 20 years, that activity could yield a gain of $41 trillion for the U.S. economy for the generation born in 2010 (Paine & Schleicher, 2011).

Since some countries with lackluster results in international testing implement methods antithetical to those with outstanding records, it is normal for educational leaders in poorly performing nations to think about borrowing the practices of the highest achievers. These leaders, however, have critics. Those who urge the use of the methods of world-class systems contend that these nations all implement similar methods.

SIMILARITIES OF WORLD-CLASS NATIONS IN EDUCATION

Some of the common practices used by high-ranking nations in education include providing high status for teachers, believing that all students can perform well, and distributing resources equitably to students (Paine & Schleicher, 2011). Nations where teachers have high status pay them well and regard them as some of the most important members of society. Parents want their children to be teachers in those countries because it is an attractive position to hold. In Finland, for example, teachers are afforded great respect because their education is analogous with that of other professionals such as doctors and lawyers (Sahlberg, 2013). Additionally, these nations offer teachers more career opportunities in education.

Having outstanding teachers without assigning them to teach disadvantaged students guarantees dismal results. In many countries with poor international test averages, good teachers are unevenly distributed, resulting in students from low socioeconomic backgrounds having fewer qualified teachers than more privileged students. One strategy used by world-class nations to avoid this detrimental practice is believing that *all* students are capable of learning at high levels. Before Finland experienced its success, for example, its system was based on the premise that talent in society is unevenly distributed, and therefore some students have more potential to learn than others. This belief created inequalities: children were separated into two streams, leading some schools to provide students with many more learning opportunities and resources than other schools. When Finland's new system replaced the old system, this detrimental belief ended, resulting in a better system with evenly distributed resources.

Honoring the premise that all students are capable of learning involves spending money on schools equitably and providing similar learning opportunities for all students. Regrettably, in some countries that score poorly on the PISA, the conditions known to improve student learning are often offered to the students who need them least.

Some poor-performing nations have higher teacher/student ratios in disadvantaged schools than in other schools, but better-performing nations sometimes do the opposite under the assumption that less fortunate students need better opportunities for success. For example, Singapore, one of the most successful countries in international testing, assigns its best teachers to the students having the most difficulty. As a result of conditions that promote equity, high-performing nations typically have lower performance variation among schools than nations lagging behind. Finland has a reputation for having the lowest performance variation among schools in the world (Sahlberg, 2012).

Another similarity among high-ranking systems relates to student engagement. Although successful school systems use different methods to motivate students, their strategies work (Stewart, 2012). Singapore utilizes community groups for children who are unengaged in school, and Finland uses a student-centered curriculum emphasizing problems and projects that aim to promote students' sense of discovery. Finland also provides strong support for students having problems learning, thereby facilitating their learning of difficult content.

Some nations react to teacher shortages resulting from teacher attrition, retirement, and the attractiveness of other professions by making it easier for teachers to enter the teaching profession, a practice that does not occur in world-class systems (Stewart, 2012). High-achieving systems typically recruit the most talented students in the country and train them well. In Finland, out of the thousands of students applying to a university program for teacher education at the primary level, only about 1 in 10 applicants are accepted. These candidates will then need to complete an advanced, 5-year master's degree program before becoming teachers (Sahlberg, 2013). Singapore uses similar methods to recruit candidates, selecting only the top one-third of its high school students and requiring them to have strong academic records (Stewart, 2012). In addition, Singapore supports these candidates financially, provides teachers with 100 hours of professional development, and offers opportunities for different careers in education such as principal, content specialist, or master teacher (Schleicher & Stewart, 2008).

High-ranking countries also use a high-quality curriculum based on standards that are rigorous and focused. Their curriculum is designed to ensure that all students learn the same content with as little overlap as possible between grades. One reason the United States underperforms relates to its curriculum. For years the United States did not implement a curriculum similar to the leading countries, but instead used standards that varied greatly among states. Now it is making an effort to implement universal high standards through the Common Core State Standards (Stewart, 2012).

While the preceding methods clearly produce favorable results for world-class nations in education, critics usually cringe at the idea of borrowing strategies from abroad to enhance the system of their own country, often without good reason.

CRITICS OF BORROWING EDUCATIONAL PRACTICES

Critics argue that each country has unique situations, and that what works in one nation's educational system does not necessarily apply to another's. This logic is not always valid, because researchers often make good points when comparing educational practices between different countries, even though these countries can vary greatly.

For example, after the PISA scores were released in 2006, critics raised concerns when the news media compared the United States with some of the countries with the highest average scores, questioning whether it is appropriate to contrast the United States, a large nation with a population of more than 300 million and a $14 trillion gross domestic product (GDP), with Singapore, a country with a population of only 4.5 million, or with New Zealand, a nation with a GDP of only $124 billion (Salzman & Lowell, 2008). However, the fact that the United States is considerably larger than Singapore or New Zealand is a poor reason for not making the comparison. Researchers can still make valid comparisons if they use a U.S. state similar in size to these smaller countries.

Tucker (2011) made such a comparison when he contrasted Wisconsin with Finland and concluded that even the highest-ranking U.S. states underperform on the PISA when compared with world-class nations. He mentioned that Wisconsin achieved less well than Finland, even though it is among the best-performing states in the United States. Other researchers made a similar comparison by contrasting the math achievement of students in high-performing U.S. states with that of students in Shanghai.

Peterson, Woessmann, Hanushek, and Lastra-Anadón (2011) felt it would be appropriate to compare student achievement in Shanghai to that in Massachusetts and Minnesota, the U.S. states with the highest math proficiency rates. Shanghai was found to have the highest proficiency rates in math in the world and is located in a prosperous area of China. When the researchers made this comparison, they concluded that Shanghai still had the highest proficiency rates.

Skeptics sometimes make good points but do not provide sufficient justification for disregarding the idea of borrowing educational policies from abroad. Sometimes they argue that cultural values, an aspect of strong-performing nations that explains their success, cannot be borrowed. Such values have been part of certain cultures for centuries and are often transmitted from parents to children at home as much as from teachers to students in school. These belief systems are difficult to borrow because they involve societal values that can differ considerably from nation to nation.

Many Asian countries' students perform better in school and on international tests as a result of attitudes parents instill in their children regarding the importance of effort. These values may conflict with cultures based on different belief systems. The idea of American children going to classes six days a week, for example, and preparing more for school during evenings and on weekends, as in Japan, would likely be objectionable to many U.S. parents (Bracey, 2009).

American parents are inclined to believe that innate ability allows their children to do outstanding work, whereas Asian parents consider hard work to be the most important factor (Stevenson & Stigler, 1992). Asian parents derive their values toward work from Confucian ideals, which emphasize the potential of creating conditions to improve moral conduct. Although Asian cultures recognize differences in innate abilities, more important is the extent to which an individual can maximize these abilities through work (Stevenson & Stigler, 1992). School systems with longer days and longer school years where teachers assign more homework fit Asian values more than American values.

Although implementing practices based on values not shared by Americans is likely to backfire in the American school system, this concern does not justify avoiding the use of practices from abroad altogether. High-performing nations can vary greatly in the way they implement schooling practices. If school leaders cannot identify a practice that can feasibly be borrowed from a particular country, they can explore other more suitable methods, or search for these practices in other top-performing nations.

Finland's system, for example, varies greatly from many high-performing Asian countries with regard to the length of time students spend in school, yet both regions produce outstanding results on international tests. In Finland, students spend only 600 hours in school per year, much less than students in the United States (Baines, 2007). One reason for this difference is that in the United States teachers spend more time on nonacademic tasks such as administrative duties. During this time, students often do "busy" work. American parents would more likely be open to using Finland's school-day structure if they understood that various studies have shown that no correlation exists between achievement levels and time spent at school. Some private schools in the United States already use this format to prepare students for universities.

Some critics feel that effective schooling practices will make little, if any, difference in the lives of poverty-stricken students. They argue that the conditions endured by children from poor families do not allow them to learn. Once again, critics make a good point, but the effects of poverty do not warrant the disregard of the dilapidated schools many disadvantaged students attend.

THE EFFECTS OF POVERTY

Poverty leads to learning problems for children in many ways. For example, higher rates of low birth weight, more common among the poor, contribute to cognitive and behavioral problems. As a result of risk factors such as the increased use of alcohol among poor pregnant women, inadequate dental and vision care, poor nutrition, and lack of a safe home environment, children from poor families experience a plethora of conditions that greatly increase their chances of learning little, if anything, in school (Berliner, 2009).

Some critics argue that blaming teachers for the poor test scores of disadvantaged students is unjustifiable. To a certain extent, these critics are right. The schools can only do so much. The educational system in Finland is one of the world's best, not only because of great schools and teachers, but also because of strong welfare programs that afford the poor basic necessities that some other countries fail to provide. Children in Finland have access to health, dental, and counseling services free of charge (Sarjala, 2013).

Although the effects of poverty have the potential to impede learning considerably, the school and its teachers can mitigate those problems. In the United States, some schools serving large numbers of disadvantaged students produce outstanding academic outcomes. Some students at these schools perform as well as students in Finland; as many as 25% of 15-year-olds in disadvantaged schools in the United States earn average scores in the same range as Finnish students in the same age category (Paine & Schleicher, 2011).

The schools in the United States that succeed in serving the disadvantaged do so because they use similar practices to those in the highest-ranked countries. For example, unlike many schools in the United States today, where teachers spend their time in isolation, teachers in high-performing disadvantaged schools meet together regularly to assess their students (Chenoweth, 2009). This collaboration benefits students because they receive help through the broader knowledge of a school's faculty; when teachers sit isolated, students are dependent on the expertise of only one individual teacher.

World-class countries in education are known for the time they allow teachers to collaborate to maximize student success. In Finland, teachers spend 2 hours per week with colleagues planning methods to improve practice (Sahlberg, 2011). High-performing Asian nations also succeed, in part, because of the opportunities available to teachers to learn from each other (Darling-Hammond, 2008).

This book will cover the education of the poor in addition to teacher recruitment, curriculum, and other factors contributing to student success. Although it covers many topics from other texts on this subject, it provides new insights and new information on high-ranking educational systems.

HOW WILL THIS BOOK DIFFER FROM OTHERS?

Although some authors have written similar books in recent years, this book differs from them in several respects. First, it offers the most recent trends in each of the countries included. World-class nations in education often make important gains as others decline or stagnate, and new leaders emerge.

Second, a unique roster of contributors with expertise in their respective regions provides new insights into this most important subject. Many authors are native to the country they are covering, and others have extensive experience and expertise regarding their region. The authors' perspectives on the practices enabling each selected country to achieve impressive results in education will undoubtedly influence educational leaders from around the world.

REFERENCES

Baines, L. (2007). Learning from the world: Achieving more by doing less. *Phi Delta Kappan, 89*(2), 98–100.
Berliner, D.C. (2009). Are teachers responsible for low achievement by poor students? *Kappa Delta Pi Record, 46*(1), 18–21.
Bracey, G.W. (2002). Another nation at risk? *Phi Delta Kappan, 84*(3), 245–247.
Bracey, G.W. (2009). PISA: Not leaning hard on U.S. economy. *Phi Delta Kappan, 90*(6), 450–451.
Chenoweth, K. (2009). It can be done, it's being done, and here's how. *Phi Delta Kappan, 91*(1), 38–43.
Darling-Hammond, L. (2008, February 25). Educating teachers: How they do it abroad. *Time, 171*(8), 34.
Darling-Hammond, L. (2010). Restoring our schools. *Nation, 290*(23), 14–20.
Darling-Hammond, L. (2011). Foreword. In M. Tucker (Ed.), *Shanghai: An agenda for American education built on the world's leading systems* (pp. ix–xii). Cambridge, MA: Harvard Education Press.
Darling-Hammond, L. (2011/12). Soaring systems. *Education Review, 24*(1), 24–33.
Duke, D. (2013). Are we pushing for greatness? *Phi Delta Kappan, 94*(5), 45–49.
Jerald, C. (2008). *Benchmarking for success: Ensuring U.S. students receive a world-class education*. Washington, DC: National Governors Association, Council of Chief State School Officers, and Achieve, Inc.
Paine, S.L., & Schleicher, A. (2011). *What the US can learn from the world's most successful education reform efforts*. New York: McGraw-Hill Research Foundation.
Peterson, P.E., Woessmann, L., Hanushek, E.A., & Lastra-Anadón, C.X. (2011). Globally challenged: Are U.S. students ready to compete? The latest on each state's international standing in math and reading. PEPG Report No. 11–03. Boston, MA: Harvard Kennedy School.
Rutkowski, D., Rutkowski, L., & Plucker, J.A. (2014). Should individual U.S. schools participate in PISA? *Phi Delta Kappan, 96*(4), 68–73.
Sahlberg, P. (2011). Lessons from Finland. *American Educator, 35*(2), 34–38.
Sahlberg, P. (2012). A model lesson: Finland shows us what equal opportunity looks like. *American Educator, 36*(1), 20–27.
Sahlberg, P. (2013). Teachers as leaders in Finland. *Educational Leadership, 71*(2), 36–40.
Salzman, H., & Lowell, L. (2008). Making the grade. *Nature, 453*, 28–30.
Sarjala, J. (2013). Equality and cooperation: Finland's path to excellence. *American Educator, 37*(1), 32–36.
Schleicher, A. (2011). Is the sky the limit to education improvement? *Phi Delta Kappan, 93*(2), 58–63.
Schleicher, A., & Stewart, V. (2008). Learning from world-class schools. *Educational Leadership, 66*(2), 44–51.

Stevenson, H.W., & Stigler, J.W. (1992). *The learning gap: Why our schools are failing and what we can learn from Japanese and Chinese education.* New York: Simon & Schuster.

Stewart, V. (2012). *A world-class education: Learning from international models of excellence and innovation.* Alexandria, VA: ASCD.

Tucker, M. (Ed.) (2011). *Surpassing Shanghai: An agenda for American education built on the world's leading systems.* Cambridge, MA: Harvard Education Press.

CHAPTER TWO

Finland

Ethos of Equality: Finnish Educational Policy and Practice

RIITTA JYRHÄMÄ AND KATRIINA MAARANEN

INTRODUCTION

One of the basic principles of Finnish education is that all people must have equal access to high-quality education and training. The same opportunities to education should be available to all citizens irrespective of their ethnic origin, age, wealth or where they live. Education policy is built on the lifelong learning principle.

The basic right to education and culture is recorded in the Constitution. Public authorities must secure equal opportunities for every resident in Finland to get education also after compulsory schooling and develop themselves, irrespective of their financial standing. In Finland education is free at all levels from pre-primary to higher education. Adult education is the only form of education that may require payment. (Ministry of Education and Culture, 2015a, para. 1–2)

This passage from the Finnish Ministry of Education and Culture's *Educational Policy in Finland* shows the core principles behind the Finnish educational system. According to the OECD, Finland has one of the highest levels of educational attainment among member countries (Organisation for Economic Co-operation and Development [OECD], 2013). Finland is also regarded as one of the world's most literate societies (Sahlberg, 2010): more than 98% of Finns attend pre-school, and 99% complete compulsory basic education. Completion rates in upper secondary school are nearly 80%, and in vocational upper secondary school 64% (Statistics Finland, 2012).

The PISA studies have shown that Finland's students are Europe's highest achievers and have scored among the top countries in mathematics, reading, and science since the studies were undertaken (Kupiainen, Hautamäki, & Karjalainen, 2009; Tirri, 2014). According to Tirri (2014), high-quality teacher education is considered one of the factors behind this success. Another reason involves the Finnish government's principle of "equal opportunity and high-quality education for all." The Finnish welfare state began developing after surviving the heavy burdens of World War II. The most important factor in the education sector was the development of comprehensive schools in the 1970s, which guaranteed equal access to education for all (Kupiainen et al., 2009; Simola, 2015).

The term "basic education" refers to grades 1–9, equating to comprehensive school. The term "general education" equates to upper secondary school (grades 10–12). Educators in early childhood, vocational, and university settings have different degree requirements from those in basic and general education (Finnish National Board of Education [FNBE], n.d.). Finnish basic education (i.e., comprehensive school) begins in the year a child turns seven and lasts for nine years, until the age of 16. Comprehensive school is divided into primary school (grades 1–6, ages 7–12) and lower secondary school (grades 7–9, ages 13–16). In primary school, teachers are responsible for teaching all subjects. In practice, however, special-subject teachers often teach languages. In lower and upper secondary school, highly specialized teachers teach all topics in the areas they have studied at the university.

After comprehensive school, students may continue their education either in an upper secondary school (high school) or in a vocational institution. Approximately half of Finnish students continue to upper secondary school, with the other half opting for vocational training. Only about 4% to 6% of all students do not continue study after completing comprehensive school. At the end of upper secondary school, students must pass a matriculation examination in order to qualify for application to a university or a polytechnic institution.

The Ministry of Education and Culture is responsible for education in Finland, and the Finnish National Board of Education (FNBE) works with the ministry to develop educational aims, content, and methods for all levels. The national education administration provides for and steers the development of education and training, mainly through funding and information.

The National Board of Education and a large group of specialists are responsible for constructing the National Core Curriculum. The Core Curriculum establishes the framework for education, but teachers and principals also create the local curricula. Local autonomy in education is widespread in Finland, with education being the responsibility of municipalities, which provide most of the pre-primary, primary, and upper secondary education and usually grant individual schools considerable autonomy in designing their own curricula and educational goals (FNBE, 2015).

There are only a few private schools in Finland. Less than 2% of children go to private schools (Ministry of Education and Culture, 2015c). These institutions must also follow the National Core Curriculum but can create their own curricula to emphasize what is important to them. As mentioned, all education is free—even private schools (Ministry of Education and Culture, 2015d).

After finishing upper secondary school, students can continue on to universities or polytechnic institutions. Polytechnics are more vocationally oriented and train engineers, nurses, and so on. This higher education is free of charge as well; however, the candidates must take an entrance examination whether they wish to attend a university or polytechnic institution. Often this examination, especially for universities, is extensive, demanding, and difficult to pass. At the University of Helsinki, acceptance into programs differs widely, depending on the field of study. The most demanding disciplines are class (basic) teacher education, law, and medicine, each with an acceptance rate (which varies yearly) of about 6%–12%. The applicants take part in the entrance examination of the subject they wish to study. Adults have the opportunity to participate in education at all levels of the system. There is, for example, so-called liberal adult education (community college) provided by adult education centers and folk high schools. At the university level, open universities and university summer schools offer education for all. These institutions charge small sums for their courses.

Teachers in Finland are highly educated, and all basic and general education teachers are required to have master's degrees, from primary school teachers to subject teachers in the comprehensive school and high school. Vocational education teachers have bachelor's degrees and sometimes master's degrees as well. The high level of education is seen as necessary because, professionally, teachers in Finland are highly autonomous. Kindergarten teachers, who teach 3-to-6-year-old olds, must have bachelor's degrees, which are attained by completing a 3-year program consisting of 180 study points (ECT credits: European Credit Transfer, each study point representing approximately 27 hours of student work). The master's degree takes 5 years to complete and consists of 300 study points.

Finnish teacher education is research based. All teachers, with the exception of kindergarten teachers, write a master's thesis as part of their degree requirements. In the course of this education, the importance of pedagogical thinking, personal practical theory, reflection, and inquiry-orientation are emphasized. Students focus on these areas in many ways during the theoretical as well as the practical studies (Maaranen & Krokfors, 2008). Finland has no auditors and no probation period for newly graduated teachers, nor is there achievement testing at the national level (Niemi, 2012).

To put this information into perspective, we want to point out some facts about Finland. The population of the country is very small: only about 5.4 million. Geographically, however, the country is relatively large, and thus on average there are only about 15.8 inhabitants per square kilometer (or 40.5 inhabitants per square mile). About one-third of the population lives in southern Finland, where the country's largest cities are located. About 91% of the people speak Finnish as their mother tongue, and 5.4% speak Swedish, Finland's second official language. Christianity is the major religion, with about 80% of Finns belonging to the Evangelical Lutheran Church. The number of immigrants (only about 4%) is fairly small, meaning that the population is largely homogeneous (Statistics Finland, 2015; *Finland in facts*, 2015).

RESEARCH-BASED TEACHER EDUCATION IN FINLAND

Finnish research-based teacher education has its roots in humanistic psychology, which was the first foundation of the new academic teacher education. In 1979, teacher education was transferred from the polytechnics to the universities, and at the same time there was a shift toward research-based education (Hytönen, 1995). As research on teaching and the idea of implementing a phenomenological paradigm and qualitative approaches gained popularity in the 1980s and 1990s, teacher educators at the University of Helsinki saw a need to direct teacher education toward a more academic track and away from a simple "how-to" focus. Humanistic psychology alone no longer met the new requirements, and the dominant themes of teacher education in the 1990s became teachers' pedagogical thinking (see Kansanen et al., 2000) and research-based teacher education (Maaranen, 2009).

While every contemporary pre-service teacher education program today would undoubtedly place its foundational principles in the theory of education rather than in practice of the craft, pre-service teacher education in Finland seeks, in addition, to be research based (Kosunen & Mikkola, 2002). The following principles have been accepted as guidelines for the research-based teacher education in Finland:

- Teachers need a profound knowledge of the most recent advances of research in the subjects they teach. In addition, they need to be familiar with the latest research on how something can be taught and learned. Interdisciplinary research on subject content knowledge and pedagogical content knowledge provides the foundation for developing teaching methods that can be adapted to suit different learners.

- Teacher education in itself should also be an object of study and research. This research should provide knowledge about the effectiveness and quality of teacher education implemented by various means and in different cultural contexts.
- The aim is that teachers internalize a research-oriented attitude towards their work. This means that teachers learn to take an analytical and open-minded approach to their work and that they develop their teaching and learning environments in a systematic way (Niemi & Jakku-Sihvonen, 2006, pp. 40–41).

Today, research-based teacher education refers, first of all, to the design of its programs, which should be organized according to logical rules, an overall theme, and the principles underlying the aims and goals of the curriculum, as well as being based on research results and research evidence concerning teacher education (Kansanen, 2006, p. 12). "Secondly, research-based teacher education aims at teacher thinking and reflection that makes it possible to justify the decisions taken and activities engaged in through research methodology" (Kansanen, 2006, pp. 12–13). In other words, research should be part of most of the courses students take. The first "official" research is the bachelor's thesis, a relatively small but independent research project carried out at the close of the first 3 years of teacher studies and a requirement for earning a bachelor's degree. The second piece of official research is a master's thesis, a larger, more demanding project written at the end of teacher studies.

The aim of teacher education at the University of Helsinki is to produce teachers who are able to make decisions in accordance with educational aims and goals. The idea is that school practice and actions can be said to be purposive (Kansanen, 1991).

> The ideal teacher is an independent professional who plans his work from the very beginning, and who also has the responsibility for the results of his pupils. He organizes his daily activities independently and, in principle, he can give pedagogical reasons for his actions. He takes his criteria from the curriculum and from the values behind it. Although the reasons may be pedagogical, that does not mean that arguments are necessarily theoretical or scientific. (Kansanen, 1991, p. 252)

The aim is also to educate inquiry-oriented teachers (Jakku-Sihvonen & Niemi, 2006, 2007). This kind of education is based on teachers' pedagogical thinking, that is, how a teacher thinks and makes decisions and, particularly, how that teacher justifies such decisions (Kansanen, 2006; Kansanen et al., 2000). On a daily basis, this means that teachers should be (1) capable of analyzing and assessing their own work, and (2) developing their work alone, as well as in cooperation with others. Reflecting on practice and developing cognitive and meta-cognitive skills are especially important considerations for managing the changing demands, environments, and surroundings of the teaching profession today all over the world. The idea is that future teachers should internalize an inquiry-oriented attitude toward their work. This means that teachers learn to take an analytical and open-minded approach, draw conclusions based on their observations and experiences, and develop their teaching and learning environments in a systematic way (Niemi & Jakku-Sihvonen, 2006, pp. 40–41). The aim is not to produce researchers but rather to provide future teachers with the skills and knowledge to enable them to apply what they have learned, observe their students, and analyze their thinking (Krokfors, 2007; Toom et al., 2010; Westbury, Hansen, Kansanen, & Björkvist, 2005).

A Twofold Approach to Teacher Education: Research & Practice

According to Krokfors (2007), the core of research-based teacher education in Finland is made up of the main principles of theory-practice integration. Krokfors (2007) views teachers' pedagogical practice as twofold: (1) to instruct or practice teaching in general, and (2) to inquire into or research one's own or other people's teaching and learning. Further on, Krokfors states that both orientations are needed to practice skills and to understand theory, reasoning, and understanding. First, theory and practice are integrated when student teachers practice and analyze teaching as part of their university study; second, theory and practice are integrated into the problem-based situations in which student teachers practice their methodological skills; finally, the teachers use research methods to solve pedagogical problems (Krokfors, 2007).

Elementary school teachers must write their theses on an educational topic that covers a research-based subject in teacher education. The topics may vary from practical dilemmas in schooling to school subject issues and philosophical, curricular, or policy matters. The master's thesis is a large project that, in most cases, takes more than a year to complete and is graded. It includes all the necessary components that a research report usually requires, such as a theoretical framework, methodology, empirical data, results, and conclusions. The average length of the master's thesis is approximately 80 to 100 pages, or about 25,000 words. Students are free to choose their topics, their theoretical backgrounds, and their research methods. Special-subject teachers usually write their theses on their principal teaching area.

Supervised Teaching Practice at the University of Helsinki

During teacher education, teaching practice comes closest to the actual work of teachers. In these situations, the candidates exercise their skills in analyzing and examining the art of teaching. Connecting school pedagogy with university study combines the academic as well as the professional points of view. The dialogic method of supervising the teaching practice with peers as well as mentors emphasizes its inquiry orientation (Jyrhämä, 2006). At the University of Helsinki, teaching practice is organized so that student teachers gain experience in both university teacher training schools and municipal teaching practice schools (Syrjäläinen & Jyrhämä, 2008). In the university teacher training school, the student teachers are usually with a peer; thus, they have the experience of teaching together yet are also responsible for teaching alone. The student teachers always have two supervisors. One is the teacher of the class in which they are practice teaching. This person is often highly educated (possibly holding a Ph.D.) and is also trained in teaching supervision. The other is a university faculty member specializing in the subject the student teachers are practicing.

The students practice teaching for 20 study points (ECT credits) during teacher education. This comprises two or three practice periods, one of which is conducted in a field school or a partner school. The recommendation is that at least one-third of teaching practice be in the field school. Their mentors, teachers of a particular class, have special training, which provides them with basic knowledge and tools in mentoring (Jyrhämä & Syrjäläinen, 2011). The student teachers are also supervised by a representative from the university faculty.

Teaching practice is an essential part of the school-university partnership. It serves as a bridge between student teachers' academic studies and their future work in the profession. Teaching practice generates implicit and practical knowledge about teaching that cannot be obtained in any other way. Awareness of the ethical, practical, and complex character of teaching requires collaboration between schools and universities to research teaching and learning. The need to integrate teachers' practical expertise into teacher education has been acknowledged on an international level (Hodkinson & Hodkinson, 1999; Sutherland, Scanlon, & Sperring, 2005). The idea behind a collaborative infrastructure between schools and universities involves the creation of a new learning community. This relationship has been one of the guiding principles in systematizing a network of teaching practice schools in Finland. The consistent and goal-oriented education of mentors and the officially ratified contractual agreement between the University of Helsinki and the schools in the Helsinki metropolitan area were the first steps in bridging the gap between academic and professional knowledge (Syrjäläinen & Jyrhämä, 2008).

Doctoral Education for Teachers

Because all Finnish basic and general education teachers hold master's degrees, they are eligible for doctoral study. It is not common for a teacher to continue on to doctoral studies, but some do. Discouragement may arise because a Ph.D. in education does not increase teachers' salaries or advance their careers. However, if a teacher intends to become a principal, an administrative official, or an academic at a university, doctoral education is advantageous. Requirements for principals are a master's degree with teaching qualifications along with a certificate in educational administration or completion of a program in educational leadership (25 credits) (Taipale, 2012). All university lecturers must hold a Ph.D. in Finnish teacher education, but for other positions, such as that of school principal or administrator, this degree is not required.

PROFESSIONAL DEVELOPMENT OF TEACHERS

Induction of Finnish Teachers

In the course of Finnish teacher education, the students acquire sound basic skills at the master's level and occupy an autonomous position in the educational system. Newly qualified teachers usually have the greatest problems in managing the diversity of the work and interacting with students, the working community, and parents (Blomberg, 2008).

Teachers' professional development can be implemented in a variety of ways. In a Finnish network called Osaava Verme, financed by the Ministry of Education and Culture, support is offered for newly qualified teachers to update their professional knowledge. In addition, Osaava Verme promotes networking at the national level to develop support at the induction phase, and it promotes research and development both nationally and internationally (Heikkinen, Jokinen, & Tynjälä, 2012).

"Verme" is a Finnish acronym that stands for peer-group mentoring. A teacher who participates in training peer-group mentors is responsible for a group of newly qualified teachers. This person is usually an experienced teacher. In training and mentoring, the principles that serve as guidelines in training as well as the project as a whole are dialogue, autonomy, narrativity, peer-experiences, constructivism, and integrative pedagogy.

Individual mentoring has also been developed, with several different practices in use. Some mentoring programs have been based on a model by the New Teacher Center at the University of California (Niemi & Siljander, 2013).

The main principles of the New Teacher Center Program include a vision of students' good learning, strong institutional commitment as well as school leaders' commitment, high-quality mentoring, and support given to teachers in a classroom. Newly qualified teachers mostly need support in matters such as home-school cooperation, working in the school community, and dealing with student misbehavior. The education for individual mentoring consists of 5 study points (ECT credits), and it is organized at the universities' continuing education centers. The employer of the mentee pays the mentor. This mentoring program is in the pilot phase in Finland (Niemi & Siljander, 2013).

Continuing Professional Education (CPE)

Finnish teachers are required to spend 3 days a year in continuing education courses, according to their collective bargaining contract. In addition, many teachers voluntarily attend courses in CPE. The employer pays some of the course fees, but sometimes the teachers pay the fees from their own salary.

The current aim in Finland is to guide teachers' professional development toward a more structured form. Different models of continuing professional education are being designed, with the main goal to connect their education to the universities. Continuing in-service education can be realized either on a research-based continuum, as a practice-based continuum for the needs of working life, as a partnership continuum, or as an updating continuum, according to Helin's (2014) outline.

EXPENDITURE ON EDUCATION

As previously mentioned, all education in Finland is free of charge. This means that from pre-school (age 6) to comprehensive school (ages 7–16) to upper secondary school or vocational training (ages 17–19) through college or university, schooling does not cost students or their families anything. Books, notebooks, pencils, and other resources are provided in the comprehensive school system. In higher education, the students must pay for them.

The school day also includes a school lunch that is a warm, two-course meal. Services by a nurse and a doctor as well as dental care are free of charge in Finland. School expenses are distributed in the following way (FNBE, 2008):

- Teaching 66%
- Accommodation and transport 4%
- School meals 8%
- Special-needs assistant services 3%
- Internal administration 5%
- Property maintenance 14%

In 2010, the financial investment in education and annual expenditure per student in pre-primary education in Finland was $5,372 (the OECD average was $6,762); for primary education, it was $7,624 (the OECD average was $7,974); for secondary education, it was $9,162 (the OECD average was $9,014); and for tertiary education, it was $16,714 (the OECD average was $13,528) (OECD, 2013).

SCHOOL LIFE IN FINLAND

Schoolwork is regulated by the laws of Finland. For example, the Basic Education Act (628/1998) states that, first and foremost, students should attend the neighborhood school closest to their home. The Basic Education Act also regulates the length of the school year, which is 190 days. Furthermore, the law (and its amendments) determines the length of the school day for students: in kindergarten and first and second grades, the school day may be no longer than 5 hours; for the older students (grades 3–9), the school day may last up to 7 hours. One hour actually means 45 minutes, but "hours" are grouped together to form longer teaching periods.

Between lessons there are usually three to five recess breaks of 15 or 30 minutes, depending on how the day is arranged. In primary school, recess is spent outdoors in the schoolyard, which is equipped with swings and other play equipment. The children often play soccer or other games during recess. The older students may sometimes stay indoors, but they usually go outside for a break at least once a day.

The teachers' working days are longer. The primary school teachers arrange divided group teaching, so that only half the class is present at a given time. Primary school teachers may also teach some subjects to other classes, especially if they are specialists in certain areas. The weekly teaching hours vary according to categories and subjects. These hours are determined through negotiations between the teachers' union and the employers' representatives, and they are stated in collective bargaining contracts. The weekly teaching hours are shown in Table 2.1. Besides their teaching hours, the teachers are also required to participate in collaborative planning 3 hours per week. No other hours are set aside for planning or evaluation, as in some countries. For many occupations and professions in Finland, the average work week is 38 hours; this number is considered an approximate total of weekly working hours for teachers as well, although it has not been specifically determined or monitored in any way.

Table 2.1. Finnish Teachers' Weekly Teaching Hours (OVTES, 2014–2016).

Teacher category	Hours/week
K–6 teachers (primary)	
Kindergarten teacher	23
Class teacher (primary teacher)	24
Special-education teacher (K–12)	24
Special-education class teacher	22
Subject teachers	
Mother tongue teacher (Finnish/Swedish)	18
Second official language teacher (Swedish/Finnish)	20
Mathematics, physics, chemistry, ICT, arts, music teacher	21
Religion, ethics, philosophy, history, social sciences, home economics, health education, biology, geography teacher	23
Crafts, physical education, student counseling teacher	24
Other	23

The total intended instruction time (in hours) per year for students in Finland in 2011 in primary education was 3,926 hours (the OECD average was 4,717 hours), and in lower secondary education, it was 2,740 hours (the OECD average was 3,034 hours). In comparison, the number of teaching hours per year in 2011 for teachers in public institutions in Finland in pre-primary education was 652 (the OECD average was 994 hours); in primary education, it was 680 hours (the OECD average was 790 hours); in lower secondary education, it was 595 hours (the OECD average was 709 hours); and in upper secondary education, it was 553 hours (the OECD average was 664 hours) (OECD, 2013).

The average classroom size in Finland (19.8 students) is slightly smaller than the average in the OECD countries (21.6 students). In upper secondary school, there is a greater difference: Finland averages 20.1 students per class, whereas the average for the OECD countries is 23.9 students per class (OECD, 2010a).

The ratio of students to teaching staff in 2011 in pre-primary school education in Finland was 11 students per teacher (the OECD average was 14); in primary education, it was 14 students per teacher (the OECD average was 15); and in secondary education it was 13 students per teacher (the OECD average was 14) (OECD, 2013).

Naturally, the fundamental task for a teacher is teaching. Classes, however, are only the most visible part of a teacher's daily life. Prior to contact with students, lessons are planned, and after class the lessons are evaluated, followed by planning for the next lessons. Teachers, especially in primary schools, are in close contact with parents and cooperate regularly with other teachers and school personnel. Besides those contacts, the teachers create relationships outside of school, depending on the surroundings and the opportunities in each particular area.

Teachers assign homework daily, but the amount of homework depends on the students' age. Schools arrange extracurricular activities (e.g., drama club, chess club, handicraft club, or home economics club). These, however, depend on yearly funding, as well as on the teachers' willingness to take on extra work for extra pay. There is no legislation regarding extracurricular activities. Most often independent actors without a connection to the school, such as sports clubs and art schools, arrange children's hobbies.

EDUCATIONAL CLIMATE AND PRACTICES IN FINLAND

Respect for Teachers and Attitudes Toward Education

The teaching profession in Finland is held in high esteem, and it continues to appeal to and attract young people. Because of its appeal, entrance into teacher education programs is highly competitive. The number of applicants for primary school teacher education programs in particular exceeds the number of available places by a considerable amount. Of every 10 applicants, only about 1 is accepted (Sahlberg, 2013).

According to statistics published by the Ministry of Education and Culture (2014), the number of applicants who took part in the phase 1 entrance test for primary teacher education, as compared to the number selected for that program, were as follows:

Table 2.2. Number of Applicants Taking Part in the Phase 1 Entrance Test for Primary Education.

	2011	2012	2013
Applicants who participated in the national test	8,856	11,976	12,493
Applicants selected for the educational program	811	879	886

The popularity of the education profession is explained by the fact that teachers in Finland are considered to be professionals and have autonomous roles not only in implementing but also in planning and evaluating activities in their classrooms. Teachers are viewed as pedagogically thinking professionals who are able to reflect on their experiences and commit to professional development. Furthermore, there is mutual trust between teachers and parents (Halinen, 2008; Laukkanen, 2008).

In Finland, teachers were traditionally "the heart of the village," the appreciated disseminators of knowledge to the entire community (Jyrhämä & Maaranen, 2012). Although society has become much more complex, what has remained is an appreciation of teachers. This is clearly shown in comparisons of nearly 400 different professions. A survey conducted by one of the largest Finnish periodicals, *Suomen Kuvalehti* (2004; 2007; 2010) [The Finnish News Magazine], on how various occupations are valued is very revealing. For instance, the most highly appreciated occupation is surgeon (ranked as number 1), whereas the least valued is door-to-door salesman (number 380). The survey shown in Table 2.3 has been carried out for several years.

Table 2.3. Popular Occupations (Examples Ranked) in *Suomen Kuvalehti*.

	2004	2007	2010
Surgeon	1	1	1
Fireman	5	2	4
Nurse	9	6	10
Special-needs teacher	23	21	22
Speech teacher	27	28	37
Psychologist	31	33	26
Professor	33	41	39
Kindergarten teacher	34	22	31
Class teacher	46	40	42
Subject teacher	72	66	62
Salesman door-to-door	380	381	380
Ranked occupations total	380	381	380

School is generally valued highly in Finland (Sahlberg, 2007), and parents support teachers in their work (Välijärvi, Linnakylä, Kupari, Reinikainen, & Arffman, 2002).

Tutoring During and After School

According to the Basic Education Act (Amendment 642/2010), teachers are required to lend support to students in need. In practice, they have several options for fulfilling this requirement. The legislation outlines a three-stage model for support as follows:

- The first level includes all students. This stage is called remedial teaching and part-time, special needs education. All students have the right to

support when they need it. The teachers can (and should) differentiate the teaching in order to provide adequate and appropriate instruction for students. If that is not enough, they can temporarily provide extra tutoring to certain students for extra pay. The amount of extra-pay tutoring depends on the school's resources. In some cases, when a student clearly needs special attention, it is possible to provide instruction by a special education teacher.
- The second level of support involves students with greater needs. This level is called enhanced support, and here the student is provided with a learning plan in collaboration with the pupil and the parents.
- At the third level—the special needs support level—the student attends a special education program, either full-time or part-time (Ministry of Education and Culture, 2015b).

Teachers are, of course, responsible for supporting learning of all students in heterogeneous classrooms and taking into account the needs of high- and low-achieving students. Depending on the nature and extent of the special needs, different support modes are available for addressing individual needs. In general, Finnish schools succeed in integrating different learners. An OECD (2010b) report mentioned that, in the 21st century, many educators began to travel annually to Helsinki to learn the secret of their favorable educational outcomes, outcomes that resulted in part from the modest gap between high and low achieving students.

In Finland there are no huge differences in citizens' socioeconomic status. Finland has been, and still is, a relatively homogeneous society (Sahlberg, 2007). Given that education is free for all, the students experience equality regardless of their economic background.

Morning and Afternoon Care for First and Second Graders

Municipalities are required to arrange afternoon care for first and second graders. This care costs the parents a small amount of money and is voluntary. Nevertheless, it is very popular, because in Finland, the school day usually ends early—at noon or 1 p.m.—for first and second graders. Most Finnish parents work outside the home; thus, without after-school care, children would face a very long afternoon alone at home. The afternoon care is often organized by independent groups such as churches, 4H clubs, sports clubs, and other interested organizations. The care includes a snack and guided activities, as well as the chance to do homework (Ministry of Education and Culture, 2015e).

Some municipalities have been able to organize morning care as well, but it is not as common as afternoon care. In the morning children can arrive at school before the school day begins, have breakfast, and participate in organized activities. This care also costs a small amount of money (FNBE, 2011).

Student Welfare in Finland

Student welfare aims at enhancing learning and physical and psychological health. It is first and foremost a form of support for the entire school community.

> Pupil welfare services mean different forms of support for pupils' learning, mental and physical health and social well-being. In pre-primary and basic education, pupils are entitled to the welfare services they need to be able to follow teaching. These include services recorded in the curriculum, health care under the Public Health Act, and support for child-rearing under the Child Welfare Act. In upper secondary schools and in vocational education and training, the education provider must see to it that the students know about the health and welfare services available to them and they use the services when needed. (Ministry of Education and Culture, 2015b, Pupil Welfare Services in Finland section, para. 1–3)

Broadly considered, student welfare comprises high-quality education that follows the National Core Curriculum as well as local curricula; it means free materials, books, and so on. It also includes support for learning, guidance (career or otherwise), safe surroundings, school health care, the services of social workers and psychologists, a hot lunch, and, in special cases, school transportation.

EDUCATION FOR STUDENTS WITH SPECIAL NEEDS

The Finnish National Core Curriculum outlines the requirements for special-needs education, which are outlined in the Basic Education Act. The principal idea is that students are entitled to attend the school closest to their home.

The support is divided into three stages: general (remedial) support, intensified (enhanced) support, and special-needs support. The student can move between these stages in either direction.

> All pupils of compulsory school age have the right to general support, that is, high-quality education, as well as guidance and support in learning and other schoolwork as soon as a need arises. A pupil who has temporarily fallen behind in studies or otherwise needs short-term support in learning has a right to remedial teaching. A pupil who has difficulties in learning or other schoolwork has a right to part-time special-needs education in connection with other teaching.

> Intensified support must be given to those pupils who need regular support measures or several forms of support at the same time. The aim is to prevent existing problems from

becoming more serious or expansive. Intensified support is in accordance with a learning plan devised for the pupil based on the pupil's own assessment or the teacher's or several teachers' pedagogical assessment.

If children cannot adequately cope with mainstream education in spite of general or intensified form of support, they must be given special support. This may come into question in cases of disability, illness, delayed development, emotional disorder or some other similar reason. The main purpose of special support is to provide pupils with broadly based and systematic help so that they can complete compulsory education and be eligible for upper secondary education. Special needs education is provided, taking into consideration the interests of the pupil and the facilities for providing education, in conjunction with mainstream instruction or in a special-needs classroom or some other appropriate facility. (Ministry of Education and Culture, 2015b, Special-Needs Education in Finland section, para. 1–3)

There is also the possibility of so-called *flexible education*, which is available for students in grades 7–9. This form of education is for unmotivated or underachieving students. It is also for those at risk of exclusion from further education and employment. The goal is to complete the basic education syllabus, possibly over a longer time period; alternatively, instruction that is organized differently is provided. This system has been an effective measure in preventing social marginalization. For immigrant children who have recently arrived in Finland, it is also possible to arrange either preparatory teaching or other support if the child is integrated into mainstream education. Such support usually requires flexibility in arranging the instruction (Eurypedia, 2015).

ROLE OF THE TEACHERS' UNION

Although membership is voluntary, more than 95% of Finnish teachers belong to the teachers' union (called *Opetusalan Ammattijärjestö*, or OAJ). OAJ, the only educational trade union in Finland, negotiates on the national level with employers (i.e., municipalities or religious organizations—private schools being mostly tied to the latter) and works closely with teachers, universities, and members of parliament, the government, and ministries. The monthly cost of membership in the union is calculated at 1.2% of a teacher's salary (OAJ, 2015).

OAJ considers the high professional status of teachers to be very important. The agency has been invited to play an active partnership role in all major reforms of teacher education and school curricula in recent decades and has promoted the policy of earning a master's degree as the basic qualification for all teachers (Niemi, 2012).

According to Niemi (2012), another initiative of OAJ was an ethical council for the teaching profession, established in 2000. "It is an independent organ and its main purpose is to advance the ethical nature of the teaching profession. The first ethical principles were published in 2000" (p. 27).

NATIONAL CORE CURRICULUM

The Finnish National Board of Education (FNBE, 2004) determines the National Core Curriculum in Finland. The curriculum includes objectives and core content for different subjects, as well as principles of pupil assessment, special-needs education, pupil welfare, and educational guidance. The principles of an optimal learning environment and teaching and learning approaches are also addressed in the National Core Curriculum. The education providers, usually the local education authorities and the schools themselves, draw up their own curricula for pre-primary and basic education within the framework of the National Core Curriculum. These curricula may be prepared for individual municipalities or institutions or both (FNBE, 2004).

Teachers play an active role in designing the local-level curriculum, which outlines schooling and implementation in more detail. In the Finnish educational system, decision-making power is decentralized and is on the local level: each municipality, along with its own teachers, is responsible for planning the local curriculum in accordance with the National Core Curriculum for Basic Education (NCCBE) (FNBE, 2004) and for monitoring the quality of education. The NCCBE defines the general and the subject-specific aims, as well as the core contents of each school subject (syllabus) only at the general level; the specific details (e.g., assessment, allocation of lesson hours, structure of the school day, and school culture) are found in the school-level curriculum (Halinen, 2015). The outline for Finnish public school education is based on the description of the aims established for teaching. The process of designing the school-level curriculum promotes teachers' awareness of and commitment to the development of schooling, which is seen as being even more important than producing the written form of the curriculum. Therefore, the design and development of the curriculum is linked to teaching practice in the classrooms and consequently to school improvement.

The decentralization process began in the 1980s, and the curriculum reform of 1994 gave the municipalities' local authorities a large degree of autonomy (Vitikka, Krokfors, & Hurmerinta, 2012). Today, the municipalities have the right to determine how they use state-provided finances, and they have the autonomy to organize schooling as they wish. Textbooks are no longer inspected, nor are there school inspectors or supervisors (Vitikka et al., 2012). Finnish teachers and schools are not controlled by external evaluation and monitoring. Schools and teachers are responsible for choosing learning and assessment materials, as well as the specific teaching methods to be used in their teaching in accordance with the requirements of the curriculum. Teachers are also free to choose the learning materials they want to use or even whether they want to use ready-made materials at all. Further, assessment is primarily designed at the school level and implemented by the teachers. This "decentralization" allows teachers to reflect on teaching and learning in their classrooms: they can choose how to use different forms of assessment suitable for each situation, such as a formative assessment of students' experimental work as well as assessment summaries. In general, teachers are valued as experts in curriculum development, teaching, and assessment at all school levels (FNBE, 2004). Education authorities and national-level education policymakers trust teachers and their professionalism: teachers themselves are able to decide how to provide the best education for all kinds of children and young people.

The National Core Curriculum is currently undergoing reform, and the new curriculum will be introduced in August 2016. The local education providers (i.e., the municipalities) are in the process of constructing their own local curricula (FNBE, 2015; Halinen, 2015).

CONCLUSION

When we examine the Finnish educational system closely, we see various reasons for its success. Stakeholders combine political decision-making and pedagogical expertise with the will to create equal educational opportunities for all children and adolescents, whatever their backgrounds may be. These kinds of decisions are value choices. In constructing the educational system and Finnish schooling, the aim has been to achieve rational, research-based arguments that serve as the basis for the National Core Curriculum. The responsibility for the latter lies with the National Board of Education, but the work itself is carried out by an array of representatives: universities, municipalities, social organizations, the teachers' trade union, parents, and so on. The draft for the reform of the National Core Curriculum of 2016 has been open to comment by any interested party through the website of the National Board of Education.

When we compare the Finnish school system to others internationally, some specific features emerge as special (Sahlberg, 2011; Simola, 2015). In Finland, there are hardly any large-scale national exams or standardized tests. Only at certain grade levels and in some subjects are students tested in order to evaluate their progress. There is no inspection of schools in Finland. The schools can design their work independently, and the teachers do not have to worry about someone auditing their skills or their ability to teach. Nor are the teachers evaluated. The principals lead the school and its teachers, but there is no evaluation or criteria for a good teacher or good teaching. Nor is there private tutoring or a track system. So far there has been hardly any such request from parents, and thus there are very few service providers for private tutoring. The Finnish school system is based on the idea of a uniform basic education. There are only a few private schools in the entire country, and their status is also based on tradition. They often have the special task of developing teaching for a special emphasis or ideology. However, the private schools must also follow the National Core Curriculum, and they are funded by the government and the municipality in the same manner as the public schools.

Finnish schools are thus founded on a high-quality basic education that is nationwide, in which the students attend the school closest to their home. Children of executives sit alongside children of lumbermen in the same classroom. In this atmosphere, the children learn to be social, respectful, and cooperative citizens. The aim of basic education is to support the children's holistic growth and to create opportunities for them to discover personal strengths and to learn from one another. Along with these reasons, the history of rapid development in the Finnish welfare state explains Finnish students' success on the PISA tests (Kupiainen et al., 2009; Simola, 2015). Finland's emphasis on educational equality is one of the most important reasons behind the nation's superior education system.

REFERENCES

Blomberg, S. (2008). *Noviisiopettajana peruskoulussa: Aloittelevien opettajien autenttisia kokemuksia ensimmäisestä opettajavuodesta*. [As a novice teacher at comprehensive school: The authentic experiences of the beginning teachers during their first year of teaching.] Research Report 291, University of Helsinki, Faculty of Behavioural Sciences, Department of Applied Sciences of Education.

Eurypedia. (2015). *Finland: Support measures for learners in early childhood and school education*. Retrieved January 20, 2015, from https://webgate.ec.europa.eu/fpfis/mwikis/eurydice/index.php/Finland:Support_Measures_for_Learners_in_Early_Childhood_and_School_Education

Finland in facts. (2015). Retrieved March 30, 2015, from http://finland.fi/Public/default.aspx?contentid=160032&nodeid=41803&culture=

Finnish National Board of Education. (n.d.). *Education system*. Accessed April 24, 2015, from http://www.oph.fi/english/education_system

Finnish National Board of Education. (2004). *The Finnish national core curriculum 2004*. http://www.oph.fi/english/curricula_and_qualifications/basic_education

Finnish National Board of Education. (2008). *School meals in Finland*. http://www.oph.fi/download/47657_school_meals_in_finland.pdf

Finnish National Board of Education. (2011). *National framework for before- and after-school activities in basic education 2011*. Publications 2011:25, National Board of Education. Retrieved March 25, 2015, from http://www.oph.fi/download/137432_national_framework_for_before_and_after_school_activities_2011.pdf

FNBE. (2015). *What is going on in Finland? Curriculum reform 2016*. Retrieved March 25, 2015, from http://www.oph.fi/english/current_issues/101/0/what_is_going_on_in_finland_curriculum_reform_2016

Halinen, I. (2008, April). *Keys to success in Finland*. Talk given at the World Education Congress: The Best Among the Best, Valencia.

Halinen, I. (2015). *General aspects of basic education curriculum reform 2016*. Presentation of the National Board of Education. Retrieved March 25, 2015, from http://www.oph.fi/download/158389_general_aspects_of_basic_education_curriculum_reform.pdf

Heikkinen, H.L.T., Jokinen, H., & Tynjälä, P. (2012). *Peer-group mentoring for teacher development*. London: Routledge.

Helin, M. (2014). *Opettajien ammatillisen kehityksen jatkumo—yliopistojen ja koulujen kumppanuus*. [Teachers' professional development as a continuum—Educational partnership between the university and schools.] Research Report 353. University of Helsinki: Department of Teacher Education.

Hodkinson, H., & Hodkinson, P. (1999). Teaching to learn, learning to teach? School-based non-teaching activity in an initial teacher education and training partnership scheme. *Teaching and Teacher Education, 15*(3), 273–285.

Hytönen, J. (1995). The role of school practice in teacher education. In P. Kansanen (Ed.), *Discussions on some educational issues VI* (pp. 77–83). Research Report 145. University of Helsinki: Department of Teacher Education.

Jakku-Sihvonen, R., & Niemi, H. (Eds.). (2006). *Research-based teacher education in Finland—Reflections by Finnish teacher educators*. Research in Educational Sciences 25. Finnish Educational Research Association.

Jakku-Sihvonen, R., & Niemi, H. (Eds.). (2007). *Education as a societal contributor: Reflections by Finnish educationalists*. Frankfurt-am-Main: Peter Lang.

Jyrhämä, R. (2006). The function of practical studies in teacher education. In R. Jakku-Sihvonen (Ed.), *Research-based teacher education in Finland—Reflections by Finnish teacher educators* (pp. 51–69). Research in Educational Sciences 25. Finnish Educational Research Association.

Jyrhämä, R., & Maaranen, K. (2012). Research-orientation in a teacher's work. In H. Niemi, A. Toom, & A. Kallioniemi (Eds.), *Miracle of education: The principles and practices of teaching and learning in Finnish schools* (pp. 97–112). Rotterdam: Sense Publishers.

Jyrhämä, R., & Syrjäläinen, E. (2011). "Good pal, wise dad and nagging wife"—and other views of teaching practice mentors. In A. Lauriala, R. Rajala, H. Ruokamo, & O. Ylitapio-Mäntylä (Eds.), *Navigating in educational contexts: Identities and cultures in dialogue* (pp. 137–149). Rotterdam: Sense Publishers.

Kansanen, P. (1991). Pedagogical thinking: The basic problem of teacher education. *European Journal of Education, 26*(3), 251–260.

Kansanen, P. (2006). Constructing a research-based program in teacher education. In F.K. Oser, F. Achtenhagen, & U. Renold (Eds.), *Competence oriented teacher training: Old research demands and new pathways* (pp. 11–22). Rotterdam & Taipei: Sense Publishers.

Kansanen, P., Tirri, K., Meri, M., Krokfors, L., Husu, J., & Jyrhämä, R. (2000). *Teachers' pedagogical thinking: Theoretical landscapes, practical challenges*. New York: Peter Lang.

Kosunen, T., & Mikkola, A. (2002). Building a science of teaching: How objectives and reality meet in Finnish teacher education. *European Journal of Teacher Education, 25*(2 & 3), 135–150.

Krokfors, L. (2007). Two-fold role of reflective pedagogical practice in research-based teacher education. In R. Jakku-Sihvonen & H. Niemi (Eds.), *Education as a societal contributor: Reflections by Finnish educationalists* (pp. 147–160). Frankfurt-am-Main: Peter Lang.

Kupiainen, S., Hautamäki, J., & Karjalainen, T. (2009). The Finnish education system and PISA. Ministry of Education. (*Opetusministeriön julkaisuja: nro* 2009:46) http://www.minedu.fi/export/sites/default/OPM/Julkaisut/2009/liitteet/opm46.pdf?lang=fi

Laukkanen, R. (2008). Finnish strategy for high-level education for all. In N. Soguel & P. Jaccard (Eds.), *Governance and performance of education systems* (pp. 305–324). Dordrecht: Springer.

Maaranen, K. (2009). *Widening perspectives of teacher education: Studies on theory-practice relationship, reflection, research and professional development.* Research Report 305. University of Helsinki: Department of Teacher Education.

Maaranen, K., & Krokfors, L. (2008). Researching pupils, schools and oneself: Teachers as integrators of theory and practice in initial teacher education. *Journal of Education for Teaching, 34*(3), 207–222.

Ministry of Education and Culture. (2014). *Teacher education in Finland 1/2014.*

Ministry of Education and Culture. (2015a). *Education policy in Finland.* Retrieved January 20, 2015, from http://www.minedu.fi/OPM/Koulutus/koulutuspolitiikka/?lang=en

Ministry of Education and Culture. (2015b). *Proudly presents: Educational support and guidance.* Retrieved January 20, 2015, from http://www.minedu.fi/OPM/Verkkouutiset/2012/09/special_education.html?lang=en

Ministry of Education and Culture. (2015c). *Education in Finland.* Retrieved March 25, 2015, from http://www.minedu.fi/pisa/piirteita.html?lang=en

Ministry of Education and Culture. (2015d). *Financing of education.* Retrieved March 25, 2015, from http://www.minedu.fi/OPM/Koulutus/koulutuspolitiikka/rahoitus/?lang=en

Ministry of Education and Culture. (2015e). *Morning and afternoon activities for the youngest pupils.* Retrieved March 25, 2015, from http://www.minedu.fi/OPM/Koulutus/perusopetus/aamu-_ja_iltapaeivaetoiminta/?lang=en.

Niemi, H. (2012). The societal factors contributing to education and schooling in Finland. In H. Niemi, A. Toom, & A. Kallioniemi (Eds.), *Miracle of education: The principles and practices of teaching and learning in Finnish schools* (pp. 19–38). Rotterdam: Sense Publishers.

Niemi, H., & Jakku-Sihvonen, R. (2006). Research-based teacher education. In R. Jakku-Sihvonen & H. Niemi (Eds.), *Research-based teacher education in Finland—Reflections by Finnish teacher educators* (pp. 31–50). Turku: Finnish Educational Research Association.

Niemi, H., & Siljander, A.M. (2013). *Uuden opettajan mentorointi: Mentoroinnilla oppilaan ja opettajan hyvinvointiin* [Mentoring a new teacher: Mentoring toward the well-being of a student and a teacher]. Helsinki: Koulutus-ja kehittämiskeskus Palmenia.

OAJ. (2015). *Union dues.* Trade Union of Education in Finland. Retrieved March 25, 2015, from http://www.oaj.fi/cs/oaj/Union%20dues

Organisation for Economic Co-operation and Development. (2010a). *Education at a glance 2010: OECD indicators.* OECD Publishing. doi:10.1787/eag-2010-en

Organisation for Economic Co-operation and Development. (2010b). *Strong performers and successful reformers in Education: Lessons from PISA for the United States.* Retrieved June 23, 2015, from http://www.oecd.org/pisa/46623978.pdf

Organisation for Economic Co-operation and Development. (2013). *Education at a glance 2013: Finland.* http://www.oecd.org/edu/Finland_EAG2013%20Country%20Note.pdf

OVTES 2014–2016. [Local Government employers.] Retrieved January 16, 2015, from http://www.kuntatyonantajat.fi/en/Pages/default.aspx

Sahlberg, P. (2007). Education policies for raising student learning: The Finnish approach. *Journal of Education Policy*, *22*(2), 147–171.

Sahlberg, P. (2010). *The secret to Finland's success: Educating teachers*. Stanford Center for Opportunity Policy in Education, Stanford University. https://edpolicy.stanford.edu/sites/default/files/publications/secret-finland%E2%80%99s-success-educating-teachers.pdf

Sahlberg, P. (2011). *Finnish lessons: What can the world learn from educational change in Finland?* New York: Teachers College Press.

Sahlberg, P. (2013). Teachers as leaders in Finland. *Educational Leadership*, *71*(2), 36–40.

Simola, H. (2015). *The Finnish education mystery: Historical and sociological essays on schooling in Finland*. London: Routledge.

Statistics Finland. (2012). Retrieved January 15, 2015, from http://www.stat.fi/til/opku/2012/opku_2012_2014-03-20_tie_001_en.html

Statistics Finland. (2015). *Population 2013*. Retrieved March 25, 2015, from http://www.stat.fi/tup/suoluk/suoluk_vaesto_en.html#foreigners

Suomen Kuvalehti. (2004; 2007; 2010). [The Finnish News Magazine.]

Sutherland, L.M., Scanlon, L.A., & Sperring, A. (2005). New directions in preparing professionals: Examining issues in engaging students in communities of practice through a school-university partnership. *Teaching and Teacher Education*, *21*(1), 79–92.

Syrjäläinen, E., & Jyrhämä, R. (2008). The network of teaching practice schools: A partnership for teachers' professional development and lifelong learning. *LLinE: Lifelong Learning in Europe*, *13*(3), 208–215.

Taipale, A. (2012). *International survey on educational leadership: A survey on school leaders' work and continuing education*. Publications 2012: 12. Finnish National Board of Education.

Tirri, K. (2014). The last 40 years in Finnish teacher education. *Journal of Education for Teaching: International Research and Pedagogy*, *40*(5), 600–609. doi:10.1080/02607476.2014.956545

Toom, A., Kynäslahti, H., Krokfors, L., Jyrhämä, R., Byman, R., Stenberg, K., Maaranen, K., & Kansanen, P. (2010). Experiences of a research-based approach to teacher education: Suggestions for future policies. *European Journal of Education*, *45*(2), 331–344.

Välijärvi, J., Linnakylä, P., Kupari, P., Reinikainen, P., & Arffman, I. (2002). *Finnish success in PISA: Some reasons behind it*. University of Jyväskylä, Institute for Educational Research.

Vitikka, E., Krokfors, L., & Hurmerinta, E. (2012). The Finnish national core curriculum: Structure and development. In H. Niemi, A. Toom, & A. Kallioniemi (Eds.), *Miracle of education: The principles and practices of teaching and learning in Finnish schools* (pp. 83–96). Rotterdam: Sense Publishers.

Westbury, I., Hansen, S., Kansanen, P., & Björkvist, O. (2005). Teacher education for research-based practice in expanded roles: Finland's experience. *Scandinavian Journal of Educational Research*, *49*(5), 475–485.

CHAPTER THREE

The United States

Schooling in the United States: What We Learn from International Assessments of Reading and Math Literacy

WILLIAM G. BROZO AND SARAH CRAIN

John Godfrey Saxe (1963), in his poetic rendition of a famous Indian legend, tells of six sightless men attempting to learn about an elephant. Each man encountered a different part of the pachyderm, and that determined his observation. Thus, the elephant was like a "wall," or like a "spear," or like a "fan," and so on. This legend is similar to the challenge of trying to capture the vast and complex character of the American school system in a single chapter. Others, like Joel Spring (2013), have written multiple editions of book-length descriptions and analyses of education in the United States. Yet even with efforts such as these, only a part of the whole is ever really accounted for.

To bring a common vision to our description and analysis, we have taken a look at the American education system through the lens of the Program for International Student Assessment (PISA) reading and math literacy results. This assessment offers expansive data on cognitive aspects of student learning as well as on a range of noncognitive factors. Thus, it is possible to link reading and math achievement of youth in the United States to such factors as race, gender, socioeconomic status, engagement, and student skills and strategies. Moreover, we argue that in order to gauge the cumulative effects of schooling, the best point at which to take a snapshot of the quality of an educational system is within its compulsory education structure. The PISA provides important insights into the academic achievement of U.S. students.

WHERE DOES THE UNITED STATES PLACE AMONG THE TOP-PERFORMING EDUCATIONAL SYSTEMS?

Depending on which metric one consults, schooling in the United States is either remarkably effective or sorely lacking. Media-grabbing pronouncements from policymakers and others that the United States is losing the race for global economic competitiveness often highlight international assessment results (Gates, 2009; Obama, 2010). Some, to rally support for their initiatives, use these results to characterize American education as being in a state of "crisis" (Ravitch, 2010). Meanwhile, broad indicators show that the U.S. economy, which remains by far the largest in the world, is not falling behind those of its competitors, including those with superior achievement levels on PISA, such as Russia and Japan (Reich, 2011). Furthermore, worker productivity in America has risen substantially since the 1990s (Chang, 2011), and the United States actually has a surplus of highly skilled workers (U.S. Bureau of Labor Statistics, 2013).

PISA data themselves can paint starkly contrasting pictures of American schooling. For example, Asian American and White students in the United States have scores that rival the best in the world, but Black and Hispanic students score at levels that are comparable to some of the lowest-performing countries. With respect to gender, girls significantly outperform boys in reading literacy, while boys continue to demonstrate superior performance in math literacy (Organisation for Economic Co-operation and Development [OECD], 2015). In both domains, however, PISA findings reinforce a vexing and persistent pattern of consistent underachievement by youth from low-income families and communities, leaving some to assert that where students live and go to school in the United States determines whether they receive a world-class education or one that is second-rate (Carnoy & Rothstein, 2013; Berliner, 2009).

What, then, can findings from international assessments such as PISA tell us about America's standard of education? When analyzed critically, PISA database information can provide a picture of the context and quality of American schooling. First and foremost, since large numbers of U.S. 15-year-olds participate, key findings for American adolescents are sure to have relevance to literacy policy, curriculum, and instruction, especially when those findings are parsed by race, gender, socioeconomic status, and other key variables. Second, we hear often in the rhetoric of national leaders that raising reading and math achievement will ensure that youth possess needed twenty-first-century literacy skills to better prepare them for the new global economy (Resmovits, 2013). This assumption appears to be supported by the results of the other OECD-sponsored global assessment, PIAAC (Program for International Assessment of Adult Competencies). Adults in the survey skilled in reading and math were more successful in their personal and professional lives compared to their less-skilled peers (OECD, 2013a). Thus, it would be prudent to learn what we can from PISA about how to prepare youth for these new global challenges, which will require sophisticated and adaptive literacy abilities (Learning Metrics Task Force, 2013; OECD, 2010a).

In the remainder of this chapter, we focus on several broad aspects of the most recent PISA cycles in reading literacy (2009) and math literacy (2012). We explore U.S. achievement relative to race, gender, socioeconomic status, engagement, and student skills and strategies. To set the stage for our discussion of these broad achievement and contextual factors, we begin the next section with a brief description of PISA, including its history and format.

WHAT DOES PISA MEASURE?

The Program for International Student Assessment, or PISA, is a study of achievement of 15-year-olds in reading, math, and science literacy from participating countries around the world. PISA occurs in 3-year cycles, with one of the three domains of literacy emphasized each cycle. Under the auspices of the Organisation for Economic Co-operation and Development (OECD), the first PISA cycle emphasized reading literacy and was launched in 2000; in 2003, math literacy; in 2006, scientific literacy; reading again in 2009; followed by math in 2012. When a particular domain is the focus of a PISA cycle, it is assessed with greater emphasis. For instance, the 2009 assessment consisted of 102 reading items, 36 math items, and 52 science items. Furthermore, PISA 2009 has yielded very rich databases of reading literacy achievement as well as of demographic, instructional, and attitudinal variables related to reading habits and practices, while the other domains—science and math literacy—produced only general data, which limits opportunities for fine-grain analysis. The findings presented here tap into the rich databases of the 2009 cycle and the more general 2012 cycle.

PISA seeks to measure how well young adults approaching the end of compulsory schooling are prepared to meet the challenges of today's knowledge societies. The assessment targets youths' ability to use their knowledge and skills to meet real-life challenges, rather than sampling content they have mastered based on specific school curricula.

The PISA test of print reading comprises both continuous (articles, essays, etc.) and noncontinuous (graphs, data tables, etc.) texts. Questions are categorized as Access and Retrieve, Integrate and Interpret, and Reflect and Evaluate. Texts and questions are distributed over four reading situations: Personal, Public, Occupational, and Educational. The digital reading test also comprises continuous and noncontinuous texts, though most electronic texts are categorized as multiple texts, which are defined as discrete texts that are juxtaposed for a particular occasion or purpose (for example, a job advertisement and a follow-up email). Similarly, digital texts include the three question types referred to above, as well as complex questions that involve multiple demands (OECD, 2009).

The PISA test defines mathematical literacy as "an individual's capacity to identify and understand the role that mathematics play in the world, to make well-founded judgments and to use and engage with mathematics in ways that meet the needs of that individual's life as a constructive, concerned and reflective citizen" (OECD, 2009, p. 14). Students demonstrate mathematical knowledge and skills on this assessment by posing and solving real-world problems, not solely by carrying out operations with numbers and symbols. PISA measures students' motivation, interest, and ability to put a range of mathematical competencies to use (e.g., mathematical language, modeling, and problem solving) in a variety of situations (personal, educational, occupational, public, and scientific) around four broad areas (quantity, space and shape, change and relationships, and uncertainty) (OECD, 2009).

PISA has its critics (see Andrews et al., 2014). However, in spite of concerns raised over language translations, gender bias, sampling procedures, and test item theory (Baird et al., 2011; Goldstein, 2004; Rauch & Hartig, 2010), it cannot be denied that OECD takes great pains to achieve valid PISA results. This goal is achieved through (1) robust quality-assurance mechanisms for translation, sampling, and test administration; (2) measures to achieve cultural and linguistic breadth in the assessment materials, particularly through countries' participation in the development and revision processes for the production of the items; and (3) state-of-the-art technology and methodology for data handling. According to OECD (2009), "The combination of these measures produces high quality instruments and outcomes with superior levels of validity and reliability to improve the understanding of education systems as well as students' knowledge, skills and attitudes" (p. 10).

RACE

Classrooms in elementary and secondary schools in the United States are becoming increasingly diverse. Recent data from the U.S. Department of Education (2013) show that the number of White students has been declining steadily over the past two decades, from 65% in 2001 to now, for the first time, just under 50% of the total share of public school enrollment. Meanwhile, Hispanic student enrollment has increased from 17% to 24% of the overall student population in pre-kindergarten through 12th grade. During this same period, Black students' share of public school enrollment has decreased from 17% to 16%, and the number of Asian/Pacific Islanders has increased from 4% to 5%.

Reading Literacy

Table 3.1 reveals a pattern of starkly contrasting scores for Asian and White American students on the one hand and Hispanic and Black American youth on the other. Immediately noticeable is the full 100-point difference in favor of Asian students (541) as compared to Black students (441). This gap is equal to a span of 2–3 years of achievement. Furthermore, Asian and White students have average scores in the upper ranges of PISA proficiency level 3 out of a 6-level reading literacy scale. Level 3 ability means students are successful at "reading tasks of moderate complexity, such as locating multiple pieces of information, making links between different parts of a text, and relating it to familiar everyday knowledge" (OECD 2010b, p. 51). Hispanic and Black students, on the other hand, have average scores at level 2, which is "considered a baseline level of proficiency" (OECD 2010b, p. 52).

Table 3.1. Average 2009 PISA Reading Literacy Scores of U.S. 15-Year-Old Students by Race/Ethnicity.

Race/Ethnicity	Score
Asian	541*
White	525*
Hispanic	466*
Black	441*
U.S. Average	500
OECD Average	493

*Significantly different from U.S. and OECD averages at .05 level

The contrast among these groups is brought into sharper focus when juxtaposing average scores by race with other countries. Asian American youth, for instance, have an average that rivals the top-performing jurisdiction in the world, Shanghai-China (556), and places them second among all 65 participating countries and jurisdictions in PISA 2009. American White 15-year-olds also fare exceptionally well in comparison with top-performing countries, ranking sixth, just one point below Singapore's average score of 526. At the same time, Hispanic youths' average score (466) looks more like those of Lithuania (468) or Turkey (464), and Black students' average score of 441 is similar to those of Serbia (442) and Chile (449).

Math Literacy

Table 3.2 further illustrates the apparent achievement gap when comparing performance by race/ethnicity. The gap between the highest-performing group (Asian)

and the lowest-performing group (Black) widens to 128 points (National Center for Educational Statistics, 2012). Furthermore, 77% of Black students and 66% of Hispanic students fall at or below level 2 which, as mentioned above, is considered a baseline for proficiency. For mathematics literacy, a level 2 performance means that students are capable of "using formulas and mathematical procedures, and making literal interpretations of mathematical contexts" (National Center for Educational Statistics, 2014, p. 1). At the opposite end of the spectrum, 60% of White students and 79% of Asian students score at level 3 or higher (National Center for Educational Statistics, 2012). At level 3, students are able to demonstrate that they are capable of "interpreting resources, constructing simple mathematical models, and engaging in basic mathematical reasoning" (National Center for Educational Statistics, 2014, p. 1). In addition, the average score for Asian students was at level 4, which suggests the ability to apply mathematical models to real-world contexts. Students at this level are also able to communicate their reasoning behind mathematical arguments and findings.

Table 3.2. Average 2012 PISA Mathematics Literacy Scores of U.S. 15-Year-Old Students by Race/Ethnicity.

Race/Ethnicity		Score
Asian		549*
White		506*
Hispanic		455*
Black		421*
	U.S. Average	481**
	OECD Average	494

*Significantly different from both the U.S. and OECD averages at the .05 level
**Significantly different from the OECD average at the .05 level

As happens with the reading literacy results, comparing U.S. students' math literacy scores by race/ethnicity to other countries highlights the extreme variance in performance. Asian American students retain a top spot, ranking sixth out of all reporting countries and jurisdictions, between Korea (554) and Macao-China (538) (National Center for Educational Statistics, 2012). White students tie Austria for 18th place, which, though considerably lower than the Asian American students' performance, is substantially above the United States' overall average ranking of 36th. However, scores for both Black and Hispanic students fall below the United States' average, with scores for Hispanic students being comparable to students in Israel (41st) and Greece (42nd), and scores for Black students identical to those of students in Malaysia, which ranks 52nd out of 65 reporting countries and jurisdictions.

What This Says About American Schooling

The No Child Left Behind Act of 2001 requires school systems to close achievement gaps wherever they are found. Although attention has been paid to closing the racial gap, Asian American and White students in the United States continue to reach achievement levels on reading and math literacy comparable to the best in the world, while Black and Hispanic students rank near the bottom in international comparisons. This leads one to ask: How did the United States do? Loveless (2011), author of one PISA report, offers a typical response: "mediocre to poor" (p. 7). When reviewers of PISA results focus only on overall averages that combine racial groups, U.S. performance appears lackluster, with scores slightly above the OECD mean in reading and below it in math.

Some, like Rueben and Murray (2008), argue that the United States runs separate and unequal schools in poorer neighborhoods, leading to ill-educated youth. They assert that the conditions of the schools and neighborhoods for poor, predominantly African American and Hispanic youth are not designed to develop high levels of literacy. Furthermore, they contend that if poverty, violence, drugs, unequal school funding, uncertified teachers, and de facto segregation are allowed to exist in the schools that serve these children and in the neighborhoods in which they live, then the United States will continue to fall short in international comparisons when the scores of ill-educated youth are combined with those of youth who enjoy better resources.

However, this gap in educational achievement between advantaged and disadvantaged students is more than an issue of social justice; it may also carry significance for the economic well-being of the nation. Raising PISA scores of Black and Hispanic youth could positively impact the U.S. economy, according to Lynch and Oakford (2014). They found that if this racial achievement gap were closed, the United States could see a cumulative increase in GDP of $20.4 trillion by the year 2050.

Eliminating racial achievement disparities and bringing all students, regardless of color, up to the level of the highest-performing racial groups, then, may be one of the most pressing social and economic goals of twenty-first-century American schooling, particularly in light of the expected continuing expansion of the nation's population of persons of color.

GENDER

As concerns about gender equality in all areas of American society have taken on increasing importance, academic performance along gender lines has also been receiving greater attention (DiPrete & Buchmann, 2013). Gender-based achievement gaps for U.S. students actually have a long history (Brozo, 2010), with trends consistently favoring girls in tasks involving verbal ability, including reading, and favoring boys in math and other STEM-related areas (U.S. Department of Education, 2012). What is new is that girls are taking rigorous high school math and science courses at comparable rates to boys and are enrolling in and graduating from colleges and universities in ever-increasing percentages over their male counterparts. In spite of these growing patterns, girls continue to choose traditional career clusters, such as education and health, in postsecondary education while avoiding the information technology and STEM fields (U.S. Department of Education, 2012).

Reading Literacy

Consistent with earlier PISA cycles, there were significant gender differences in favor of girls on overall print reading in all 65 countries in the 2009 cycle (OECD, 2010b). These results reinforce what has now become a clear and dominant pattern in academic achievement in the United States. For example, the Center on Education Policy (2010) found that girls have significantly superior scores on virtually every state test of reading. Girls in the United States also outperformed boys by a wide margin on the 2009 PISA and have done so since the original PISA cycle in 2000 (Fleischman, Hopstock, Pelczar, & Shelley, 2010). There was a 25-point difference in overall achievement favoring girls, which represents a slight decline from the 28-point difference in 2000, though the reported gap rose again on the 2012 PISA cycle to 31 points. As large as this difference between the genders is, it is significantly lower than the OECD average of 40 points, with some countries, such as Finland, experiencing a staggering 55-point gender-based disparity in the 2009 cycle.

Unlike other OECD countries, the United States has for many years had a higher level of awareness of gendered achievement in reading (Brozo, 2010). And even though programs to close this achievement gap have not been national in scope or systematic in nature, an overall heightening of sensitivity to practices and texts that engage boys as readers may be having a positive effect (Brozo et al., 2014). Finland, on the other hand, has been slow to respond to mounting evidence that boys are overrepresented among the low performers in reading. In fact, the gender issue only made it onto the national education agenda in Finland after the first indications of a decline in overall reading performance on the 2009 PISA assessment (Ministry of Education and Culture, 2012).

A closer look at gender differences in the PISA 2009 results reveals the profiles of U.S. boys and girls performing well and those who are not. Among the total number of boys, 21% scored below Proficiency Level 2, the minimal acceptable level, on the PISA 6-level scale; 14% of girls were found in this category. The highest scores are achieved by Asian American 15-year-old females from the upper socioeconomic strata (Hopstock & Pelczar, 2011). The next-highest achievers are White girls from similarly high SES backgrounds. The lowest performers are Black boys from low SES backgrounds, followed by Hispanic boys with lower SES levels (Hopstock & Pelczar, 2011).

Boys also perform less well than their female peers on the reading and writing tests of the National Assessment of Educational Progress (NAEP) (Klecker, 2006). Girls at the 13- and 17-year-old levels have held an advantage in reading ranging from 8 to 12 scale score points over the 4 decades since NAEP was launched in 1971 (National Center for Education Statistics, 2013).

Math Literacy

As the reading assessment favors girls, the mathematics assessment typically favors boys, with only Thailand, Qatar, and Jordan reporting statistically significant scores that favor girls. The United States' overall averages by gender point to only a modest advantage for boys (484) over girls (479) (OECD, 2014). These findings are consistent with the most recent NAEP results for 12th-grade mathematics, which reported a significant 3-point difference in favor of boys in mathematics (National Center for Education Statistics, 2013). Furthermore, this trend has not changed in the last three NAEP testing cycles.

What This Says About American Schooling

Because the patterns of achievement for U.S. students in reading and math on PISA are not consistent between the genders, their implications about the influence and role of American education need to be parsed. Female dominance in reading literacy has been speculatively linked to school conditions in the United States such as girl-friendly language curricula, a feminized teaching force, and even the Pygmalion effect in the classroom (Brozo, 2010). On the math side, greater opportunity for girls in the United States—starting with Title IX in the 1970s, which established a legal foundation for gender equality in education through numerous national, state, and local initiatives to increase girls' participation in STEM-related fields and careers—has led to substantial progress over the past decade. However, while girls have reached parity with boys and even surpassed them when it comes to enrolling in and successfully completing algebra and advanced placement math courses in high school (U.S. Department of Education, 2012), their lower math scores and underrepresentation in math-related degree programs persist (Stoet & Geary, 2013).

Although achievement gaps should be addressed, as mandated by NCLB, gender differences in reading have not received the attention they deserve (Brozo, 2010). To reduce girls' large and ongoing advantage in reading literacy over boys, it seems clear that more needs to be done to address boys' lower reading achievement and motivation, particularly for boys of color and with immigrant backgrounds.

Language curricula in American schools need to include texts and instructional practices orchestrated in ways that capture boys' imaginations, sustain their attention, and build reading competence.

With respect to math, girls in the United States—a country that ranks high in terms of standard of living and equality policies—appear to need more than privilege and opportunity to make up for the achievement gap (Stoet & Geary, 2013). Researchers have found that girls' decisions about whether to pursue a STEM-related field may have more to do with individual interest than with opportunity (Su, Rounds, & Armstrong, 2009). Thus, studying and determining other factors that contribute to girls' underachievement in math—such as their preferences and interests—and how these variables might be shaped to guide females into coursework and fields that foster advanced knowledge and skills in math is as crucial as understanding boys' underachievement in reading.

SOCIOECONOMIC STATUS

Socioeconomic status (SES) is a metric that combines economic and sociological factors to gauge a person's social position in relation to others. For individuals and families, factors typically included in SES are household or combined income, education attainment, and occupation (Marmot, 2004). Individual and family economic well-being has been linked to a variety of benefits for children and youth, including overall academic achievement (Ladd, 2012), early word learning and language development (Farrant & Zubrick, 2012; Schiff & Lotem, 2011), reading achievement and growth (Aikens & Barbarin, 2008; Benson & Borman, 2010), and even physical and psychological health (Marmot, 2004).

Since societies both in the United States and across the globe stand to benefit from increasing the socioeconomic status for all citizens, it is important to consider SES in relationship to cognitive skills in reading and math literacy. Hanushek and Woessmann (2010) build a compelling case for leavening the economic health and overall well-being of a nation by raising PISA scores. They argue that "A modest goal of having all OECD countries boost their average PISA scores by 25 points over the next 20 years implies an aggregate gain of OECD GDP of $115 trillion over the lifetime of the generation born in 2010" (p. 6). The researchers further claim that GDP benefits up to $200 trillion could accrue to the global economy if all students were brought to just a minimal level of proficiency (i.e., reaching a PISA score of 400).

The implications of Hanushek and Woessmann's analysis of cognitive skills and the economy are staggering, particularly for the United States, which, according to the researchers, stands to make by far the most dramatic gain in GDP—over $40 trillion—compared with other OECD countries.

Reading Literacy

Although state, district, and individual information related to SES is not available in the PISA databases, analysis of SES can be achieved using proxy variables. For instance, reading scores can be correlated with free and reduced-price lunch rates, which represent students' family income. Table 3.3 confirms the linear relationship between these two variables. American students from the most privileged backgrounds, attending schools with a subsidized-meal rate of 10% or less, have an average PISA score (551) that is second in the world, just shy of the top-performing jurisdiction, Shanghai-China (556). The score achieved by students who fall into the next category (those attending schools with 10–29.9% of enrolled students qualifying for free and reduced-price lunch) would rank them fifth in the world, just ahead of Singapore (526) and a few score points below Hong Kong-China (533).

A very different outcome is evident for groups of students attending schools with high eligibility rates for free and reduced-price lunches. Students in schools with 50–74.9% of enrolled pupils qualifying for free and reduced-price lunch, for example, have an average score of 471, a score comparable to a rank of about 31st among the 34 OECD countries participating in the 2009 assessment. The lowest score, 446, associated with students who are enrolled in schools with at least 75% of the student body eligible for subsidized meals, ranks 33rd among the OECD countries, higher only than Mexico at 425.

Table 3.3. Relationship Between Eligibility Categories for Free and Reduce-Priced Lunch and 2009 PISA Scores for U.S. Students.

Schools' Subsidized-Meal Rate as Percentage of Eligible Students	PISA Score
Less than 10%	551*
10–29.9%	527*
25–49.9%	502
50–74.9%	471**
75% or more	446**

*Significantly higher than U.S. average of 500
**Significantly lower than U.S. average of 500

We also learn from the PISA 2009 database that nearly one-fourth of the U.S. students were from single-parent families. This is representative of the population of youth as a whole. Additionally, households with a single parent, especially if the parent is the mother, are much more likely to have low incomes than two-parent families (Ladd, 2012). Students living with one parent achieved scores that averaged

45–50 points lower than their peers from other types of families. A further telling indicator of achievement related to SES is immigrant status. This variable often links closely to family income as well as the level of academic support and preparation for school students provided at home. For instance, immigrant children in the United States are nearly twice as likely to be living in poverty (21%) as compared with their native peers (14%) (Hernandez, 2004). As a consequence, low-income immigrant families lack the resources to purchase material goods, services, and experiences that promote children's educational development (Mistry, Biesanz, Chien, Howes, & Benner, 2008). The point is that the greater socioeconomic risks experienced by children of immigrants undoubtedly exacerbate the linguistic challenges they face. While about 16% of all U.S. students from nonimmigrant backgrounds scored below proficiency level 2, close to 20% of second-generation immigrants and nearly 25% of first-generation students scored below this level.

Math Literacy

With regard to socioeconomic status, the math data paint a picture similar to the reading data. Table 3.4 demonstrates that students from more affluent areas, in which less than 10% of the population qualifies for free or reduced-price lunch, have an average math score that would rank second only to that of South Korea. Meanwhile, students from the most impoverished areas, in which 75% or more students qualify for free or reduced-price lunch, rank above only Chile and Mexico.

Table 3.4. Relationship Between Eligibility Categories for Free and Reduced-Price Lunch and 2012 PISA Scores for U.S. Students.

Schools' Subsidized-Meal Rate as Percentage of Eligible Students	PISA Score
Less than 10%	540*
10–24.9%	513*
25–49.9%	506*
50–74.9%	464**
75% or more	432**

* Significantly higher than the U.S. average of 481
** Significantly lower than the U.S. average of 481

Furthermore, in 2012, 20% of students reported being from single-parent families. Although the difference in scores was not as drastic as with reading, students from single-parent homes scored 24 points lower in mathematics overall than their peers from other home environments (OECD, 2013c).

The data regarding immigrant status are not as linear. In 2012, 21.5% of students identified themselves as immigrants. When compared to nonimmigrants, first-generation immigrants scored 24 points lower in overall mathematics performance, and second-generation immigrants scored 9 points lower (OECD, 2013c). One explanation for this difference could be related to the individual's degree of English proficiency at the time of the test. Of the students who identified themselves as immigrants, 9% reported speaking English in the home, while slightly more than 12% reported speaking a language other than English in the home (OECD, 2013c). When considering immigrant status and language use in the home, the lowest-performing group of students classified themselves as nonimmigrants who spoke a language other than English at home (443). Accounting for less than 2% of the total population tested, this group could represent a subset of students who were born in the United States to immigrants who spoke a language other than English. For nonimmigrants, whether English was the language used in the home had almost as much of an impact on students' scores as did their socioeconomic status. The highest-performing subgroup was students who classified themselves as immigrants who spoke English at home (494).

What This Says About American Schooling

Social mobility has been an idealized, if not always a realized, goal of American schooling going as far back as the founding of common or public schools shortly after the American Revolution (Spring, 2013). Education, particularly for immigrants and the less privileged, was thought to be the answer to problems related to inequities in wealth and resource distribution and quality of life (Bowles & Gintis, 2002). However, we have been forced to realize that unjust conditions in society are not readily ameliorated by schools. Inequalities of social position can have a cumulative effect, influencing opportunities for individuals across generations. For example, the effect of large inequalities in parental educational attainment can lead to significant differences in their children's chances in school (Van de Werfhorst & Mijs, 2010).

This seems to be what the PISA results are telling us. Students from privileged families have much higher scores in reading and math than students from low-income backgrounds. Furthermore, the test score difference associated with moving one standard deviation on the PISA's Economic, Social, and Cultural Status index equates to about one year of schooling. Thus, PISA data convincingly reveal that SES has a powerful association with reading and math achievement (OECD, 2013c). This influence of SES also extends to schools. Education systems in low-SES communities often lack the resources of those in more privileged areas; this lack links directly to students' academic outcomes and progress (Aikens & Barbarin, 2008).

Research findings make clear that SES matters when it comes to children's and youth's academic development (Morgan, Farkas, Hillemeier, & Maczuga,

2009). Efforts to reduce the wide gaps between the haves and the have-nots, between those with wealth and those in poverty, can benefit society (Milanovic, 2012). Improving school systems through equitable distribution of resources and targeting students with early intervention and responsive literacy and math programs may help to reduce the academic risk factors associated with low income (Berliner, 2009). Another promising approach to narrowing the achievement gap for low-SES students is to discover factors that contribute to academic success for those who "beat the odds" and to implement aggressive programming for caregivers based on these insights (Milne & Plourde, 2006).

ENGAGEMENT

Nobel Prize–winning economist James Heckman argues in favor of what he refers to as "soft skills"—those personality traits that may be even more essential to successful learning and achievement inside and outside the classroom than cognitive abilities (Heckman & Kautz, 2012). According to Heckman and his colleagues (Heckman, Stixrud, & Urzua, 2006), traits such as curiosity and perseverance might have greater predictive power for success in life than cognitive skills.

Engagement for learning, like perseverance, is a soft skill that has been shown to be a potent predictor of academic success (Pintrich & Schunk, 2002). Generally speaking, learning improves when students are inquisitive, interested, inspired, or otherwise "engaged." Above all other variables, engagement has the greatest shared variance with performance on PISA (OECD, 2013b).

Reading Literacy

Reading engagement is a multidimensional factor in PISA related to overall attitude toward reading, time spent reading, and breadth of reading preferences. To derive composite indices comparable to achievement and other variables, the reading literacy tasks of PISA 2009 were accompanied by a student questionnaire that gathered data on these three aspects of reading engagement.

The pattern for U.S. 15-year-olds is similar to the pattern for all students on PISA. Higher reading engagement—as indicated by reading enjoyment, extensive daily and weekly reading time, and reading a wide variety of fiction and nonfiction texts—is related to higher achievement (Brozo et al., 2014). American students who read one or more hours per day had average scores from 541 to 544, while those who do not read for enjoyment at all had an average score of 467. Similarly, students who strongly agree with the statement "I read only if I have to" averaged 459, while those who strongly disagree averaged 552. Students who view reading as a favorite hobby scored 562 on average, whereas those who do not had an average score of 466. The difference in performance in each of these cases ranges from near 80 to 100 score points, or the equivalent of nearly 2 years of schooling between highly engaged and disengaged readers.

As might be expected, given their overall superior performance on PISA, girls from the United States had significantly higher indices of reading engagement compared with boys. Girls enjoyed reading more, spent a greater amount of time reading, and had a wider range of reading preferences compared with their male peers (Brozo et al., 2014).

Math Literacy

As with reading, multiple indicators determine the degree of student engagement in mathematics. Although all of these components contribute to engagement, individual student motivation—both intrinsic and extrinsic—appears to be a significant contributor to overall engagement and presents some interesting findings.

Even though nearly 50% of students reported that they were "interested in the things [they] learn in mathematics" (OECD, 2013b), only about one-third of them reported that "[they] enjoy reading about mathematics" or that they "do mathematics because [they] enjoy it." In each of these categories, the percentage of boys who agreed with these statements exceeded the percentage of girls; most notably, boys reported being more interested in the learning of mathematics (6.7%) and enjoyed reading about mathematics more (11.1%).

Somewhat surprisingly, only slight differences were reported between socioeconomic groups. For example, about 52% (OECD, 2013b) of socioeconomically advantaged students reported an interest in learning mathematics compared to 48% of socioeconomically disadvantaged students. Furthermore, a greater percentage (49%) of socioeconomically disadvantaged students indicated that they looked forward to their math lessons compared to 45% of socioeconomically advantaged students. Given the performance gap between these two groups on the PISA assessment, it does not seem that intrinsic motivation to learn mathematics is the principal cause of the disparity between the groups.

Despite low levels of intrinsic motivation for math, a majority of students across genders and socioeconomic groups reported that math would be helpful to them in the future when they consider career opportunities and continue their studies. Both genders responded similarly to questions about the importance of mathematics as it related to job prospects; however, boys were more inclined (5%) (OECD, 2013b) to agree that math was important because of what they planned to study in the future. That question also yielded the greatest difference in response when considering socioeconomic status. Socioeconomically advantaged students were 6% (OECD, 2013b) more likely than their counterparts to consider math playing an important role in future studies.

What This Says About American Schooling

PISA results for both reading and math make clear the power of engagement. American 15-year-olds who are engaged learners demonstrate higher achievement than their less-motivated peers. Overall, 58% of U.S. students indicated they read for enjoyment, whereas only 50% reported interest in learning about and doing math. The percentages favor girls who had higher scores in reading literacy and boys who had higher scores in math literacy.

Researchers (Pintrich & Schunk, 2002) concerned with student engagement urge closer scrutiny of the curriculum (what is to be taught) and pedagogy (how it is to be taught) to ensure that content is meaningful, relevant, and authentic, and that it is offered to students through interesting and challenging instructional approaches (Meyer & Turner, 2006). Rethinking curriculum and instruction in this way will be especially critical for discovering responsive texts and practices for boys who are unmotivated to read and for girls who are disengaged students of math.

It is important to bear in mind that engagement is vital to the maintenance and further development of skills beyond adolescence and throughout life (OECD, 2013a). Thus, finding and implementing approaches that have shown evidence or promise for increasing student engagement for learning in reading and math should be a central goal of American education. Researchers focusing on student motivation advocate for practices that include (a) providing youth with numerous opportunities to read and problem solve with a variety of high-interest texts and tasks; (b) linking inside and outside of school learning to ensure relevance and meaningful application of reading and math skills; (c) bringing disengaged students together with motivating mentors who can serve as role models; and (d) employing creative outreach efforts to involve caregivers and other family members in nurturing students' motivation to learn (Brozo, 2010; Martin, Anderson, Bobis, Way, & Vellar, 2012; Singh, Granville, & Dika, 2002; Taylor & Parsons, 2011; Turner & Meyer, 2009).

STUDENT SKILLS AND STRATEGIES

All demanding cognitive processes require sophisticated skills and strategies. We know that proficient readers enhance comprehension and elaborate understandings by using their prior knowledge as they interact with text (Best, Rowe, Ozuru, & McNamara, 2005). Good readers also construct meaningful summaries of text (Pressley & Hilden, 2004), actively monitor comprehension (Kintsch & Kintsch, 2005), and employ a host of other possible actions to ensure retention and recall of important information (Caccamise & Snyder, 2005).

Mathematical proficiency also entails several critical underlying skills (Cragg & Gilmore, 2014). The literature points to the significance of such metacognitive functions as (a) turning real-world problems into mathematical equations for solving; (b) using representational knowledge for interpreting and generating symbols and graphic content; (c) finding or forming logical arguments for reasoning processes in problem solving; (d) devising strategies needed for specific problem-solving contexts; (e) understanding and using symbolic and technical language and operations; and (f) reading, decoding, and interpreting statements, questions, and tasks (Gersten et al., 2009; Rosli, Capraro, & Capraro, 2014).

Reading Literacy

Fifteen-year-olds in the United States who reported using reading strategies and processes regarded as effective ways of aiding comprehension had higher scores on PISA 2009 than those who did not. Executive control strategies such as monitoring comprehension, determining importance, connecting new information with prior knowledge, summarizing, and questioning were all associated with higher achievement.

A closer analysis of the PISA results related to skills and strategies for U.S. students (see Table 3.5) reveals that those who almost always check their understanding after reading had a significantly higher score (521) than those who almost never do this (465). Similarly, those who almost always try to identify the important points while reading had a score nearly 100 points higher (532) than those who almost never do (436). This same pattern is evident for students who relate new information to what they've already learned (526) versus those who almost never do this (480); for students who summarize what they read (519) compared to those who rarely do this (460); and for students who always ask their own questions while reading (519) and for those who almost never do this (445).

Table 3.5. Comparison of 2009 PISA Scores Between U.S. Students Who Use Reading Comprehension Strategies and Those Who Do Not.

Reading Comprehension Strategy	Frequently/Always	Rarely/Never
Check understanding after reading	521	465
Identify important points while reading	532	436
Relate new information to prior knowledge	526	480
Summarize what has been read	519	460
Ask questions while reading	519	445

Math Literacy.

PISA categorizes skills in mathematics as either process or content. The trend of boys outperforming girls continues in both of these categories. The most fundamental means of assessing mathematics on PISA is through an evaluation of students' proficiency with three processes involved in analyzing mathematical situations: formulating situations mathematically; employing mathematical concepts, facts, procedures, and reasoning; and interpreting, applying, and evaluating mathematical outcomes. While the results of students in the United States fell into the lower half of the 65 participating countries and jurisdictions in all three categories, their strongest performance was in the interpreting category.

However, the ability to interpret, apply, and evaluate in math wasn't consistently related to higher overall math achievement. For example, the five countries with the highest overall mathematics scores each had results more than 10 points lower on the interpreting scale; similarly, the countries with the lowest overall scores each had significantly higher scores on this subscale. This could indicate that the interpreting process strand may not be a direct measurement of a student's mathematical ability, or at least that other learning and reasoning factors should be considered (OECD, 2014).

What This Tells Us About American Schooling.

Proficient reading and math performance requires knowledge of and facility with complex learning processes and strategies. This means that foundational reading and computational skills mastered in the early grades, while important for initial success, are not nearly enough for increasingly sophisticated texts and problem-solving tasks that students will encounter in academic and workplace contexts. American middle and high school teachers must develop the capacity to infuse the secondary curriculum and instructional routines with strategic reading and math processes (Brozo & Simpson, 2007).

In reading, secondary teachers can use a variety of strategies to help students move toward a more sophisticated level of thinking about texts. As expert readers, teachers can model processes of thinking, present scaffold strategies for comprehension, and engage youth in interactive experiences that require them to go beyond mere memorization. Along with their apprenticing role, students can also be challenged to accept greater levels of responsibility for their own critical and elaborative thinking.

In math as well, teachers can employ several critical instructional practices to improve students' strategic math abilities. Students can be encouraged to seek various solutions and then be allowed to defend their decisions. They can be shown how to construct visual and graphic representations of problems. Teachers can model problem-solving approaches using think-alouds that students can imitate when working through problems with peers. Teachers can ask higher-order questions about problems and elicit similar questions from students, resulting in students developing their own heuristics for solving problems. Finally, just as all teachers can support students' strategic thinking about texts, all teachers can integrate problem-solving strategies throughout the curriculum to reinforce these important independent literacy processes.

CONCLUSION

In this chapter we have highlighted findings for U.S. students in the 2009 and 2012 PISA databases to explore the contours of the American educational landscape. Although these data can reveal a great deal about the nature of schooling and learning, like the blind men of Indostan we run the risk of describing only what we can see in these assessment results, while so much more is left out. The challenge has been finding a suitably efficient and yet broad way to understand the system of education in the United States.

Since PISA is intended for adolescents who are approaching the end of compulsory education, it offers one way to gauge the impact of schooling by considering its cumulative effects on American youth. What we learned is that, overall, the American educational system has proven it can endow many of its future citizens with the critical twenty-first-century skills necessary to compete in the global economy and to actively participate as citizens of the world. However, this same system has also revealed its limitations in addressing the needs of a large segment of youth through education. As we have pointed out, any system that elevates the reading and math literacy achievement of its students on such measures as PISA stands to reap economic and societal benefits for decades to come. The United States may be one of the biggest beneficiaries of that kind of systemic effort, not only in large part because of its particularly great divide between the economic haves and have-nots, but also because of the economic potential to be realized through higher achievement in the unquestionably richest of all OECD countries. Thus, those students coming from the lower rungs of the economic ladder are likely to climb the highest and claim a larger share of the nation's vast wealth as their cognitive abilities expand.

REFERENCES

Aikens, N.L., & Barbarin, O. (2008). Socioeconomic differences in reading trajectories: The contribution of family, neighborhood, and school contexts. *Journal of Educational Psychology, 100*(2), 235–251.

Andrews, P., et al. (2014, May 6). OECD and PISA tests are damaging education worldwide. *The Guardian.* Retrieved from http://www.theguardian.com

Baird, J.A., Issacs, T., Johnson, S., Stobart, G., Yu, G., Sprague, T., & Daugherty, R. (2011). *Policy effects of PISA.* Oxford, UK: Oxford University Centre for Educational Assessment.

Benson, J., & Borman, G. (2010). Family, neighborhood, and school settings across seasons: When do socioeconomic context and racial composition matter for the reading achievement growth of young children? *Teachers College Record, 112*(5), 1338–1390.

Berliner, D. (2009). *Poverty and potential: Out-of-school factors and school success.* Boulder, CO: National Education Policy Center.

Best, R., Rowe, M., Ozuru, Y., & McNamara, D. (2005). Deep-level comprehension of science texts: The role of the reader and the text. *Topics in Language Disorders, 25*(1), 65–83.

Bowles, S., & Gintis, H. (2002). Schooling in capitalist America revisited. *Sociology of Education, 75*(1), 1–18.

Brozo, W.G. (2010). *To be a boy, to be a reader* (2nd ed.). Newark, DE: International Reading Association.

Brozo, W.G., & Simpson, M.L. (2007). *Content literacy for today's adolescents: Honoring diversity and building competence.* Upper Saddle River, NJ: Pearson.

Brozo, W.G., Sulkunen, S., Shiel, G., Garbe, C., Pandian, A., & Valtin, R. (2014). Reading, gender, and engagement: Lessons from five PISA countries. *Journal of Adolescent & Adult Literacy, 57*(7), 584–593.

Caccamise, D., & Snyder, L. (2005). Theory and pedagogical practices of text comprehension. *Topics in Language Disorders, 25*(1), 5–20.

Carnoy, M., & Rothstein, R. (2013). *What do international tests really show about U.S. student performance?* Washington, DC: Economics Policy Institute.

Center on Education Policy. (2010). *State test score trends through 2007–08, Part 5: Are there differences in achievement between boys and girls?* Washington, DC: Author.

Chang, H.J. (2011). *23 things they don't tell you about capitalism.* New York: Bloomsbury.

Cragg, L., & Gilmore, C. (2014). Skills underlying mathematics: The role of executive function in the development of mathematics proficiency. *Trends in Neuroscience Education, 3*(2), 63–68.

DiPrete, T.A., & Buchmann, C. (2013). *The rise of women: The growing gender gap in education and what it means for American schools.* New York: Russell Sage Foundation.

Farrant, B., & Zubrick, S. (2012). Early vocabulary development: The importance of joint attention and parent-child book reading. *First Language, 32*(3), 343–364.

Fleischman, H.L., Hopstock, P.J., Pelczar, M.P., & Shelley, B.E. (2010). *Highlights from PISA 2009: Performance of U.S. 15-year-old students in reading, mathematics, and science literacy in an international context* (NCES 2011-004). U.S. Department of Education, National Center for Education Statistics. Washington, DC: U.S. Government Printing Office.

Gates, B. (2009, July 21). *Address to the National Conference of State Legislatures.* Retrieved from www.gatesfoundation.org/media-center/speeches/2009/07/bill-gates-national-conference-of-state-legislatures-ncsl

Gersten, R., Chard, D., Jayathi, M., Baker, S., Morphy, P., & Flojo, J. (2009). *A meta-analysis of mathematics instructional interventions for students with learning disabilities: A technical report.* Los Alamitos, CA: Instructional Research Group.

Goldstein, H. (2004). International comparisons of student attainment: Some issues arising from the PISA study. *Assessment in Education, 11,* 319–330.

Hanushek, E.A., & Woessmann, L. (2010). *The high cost of low educational performance: The long-run economic impact of improving PISA outcomes.* Paris: OECD. Retrieved from www.sourceoecd.org/education/9789264077485

Heckman, J.J., & Kautz, T. (2012). *Hard evidence on soft skills.* Bonn, Germany: Institute for the Study of Labor.

Heckman, J.J., Stixrud, J., & Urzua, S. (2006). The effects of cognitive and noncognitive abilities on labor market outcomes and social behavior. *Journal of Labor Economics, 24*(3), 411–482.

Hernandez, D.J. (2004). Demographic change and the life circumstances of immigrant families. *The Future of Children, 14*(2), 17–47.

Hopstock, P., & Pelczar, M. (2011). *Technical report and user's guide for the Program for International Student Assessment (PISA): 2009 data files and database with U.S. specific variables* (NCES 2011-025). National Center for Education Statistics, Institute of Education Sciences, U.S. Department of Education. Washington, DC: U.S. Government Printing Office. Retrieved from http://nces.ed.gov/surveys/pisa/pdf/2011025.pdf

Kintsch, W., & Kintsch, E. (2005). Comprehension. In S. Paris & S. Stahl (Eds.), *Current issues on reading comprehension and assessment.* Mahwah, NJ: Lawrence Erlbaum.

Klecker, B.M. (2006). The gender gap in NAEP fourth-, eighth-, and twelfth-grade reading scores across years. *Reading Improvement, 43*(1), 50–56.

Ladd, H.F. (2012). Education and poverty: Confronting the evidence. *Journal of Policy Analysis and Management, 31*(2), 203–227.

Learning Metrics Task Force. (2013). *Toward universal learning: What every child should learn.* Montreal and Washington, DC: UNESCO Institute for Statistics/Brookings.

Loveless, T. (2011). *How well are American students learning?* Washington, DC: Brookings Institution.

Lynch, R.G., & Oakford, P. (2014). *The economic benefits of closing educational achievement gaps: Promoting growth and strengthening the nation by improving the educational outcomes of children of color.* Washington, DC: Center for American Progress. Retrieved from https://cdn.americanprogress.org/wpcontent/uploads/2014/11/WinningEconomyReport2.pdf

Marmot, M. (2004). *The status syndrome: How social standing affects our health and longevity.* New York: Owl Books.

Martin, A.J., Anderson, J., Bobis, J., Way, J., & Vellar, R. (2012). Switching on and switching off in mathematics: An ecological study of future intent and disengagement among middle school students. *Journal of Educational Psychology, 104*(1), 1–18.

Meyer, D.K., & Turner, J.C. (2006). Re-conceptualizing emotion and motivation to learn in classroom contexts. *Educational Psychology Review, 18*(4), 377–390.

Milanovic, B. (2012). *The haves and the have-nots: A brief and idiosyncratic history of global inequality.* New York: Basic Books.

Milne, A., & Plourde, L.A. (2006). Factors of a low-SES household: What aids academic achievement? *Journal of Instructional Psychology, 33*(3), 183–193.

Ministry of Education and Culture. (2012). *Announcement of the Joyread program.* [In Finnish]. Retrieved from www.minedu.fi/OPM/Tiedotteet/2012/08/lukuinto.html

Mistry, R.S., Biesanz, J.C., Chien, N., Howes, C., & Benner, A.D. (2008). Socioeconomic status, parental investments, and the cognitive and behavioral outcomes of low-income children from immigrant and native households. *Early Childhood Research Quarterly, 23*(2), 193–212.

Morgan, P.L., Farkas, G, Hillemeier, M.M., & Maczuga S. (2009). Risk factors for learning-related behavior problems at 24 months of age: Population-based estimates. *Journal of Abnormal Child Psychology, 37*(3), 401–413.

National Center for Education Statistics. (2012). *Program for international student assessment (PISA): Mathematics literacy*. Institute of Education Sciences, U.S. Department of Education, Washington, DC. Retrieved from http://nces.ed.gov/surveys/pisa/pisa2012/pisa2012highlights_3.asp

National Center for Education Statistics. (2013). *The nation's report card: Trends in academic progress 2012* (NCES 2013 456). Institute of Education Sciences, U.S. Department of Education, Washington, DC Retrieved from http://nces.ed.gov/nationsreportcard/subject/publications/main2012/pdf/2013456.pdf

National Center for Education Statistics. (2014). *PISA 2012: Data tables, figures, and exhibits*. U.S. Department of Education, Washington, DC. Retrieved from http://nces.ed.gov/pubs2014/2014024_tables.pdf

Obama, B. (2010, February 22). *Address to the National Governors Association*. Washington, DC.

Organisation for Economic Co-operation and Development. (2009). *PISA 2009 assessment framework: Key competencies in reading, mathematics and science*. Paris: Author.

Organisation for Economic Co-operation and Development. (2010a). *The high cost of low educational performance: The long-run economic impact of improving PISA outcomes*. Paris: Author.

Organisation for Economic Co-operation and Development. (2010b). *PISA 2009 results: What students know and can do: Performance in reading, mathematics and science (Volume I)*. Paris: Author.

Organisation for Economic Co-operation and Development. (2013a). *OECD skills outlook 2013: First results from the survey of adult skills*. Paris: Author.

Organisation for Economic Co-operation and Development. (2013b). *PISA 2012 results: Ready to learn (vol. III): Students' engagement, drive and self-beliefs*. Paris: Author.

Organisation for Economic Co-operation and Development. (2013c). *PISA 2012 results: Excellence through equity: Giving every student the chance to succeed (Volume II)*. Paris: Author.

Organisation for Economic Co-operation and Development. (2014). *PISA 2012 results: What students know and can do: Student performance in mathematics, reading and science* (Vol. 1, rev. ed., February 2014). Paris: Author.

Organisation for Economic Co-operation and Development. (2015). *The ABC of gender equality in education: Aptitude, behaviour, confidence*. Paris: OECD Publishing.

Pintrich, P.R., & Schunk, D.H. (2002). *Motivation in education: Theory, research, and applications* (2nd ed.). Englewood Cliffs, NJ: Merrill.

Pressley, M., & Hilden, K. (2004). Toward more ambitious comprehension instruction. In E. Silliman & L. Wilkinson (Eds.), *Language and literacy learning in schools*. New York: Guilford.

Rauch, D.P., & Hartig, J. (2010). Multiple-choice versus open-ended response formats of reading test items: A two-dimensional IRT analysis. *Psychological Test and Assessment Modeling, 52*(4), 354–379.

Ravitch, D. (2010). *The death and life of the great American school system: How testing and choice are undermining education*. New York: Basic Books.

Reich, R. (2011). *Aftershock: The next economy and America's future*. New York: Vintage.

Resmovits, J. (2013, October 8). *OECD skills test: U.S. adults lag in practical workplace skills*. Retrieved from http://www.huffingtonpost.com

Rosli, R., Capraro, M.M., & Capraro, R.M. (2014). The effects of problem posing on student mathematical learning: A meta-analysis. *International Education Studies, 7*(13), 227–241.

Rueben, K., & Murray, S. (2008). *Racial disparities in education finance: Going beyond equal revenues.* Washington, DC: The Urban Institute. Retrieved from http://www.urban.org/Uploaded-PDF/411785_equal_revenues.pdf

Saxe, J.G. (1963). *The blind men and the elephant.* New York: McGraw-Hill.

Schiff, R., & Lotem, E. (2011). Effects of phonological and morphological awareness on children's word reading development from two socioeconomic backgrounds. *First Language, 31*(2), 139–163.

Singh, K., Granville, M., & Dika, S. (2002). Mathematics and science achievement: Effects of motivation, interest, and academic engagement. *Journal of Educational Research, 95*(6), 323–332.

Spring, J. (2013). *American education.* New York: McGraw-Hill.

Stoet, G., & Geary, D.C. (2013). Sex differences in mathematics and reading achievement are inversely related: Within- and across-nation assessment of 10 years of PISA data. *PLoS ONE, 8*(3), 1–10: e57988. doi:10.1371/journal.pone.0057988

Su, R., Rounds, J., & Armstrong, P.I. (2009). Men and things, women and people: A meta-analysis of sex differences in interests. *Psychological Bulletin, 135*(6), 859–884.

Taylor, L., & Parsons, J. (2011). Improving student engagement. *Current Issues in Education, 14*(1). Retrieved from http://cie.asu.edu/

Turner, J., & Meyer, D. (2009). Understanding motivation in mathematics: What is happening in classrooms? In K.R. Wenzel & A. Wigfield (Eds.), *Handbook of motivation at school* (pp. 527–552). New York: Routledge.

U.S. Bureau of Labor Statistics. (2013). *Employment projections: Fastest growing occupations.* Washington, DC.

U.S. Department of Education. (2012). *Gender equity in education: A data snapshot—June 2012.* Retrieved from http://www2.ed.gov/about/offices/list/ocr/docs/gender-equity-in-education.pdf

U.S. Department of Education. (2013). *Digest of education statistics.* Retrieved from http://nces.ed.gov/programs/digest/d13/tables/dt13_203.50.asp?current=yes

Van de Werfhorst, H.G., & Mijs, J.J.B. (2010). Achievement inequality and the institutional structure of educational systems: A comparative perspective. *Annual Review of Sociology, 36*(1), 407–428.

CHAPTER FOUR

Japan

The High-Achieving Educational System of Japan

LAWRENCE BAINES AND MANO YASUDA

For many years, students from Japan have been among the highest-performing students in the world on international tests, particularly in mathematics and science. "Among OECD countries, Japan is now ranked second in mathematics performance and first in...science performance" (Organisation for Economic Cooperation and Development [OECD], 2014c, p. 1). Recently, the scores posted by Japanese students in reading and problem solving have improved to the extent that they now also rank among the highest in the world in those areas (OCED, 2014a).

Similarly, on the 2011 administration of the TIMSS international mathematics test for fourth and eighth graders, Japanese students ranked among the top performers, just below marks set by students from Singapore, Hong Kong, Korea, and Taipei (Mullis, Martin, Foy, & Arora, 2012). Perhaps one of the most remarkable aspects of Japanese success is that high performance is not the result of a few high achievers but is distributed throughout the system. For example, in the most recent administration assessing problem-solving skills of 15-year-olds, PISA found that only 7% of Japanese students scored below level 2 on the assessment, compared to 18% of American students (National Center for Education Statistics, 2014). Of Japanese 15-year-olds, 22% scored level 5 or above, compared to 12% of American 15-year-olds.

As the Center on International Education Benchmarking (2014) notes, "As long as there have been international comparisons of national student achievement, Japan has placed at or near the top" (p. 1). Over the past decade, East Asian countries have consistently dominated international rankings, with Singapore and Korea typically in the lead, and Japan and China Taipei not far behind (Mullis et al., 2012).

In terms of global competitiveness, the World Economic Forum ranked Japan 6th (Schwab, 2014, p. 13), and Cornell University ranked Japan 21st of 143 countries on the global innovation index (Cornell University, INSEAD, & WIPO, 2014, p. xxiv). Despite such lofty levels of achievement, many Japanese are highly critical of the nation's educational policies. Fujita and Dawson (2007) comment: "Japanese schools and teachers, especially public schools and their teachers, have been under relentless attack from various stakeholders since the 1980s" (p. 50). Willis, Yamamura, and Rappleye (2008) note that criticisms over "lack of creativity and imagination, not to mention the dearth of Nobel Prizes, a point of wounded national pride, has people seriously worried" (pp. 496–497). Even a recent report from OECD (2010) on the highest-achieving school systems in the world acknowledged the furor over the state of public education in Japan:

> Over the last two decades, there has been a rising chorus of criticism about Japan's education system, especially concerns over a deficit in encouraging creativity and innovation and whether Japan can maintain its top place in the international league table of student achievement. Other concerns center on an apparent erosion of moral and group values. (p. 147)

Data on the attitudes of Japanese students indicate that they experience more anxiety, enjoy learning less, and have lower confidence in their abilities than students in other countries. In contrast, students in the United States are less anxious, enjoy learning more, have higher confidence in their abilities, but perform at lower levels (OECD, 2013).

As a recent document states, one of the functions of the Ministry of Education, Culture, Sports, Science, and Technology (MEXT) is to inculcate in students the importance of exerting great individual effort for the betterment of the local community and the nation:

Through the steadfast efforts of each and every individual citizen, education in Japan realizes the ideal of equal opportunity, raises the education standards of the nation, and responds to the needs of the times while making significant contributions to the development of society. (Ministry of Education, Culture, Sports, Science, and Technology [MEXT], 2014c, p. 1)

ATTITUDES TOWARD EDUCATION

When students do not perform well in school in Japan, their failure is more than just an individual disappointment; it is a blow to the stature of the entire family, especially the mother. Conversely, when students do well, they advance the family name and reputation. As a professor of sociology at Komazawa University in Tokyo has noted, "The social status of parents is related to their child-rearing and child's education" (Pasion, 2014, p. 1). In this way, academic success is inextricably linked to "saving face."

Perhaps as a result of the importance of performance in school, truancy in Japan is rare. Students in Japanese schools tend to be punctual and are unlikely to be disruptive. Most Japanese students reported that they listen to what the teacher says; 90% of Japanese students agree that noise or disorder never or rarely disrupts learning (OECD, 2009). Overall, Japan has the "best disciplinary climate...among students in all other OECD countries," and it continues to improve (OECD, 2013, p. 7). The remarkable compliance among students derives not only from pressure from parents, but also from the meticulous record keeping of teachers. In Japan, a student's record describes not only grade point average and academic performance, but also detailed comments on attendance, participation in extracurricular activities, behavior, and attitude. At every level of schooling, schools require students to submit school reports as part of the admission process. Thus, students who misbehave, who do not participate in extracurricular activities, or who exhibit poor manners significantly decrease their chances of getting into the better schools.

The Japanese constitution states that education is both a right and a duty. Children have the right to receive an education, and it is the parents/guardians who should provide the best education possible. Homeschooling does not exist in Japan, unless extreme circumstances require a child to be housebound.

Education is compulsory for grades 1–9 (Ellington, 2005), and public schools are free except for the cost of lunch or extracurricular activities such as field trips. Municipalities and private sources pay for kindergarten, but national, prefectural (similar to state or provincial), and local governments pay almost equal shares of costs for students in grades 1–9.

Textbooks are free as well. Interestingly, MEXT pledges to provide free textbooks to Japanese children, no matter where they might live. Thus, a Japanese family living in the United States could contact the nearest Japanese Embassy and request that textbooks be sent to them.

EARLY CHILDHOOD EDUCATION

Although compulsory education officially starts at age 6, children are introduced to schooling at a relatively young age. Of Japanese 3-year-olds, 77% attend half-day kindergarten or go to childcare centers, and 93% of 4-year-olds attend kindergarten or childcare centers (OECD, 2013). Japanese kindergartens have distinctive programs with classes grouped by age: 3-year-olds, 4-year-olds, and 5-year-olds. Kindergartens are regulated by the Ministry of Education, Culture, Sports, Science, and Technology and are inclined to be concerned with academic preparation for elementary schools. Most students in MEXT-regulated kindergartens attend for only half a day.

On the other hand, most childcare centers in Japan offer all-day programs and tend to focus on "general care." The Ministry of Health, Labor, and Welfare (MHLW) monitors these centers. See Table 4.1 for a comparison of kindergarten and childcare centers in Japan.

Table 4.1. Comparison of Kindergarten and Childcare Centers (OECD, 2014b).

Variable	Kindergarten	Childcare center
Age	From age 3 to 6 (before entering primary school)	From age 0 to 6 (before entering primary school) Eligibility for children with needs for care is determined by municipal governments.
Childcare Time	4 hours a day	8 hours a day
Legal Foundation	School Education Act	Child Welfare Act
Governing Body	Ministry of Education, Culture, Sports, Science and Technology (MEXT)	Ministry of Health, Labor and Welfare (MHLW)
Standards	National Curriculum Standards for Kindergartens	Day Care Guidelines
Number of Children	1,706,000 (2007) Public: 338,000 Private: 1,368,000	2,016,000 (2007) Public: 945,000 Private: 1,071,000
Number of Facilities	14,000 (2007) Public: 5,500 Private: 8,500	23,000 (2007) Public: 12,000 Private: 11,000

Parents usually apply to the local municipality for licensed childcare centers and pay 40% of the costs, while the government pays the remaining 60% (OECD, 2012b). Despite Japan's having over 37,000 facilities, some families, particularly in urban areas such as Tokyo, have difficulty finding openings for their children in government-approved centers. "Because of the shortage of licensed facilities,

233,000 children were cared for in 11,153 unlicensed centers (recognized and unrecognized) in 2009" (Jones, 2011, p. 11). However, a facility being unlicensed does not necessarily mean that the quality of care is subpar. Instead, being unlicensed means that the facility does not meet all of the criteria set by the government, such as the size of the property, location, or recommended student/teacher ratio.

In 2006, the government began to develop Centers for Early Childhood Education and Care (ECEC), a program that merges academic preparation with more holistic approaches to childcare and is jointly regulated by MEXT and MHLW. One of the purposes of the ECEC was to provide all-day care and flexible hours for a family in which either or both parents work. Although parents generally give high marks to ECECs, such centers are more complicated to operate and have thus been slow to launch (OECD, 2012b).

In general, kindergartens and childcare centers that offer early care in Japan are well equipped with gymnasiums, swimming pools, pianos, and televisions, and they are generally of good quality. All kindergartens and childcare centers require that teachers hold teaching certificates. In a comparative study of approaches to early childhood education, Nagayama and Gilliard (2005) found that American early childhood teachers focused on creating activities based on the needs and talents of the individual child, while Japanese early childhood teachers focused on "promoting community and regard for others" (p. 137).

PRIVATE SCHOOLS

Despite large numbers of young children under the age of six enrolled in private kindergarten or daycare centers, only 1% of primary and 7% of middle-grade students attend private schools. Enrollments in private schools surge again during the teen years, when about one-third of students go to private high schools. Private school enrollment increases to 80% for students enrolling in universities and junior colleges, and to 90% for students enrolling in specialized training colleges (MEXT, 2014a). In urban areas such as Tokyo, private schools may be chosen because they feature a specific curriculum or have a more prestigious reputation than public options. In rural areas, however, private schools tend to be for students who cannot meet the rigorous criteria of nearby public schools (M. Yasuda, personal communication, January 15, 2015).

The government pays about half the salaries of all teachers in private schools. According to MEXT (2014a):

> Private schools play important roles, both qualitatively and quantitatively, in the development of Japan's school education. Accordingly, MEXT positions the promotion of private

schools as an important policy goal, under which it strives to maintain and improve these schools' educational and research conditions and reduce the financial burden of learning for students and pupils enrolled there. (p. 5)

Indeed, private schools perform an essential role in the Japanese educational system. Perhaps the biggest problem with regard to private schools is that they are not available in all parts of Japan.

STRUCTURE OF THE SCHOOL

As in most OECD member countries, students in Japan enter first grade around age six. In most schools, the day begins around 8:30 a.m. with 15 minutes of announcements in homeroom or a school assembly. Because schools do not provide transportation, students walk, ride with their parents, or take public trains or buses from home to school. Classes last around 45 minutes, and students receive breaks of 5 or 10 minutes between classes. Lunch usually begins around 12:30 p.m. and lasts for 40 minutes. Many elementary schools include a 20-minute recess every day, although sometimes recess is combined with time spent cleaning and organizing the classroom. (Japanese children are expected to clean their classrooms every day.)

For most students in grades 1–3, school ends after lunch. Students in grades 4–6 take an additional class or two, so school lasts until 3:00 or 4:00 p.m. Students in elementary school usually participate in a club or extracurricular activity after school once or twice per week. In middle school (grades 7–9) and high school (grades 10–12), students often stay longer and more frequently after school to participate in sports and clubs. In most schools, students remain in one classroom and teachers rotate from room to room over the course of the school day.

Prior to April 2002, students in public schools in Japan (from elementary to high school) attended school 6 days per week, Monday to Saturday. In 2002, in an effort to reduce student stress and increase innovation, MEXT announced a policy of *Yutori Kyoiku*, meaning "pressure-free education." This translated into no formal study at school on Saturdays, though students and teachers continued to participate in extracurricular activities such as sports (baseball, soccer) or clubs (band, dance) on Saturdays (Takayama, 2007).

Despite the prohibition against academic classes on Saturdays, as many as half of the public schools in Tokyo have held classes at least one Saturday per month since 2010, using the loophole that a school could hold Saturday school if there existed a "special need" (Shimbun, 2013). An advantage of private schools is that they could legally ignore the "five-day rule" imposed on public schools. Many private schools never shifted to the 5-day school week (Fish, 2014).

Japanese students spend many days at school, and holidays tend to be brief. In 1971, Japanese law established that "the minimum number of school days per year is prescribed as 240" (Ministry of Education, Culture, Sports, Science, and Technology, 2014b). Although the number of days that Japanese children attend school remains among the highest in the world, students do not spend all of their time listening to class lectures. One goal of the Second Basic Plan, ratified in 2013, was for "each and every individual to engage proactively with learning aimed at independence, collaboration and creativity" (MEXT, 2014c, p. 15).

In 2011, MEXT set the maximum size of a first-grade class in elementary school at 35 students (Ministry of Education, Culture, Sports, Science, and Technology, 2014a, p. 3). Average class size in all grades of elementary school is around 26 students; average class size at the secondary level is around 31 students (Jones, 2011, p. 12), though the number of students per classroom is frequently higher in urban schools.

THE CURRICULUM

All aspects of the curriculum are regulated in Japan, from the activities suggested for 3-year-olds in public kindergarten to the teaching of advanced mathematics in high school. MEXT, in collaboration with faculty in higher education and the Central Council for Education, establishes the content of what is taught in Japanese schools. "The curriculum for each grade level is carefully calibrated to pick up each year where the previous grade left off, and to ensure preparation for the following grade" (National Center on Education and the Economy, 2014, p. 1). As a result, Japanese schools do not face abrupt changes to the curriculum, common in some American schools, when budget cuts force the closure of "nonessential" programs in art, music, and physical education.

In the primary grades, the required curriculum includes moral education, the Japanese language, social studies, mathematics, and science. Art, music, homemaking, physical education, and literature are also mandated. A new law ratified in 2011 required that English be taught beginning in grade five, though subsequently MEXT has recommended that the teaching of English be moved down to grade three by 2020. A typical schedule for primary school is described in Table 4.2.

Table 4.2. Typical Schedule for Primary School (National Institute for Educational Policy Research, 2012, p. 2).

Time	Event
8:00–8:30	Arrive at school
8:30–8:40	Morning assembly for the entire school
8:40–9:25	1st class
9:30–10:15	2nd class
10:15–10:35	Break
10:35–11:20	3rd class
11:25–12:20	4th class
12:25–12:55	Lunch
12:55–1:35	Lunch break (students clean the classroom and/or building)
1:35–2:20	5th class
2:25–3:10	6th class
2:20–2:30	End of the day homeroom for students with 5 classes
3:10–3:20	End of the day homeroom for students with 6 classes
3:30	Dismissal
3:30–5:00	Clubs or extracurricular activities

The National Institute for Educational Policy Research (2012) states the following:

> In most cases, a first-grader's school week consists of four days with five school hours and one day with four school hours, and for second-graders, every school day has five school hours. Generally, a third-grader's week has three days with five school-hours and two days with six school-hours, and fourth- to sixth-graders usually have two days with five school hours and three days with six school hours. The number of classes varies in accordance with the difference in total school hours laid out in the Course of Study. (p. 2)

The number of hours spent per subject is also regulated by MEXT. The annual number of hours spent per subject is established by grade level and is shown in Table 4.3.

Table 4.3. School Hours by Subject and Grade in Japanese Primary Schools (National Institute for Educational Policy Research, 2012, p. 9)

Subject	Grade 1	Grade 2	Grade 3	Grade 4	Grade 5	Grade 6
Japanese (language)	306	315	245	245	175	175
Social studies	0	0	70	90	100	105
Mathematics	136	175	175	175	175	175
Science	0	0	90	105	105	105
Living environment studies	102	105	0	0	0	0
Music	68	70	60	60	50	50
Arts and handicrafts	68	70	60	60	50	50
Home economics	0	0	0	0	60	55
Physical education	102	105	105	105	90	90
Moral education	34	35	35	35	35	35
Special activities	34	35	35	35	35	35
Integrated studies	0	0	70	70	70	70
Foreign language activities (usually English)	0	0	0	0	35	35
Total school hours	850	910	945	980	980	980

Education reforms established in 2002 (*yutori*) reduced the amount of time devoted to core subjects, shortened the school day, and introduced "integrated studies," which offered contemporary, often multidisciplinary approaches to learning. Subsequent reforms in 2011 increased the amount of time devoted to core subjects, lengthened the school day, and reduced the time allotted to integrated studies (Fish, 2014).

SPECIAL EDUCATION

The Japanese education system tends to segregate students with disabilities (Jordan, 2009). Most Japanese children with special needs are taught in designated schools exclusively for them (*Tokubetsu-Shien-gakko*), though since the establishment of new policies in 2007, there seems to be some effort to provide services for select special-needs students in separate classrooms within schools or, in cases of mild disability, in regular classrooms.

In a recent qualitative study of special-needs students with mild disabilities, all the children who were observed asked to be removed from the regular classroom and placed in an environment with other special-needs children (Kayama & Haight, 2012). The researchers attributed the children's decision to attend classes apart from their peers in mainstream classrooms to an awareness of each child's *kokoro* (heart and mind). However, the pressure to conform to norms within a classroom and the disgrace associated with failing to do well in school certainly contribute to the motivation of these students to leave the highly competitive classroom.

THE LIFE OF A TEACHER

It is telling that, when the idea of public education emerged in Japan, most of the nation's first teachers were samurai, or came from the samurai class. Perhaps this heritage is one reason that the job of a teacher has always carried very high status (National Center on Education and the Economy, 2014). Having samurai roots may be one reason that more Japanese males choose the teaching profession in comparison to men in other countries. In 2011, men comprised 35% of teachers in primary schools, 58% of teachers in lower secondary schools, 72% of teachers in upper secondary schools, and 81% of faculty in postsecondary institutions (OECD, 2013). The prestige of the profession is enhanced by a law that requires teachers to be among the highest-paid civil servants in Japan. As a result, beginning teachers are paid about the same as beginning engineers (OECD, 2013). The usual career trajectory is from teacher to head teacher and from head teacher to principal. MEXT has established 36 steps leading to salary increases for teachers; 20 steps within the rank of head teacher; and 15 different salary steps for principals. In general, teachers' salaries rise sharply as years of experience increase (OECD, 2013, p. 10).

The process of becoming a teacher is highly competitive and quite rigorous. Only about 14% of applicants gain admission to schools of education. The National Entrance Exam for admission to undergraduate teacher preparation programs assesses five fields: Japanese language, foreign language (usually English), mathematics, science, and social studies. In addition to the requisite admission tests, teachers must pass exams on subject-area knowledge and pedagogical techniques once they complete their course of study. Students who successfully pass exams and manage to graduate serve a 3-week teaching internship before graduation. Elementary/middle school teachers serve an additional weeklong nursing internship. Because of the tight job market and falling birth rates, only about one in three graduates of teacher preparation programs actually lands a job as teachers after the internship (Ikuo, 2014). Aspiring teachers must also pass a battery of exams created by prefectural school boards as part of their consideration for employment. Most school boards also require interviews, the submission of essays, and demonstration lessons before an offer of employment is made (OECD, 2013).

Once hired, all first-year teachers are required to spend a year under the mentorship of a veteran teacher, who is relieved of additional duties to focus on the professional development of the first-year teacher. Prefectural boards of education may require daily in-service training and further education for teachers at 5, 10, and 20 years of service. A new system implemented by MEXT in 2009 requires teachers to demonstrate that they are current in their content knowledge.

While teachers in Italy, the Netherlands, and the United States typically spend more than 1,000 hours teaching over the course of a year, teachers in Japan, on average, teach for 731 hours at the primary level, 602 hours at the lower secondary level, and 510 hours at the upper secondary level (OECD, 2013). Despite teaching for fewer hours, Japanese teachers spend more total time at school than teachers in almost any other country. Japanese teachers usually spend additional hours supervising student activities, completing administrative chores, planning lessons with colleagues, and counseling students (Arani, Fukaya, & Lassegard, 2010). Instead of having desks in individual classrooms or in private offices, teachers share space in a large, comfortable community room. This faculty room (*shokuin shitsu*) is a designated space where teachers congregate to plan lessons, grade papers, call parents, and get "advice from administrators and veteran colleagues" (Ahn, 2014, p. 50).

Attrition among teachers in Japan is quite low, with only about 1% leaving the profession at the end of their first year. The relatively high pay and high prestige of the occupation in Japan help keep the profession attractive. However, the workload of teaching can sometimes be staggering. For example, when an adolescent has a run-in with the police, the teacher and the parents are likely to be contacted, and all are expected to respond. As Tsuneyoshi (2001) has noted, "when the classroom teacher is in charge of the entire child, both mind and body, with the added pressures of new problems, the load can be overwhelming" (p. 113). Regarding the workload of a teacher, a recent blog by a teacher in rural Japan commented, "Teachers are here by 7 a.m. and don't leave until 6:30–7 p.m. Then there's Saturday...4 hours on Sat. So, it's more like 55–60 hour work weeks" (Kairosity, 2014, p. 1).

ENTRANCE EXAMS

One reason that students take school so seriously in Japan is the presence of high stakes at every level. Passing tests determines admission to secondary and post-secondary institutions, which in turn clarifies possible career options, which in turn determines salary and social class. Although entrance exams are required for most schools, including private elementary schools or kindergartens, the two most important exams that everyone takes are for admission into high schools and universities.

Public high schools are ranked by academic reputation, with the most prestigious high schools admitting only students with the highest scores on the exams prepared by the board of education of the prefectural regions. Private high schools prepare their own exams for students. In general, the complexity and difficulty of exams correspond to the individual school's academic ranking. Similarly, universities are ranked according to their reputation, with the University of Tokyo having the most stature and, thus, the most stringent admission requirements.

There are seven possibilities for students after completing the high school entrance exam at age 15 (MEXT, 2014b):

1. A student enrolls in a public high school (about 62%)
2. A student enrolls in a private high school (about 27%)
3. A student takes courses online or through correspondence (about 5%)
4. A student enrolls in a school for students with special needs (about 2%)
5. A student enrolls in a college of technology, specializing in a program such as engineering (about 1%)
6. A student enrolls in a specialized training college that might emphasize job preparation in the fields of health/medicine, technology, business, personal care and nutrition, fashion and home science, or agriculture (about 1%)
7. A student starts working in a job or becomes unemployed (about 2% of Japanese students leave school at age 15)

Because so much depends upon the students' performance on tests, after-hours tutoring for students, or *juku*, is a common practice. The most popular subject areas for *juku* are the Japanese language, mathematics, and English (*The Economist*, 2011). *Juku* extends the curriculum well beyond what is covered in schools and is designed to help students perform well on entrance exams, especially those of high-ranking high schools. Since students are required to submit transcripts when applying for schools, it is important for them to maintain high grades and good behavior.

More than 20 business firms that offer *juku* are large and wealthy enough to issue shares of stock that are traded on the Tokyo stock exchange. About the widespread acceptance of *juku*, *The Economist* (2011) comments:

> Almost one in five children in their first year of primary school attends after-class instruction, rising to nearly all university-bound high schoolers. The fees are around ¥260,000 ($3,300) annually. School and university test-scores rise in direct proportion to spending on juku. (para. 2)

Of course, the intensity and duration of *juku* are widely variable, depending upon the student, parents, and family income. Nevertheless, most Japanese students devote long hours to study after the school day officially ends (*The Economist*, 2011).

CONCLUSION

A visitor to Japanese schools from Europe or North America would find much on the surface that seems familiar. Students wear uniforms, sit in rows, and listen to a teacher, who typically directs instruction from the front of a classroom. Class periods usually last between 45 and 60 minutes. The system is set up so that students participate in a logical progression from one grade level to another, based upon their age and relative performance. Early childhood education segues into elementary, which transitions to secondary and postsecondary schooling with crucial, high-stakes exams as gatekeepers in between.

Despite superficial resemblances, schools in Japan are distinctively and irrepressibly Japanese. Unlike the relatively chaotic and decentralized systems of education in the United States, the Japanese system, reliant upon the rulings of MEXT, is stable and centralized. As a result, the delivery of curriculum, the education of teachers, and the expectations for students are set at the national level. In most states in the United States, the quality of education varies by the income of the parents who live in the neighborhoods near a school. Consequently, a child who grows up in Silicon Valley in California can attend a posh, well-manicured neighborhood school that regularly knocks the top off exam scores and sponsors field trips to the Galapagos, while a child who grows up in the ranchlands only a few miles to the east may be educated in dilapidated buildings and have no access to drinkable water (Baines, 2014).

Such blatant discrimination against poor children would not be tolerated in Japan. In fact, Japan is one of only 16 OECD countries in which socioeconomically disadvantaged schools actually have lower student-teacher ratios than socioeconomically advantaged schools (OECD, 2012a, p. 6). In addition, teachers in Japan rotate to different schools over the course of their careers, usually every 7 years or so (OECD, 2013). In this way, brilliant teachers are not concentrated in the richest schools, as sometimes happens in the American and European systems of schooling. Rather, brilliant teachers are distributed among rich and poor areas throughout the country.

In the United States, charter schools are proliferating (Powell, 2014). In San Diego, the Iftin Charter School admits students who are of the Muslim faith and mostly from Somalia. The By the Hand Charter School in Chicago is funded by an evangelical Christian organization that provides both Bible lessons and after-school snacks. Although the state of Michigan has struggled with budgetary shortfalls over the past few decades, it spent over $1 billion supporting charter schools in 2014, though many of the publicly supported charter schools are among the lowest-performing schools in the nation and have been among the lowest-performing schools in the nation for more than a decade (*Detroit Free Press*, 2014).

The Chief Executive Officer of the largest charter school operator in the United States paid himself about $3.6 million in 2014 and hired his wife as chief academic officer (Education Matters, 2014). Yet state governments, with the fiscal support of the federal government, continue to urge the fragmentation of public education through charter school expansion.

Of course, any Japanese educator would be aghast at both the disjointed, wildly variable forms of schooling funded through taxpayer dollars and the way that legislators in the United States have subcontracted the education of children to profiteers. MEXT ensures that all children have access to quality teachers, stresses the importance of community, and promotes the power of individual student effort. On the other hand, in the United States, charter schools create their own curriculum, stress widely divergent goals, and focus upon the predilections of their founders.

Another striking difference between education in Japan and education in other countries is the difference in expectations for teachers. In Japan, only the best students are accepted into teacher preparation programs. Prospective teachers in Japan must pass rigorous tests, repeatedly demonstrate their teaching skills, and undergo several high-pressure interviews. Even if they succeed in all these areas, however, they still might not get hired. All teachers in Japan, no matter where or what they teach, are well educated and well paid (National Center on Education and the Economy, 2014).

In some parts of the United States, any college graduate can become a teacher—and can do so almost instantaneously. In Texas, more than half of all new teachers are alternatively certified, and alternative certification is sold on the open market by for-profit businesses as if it were laundry detergent (Baines, 2010b). Billboards along the highways in Texas compete to sell their online teacher certification as the cheapest and easiest route available with slogans like "Want to teach? When can you start?" Recent laws passed in Indiana and New Mexico allow anyone with a bachelor's degree in any discipline to teach; in Kentucky, veterans with bachelor's degrees who want to teach are offered teaching certificates without having to take a course in pedagogy or engage in any sort of teacher training (Baines, 2010a).

Stellar teacher preparation programs exist in the United States, and they are usually similar in length and rigor to teacher preparation programs in Japan, which means that they are also relatively costly. As teacher pay remains low in most parts of the United States, quick and easy alternative certification programs continue to grow in popularity, despite the evidence that alternative certification brings with it corresponding decreases in student performance and trivialization of the teaching profession (Baines, 2010b; Vasquez Heilig & Jez, 2014).

Of course, not everything about education in Japan is ideal. By its nature, MEXT is a huge bureaucracy that must serve multiple constituents and fulfill manifold responsibilities. Any change in curriculum or policy must be communicated years in advance and implemented gradually. Thus, the Japanese government announced in 2013 that it would move the beginning of English instruction from fifth grade to third grade in 2020 (Yoshida, 2013). That is, MEXT gave teachers 7 years' warning of the possible change in curriculum. While consistency is important, one of the shortcomings of a large bureaucracy is that it may not be particularly nimble.

Although MEXT's heavy emphasis on high achievement promotes high performance, it is less effective in other areas. For example, bullying is a widespread problem in Japanese schools, despite repeated efforts by MEXT to cultivate tolerance and acceptance among children (McCurry, 2013).

Finally, the complaint that Japanese students are relatively less creative than some of their counterparts in other parts of the world probably has some legitimacy. After all, Japanese students in general study diligently while at school, participate in a variety of extracurricular activities, and then spend myriad hours in *juku*, sometimes until 9 or 10 p.m., 5 or 6 nights a week (*The Economist*, 2011). Surviving the workload and the mounting pressures of academic performance are sufficiently taxing. There may be little time or energy left for chasing the ephemeral muse of creativity.

After World War II, the United States acted as Japan's advisor as that nation created a new K–12 educational system. The *Report of the United States Education Mission to Japan* (U.S. Department of State, 1946), published shortly after the end of the war, excoriated Japan's previous educational system as elitist and restrictive and chastised the Japanese for allowing the intrusion of religion and politics into schools. In particular, the *Mission Report* criticized the Japanese because their previous system of education

1. "Prepared different types of education for the masses and the privileged minority class,"
2. Ignored "differences of ability and interest among students,"
3. "Reduced the opportunities for teachers to exercise their professional freedom," and
4. Established a "yardstick of efficiency" based upon "how far standardization and uniformity was ensured" (Aso & Amano, 1972, pp. 64–65).

Over the past 70 years, Japan's new democratic educational system has flourished and become one of the strongest in the world. On the other hand, the United States has taken four practices characterized as "malicious" by American consultants in the *Mission Report*—elitism, lack of differentiated instruction, reduced freedom for teachers, standardization and uniformity—and made them the cornerstone of American education reform for the twenty-first century. In response to waning American achievement and fading student enthusiasm, politicians in the United States have chosen not to abandon these four reprehensible practices, but to "double down" on them, with predictably disastrous results.

REFERENCES

Ahn, R. (2014, May). How Japan supports novice teachers. *Educational Leadership*, 49–53.

Arani, M., Fukaya, K., & Lassegard, J. (2010). "Lesson study" as professional culture in Japanese schools: An historical perspective on elementary classroom practices. *Japan Review*, 22, 171–200.

Aso, M., & Amano, I. (1972). *Education and Japan's modernization*. Tokyo: Ministry of Foreign Affairs.

Baines, L.A. (2010a). The disintegration of teacher certification. *Educational Horizons*, 88(3), 152–163.

Baines, L.A. (2010b). *The teachers we need, the teachers we have*. Lanham, MD: Rowman & Littlefield.

Baines, L.A. (2014). Public education: For richer, for poorer. *Teachers College Record*. Retrieved from http://www.tcrecord.org, ID Number: 17707.

Center on International Education Benchmarking. (2014). *Japan overview*. Retrieved from http://www.ncee.org/programs-affiliates/center-on-international-education-benchmarking/top-performing-countries/japan-overview/

Cornell University, INSEAD, and WIPO. (2014). *The Global innovation index 2014: The human factor in innovation*. Geneva, Switzerland: World Intellectual Property Organization (WIPO).

Detroit Free Press. (2014). *State of charter schools: How Michigan spends $1 billion but fails to hold schools accountable*. (*Free Press* special report). Retrieved from http://www.freep.com/article/20140622/NEWS06/140507009/State-of-charter-schools-How-Michigan-spends-1-billion-but-fails-to-hold-schools-accountable

The Economist. (2011, December 31). *Japan's cramming schools: Testing times*. Retrieved from http://www.economist.com/node/21542222

Education Matters. (2014). *Sherry Hage stands up for her man and for her charter schools too*. Retrieved from http://jaxkidsmatter.blogspot.com/2014/06/sherry-hage-stands-up-for-her-man-and.html

Ellington, L. (2005). *Japanese education*. National Clearinghouse for United States-Japan studies. Retrieved from www.indiana.edu/~japan/digest5.html

Fish, R. (2014). *Japan: Recent trends in education reform*. Asia Society website. Retrieved from http:asiasociety.org/japan-recent-trends-education-reform

Fujita, H., & Dawson, W. (2007). The qualifications of the teaching force in Japan. In R. Ingersoll (Ed.), *A comparative study of teacher preparation and qualifications in six nations* (pp. 41–54). Philadelphia, PA: Consortium for policy research in education.

Ikuo, A. (2014, March 11). *Globalization and higher education reforms in Japan*. Nippon.com. Retrieved from http://www.nippon.com/en/in-depth/a02801/

Jones, R. (2011). *Education reform in Japan*. OECD Economics Department Working Papers, no. 888. Paris, France: OECD.

Jordan, S. (2009, June 24). Perspectives on special education in Japan. *Teacher Magazine*. Retrieved from http://www.edweek.org/tm/section/first-person/2009/06/24/tm_sjordan_web.h20.html

Kairosity. (2014). *On the Asian school structure: Or, why 6-day weeks would be bad*. Retrieved from http://kairosity.tumblr.com/post/44271823031/on-the-asian-school-structure-or-why-6-day-weeks

Kayama, M., & Haight, W. (2012). The experiences of Japanese elementary-school children living with "developmental disabilities." *Qualitative Social Work, 12*(5), 555–571.

McCurry, J. (2013, May 9). Long troubled by school bullying, Japan now eyes zero tolerance. *Christian Science Monitor*. Retrieved from http://www.csmonitor.com/World/Asia-Pacific/2013/0509/Long-troubled-by-school-bullying-Japan-now-eyes-zero-tolerance

Ministry of Education, Culture, Sports, Science, and Technology. (2014a). *2012 white paper on education, culture, sports, science and technology*. Retrieved from http://www.mext.go.jp/b_menu/hakusho/html/hpab201201/detail/1345171.htm

Ministry of Education, Culture, Sports, Science, and Technology. (2014b). *Table 26. Number of weekly teaching hours, and number of school weeks and days a year in various major countries*. Retrieved from http://www.mext.go.jp/b_menu/hakusho/html/hpae197101/hpae197101_2_035.html

Ministry of Education, Culture, Sports, Science, and Technology. (2014c). *2012 white paper on education, culture, sports, science and technology*: Special feature 1: Toward implementation of educational rebuilding. Retrieved from http://www.mext.go.jp/b_menu/hakusho/html/hpab201201/detail/1344908.htm

Mullis, I., Martin, M., Foy, P., & Arora, A. (2012). *TIMSS 2011 international results in mathematics*. Chestnut Hill, MA: TIMSS & PRILS International Study Center, Lynch School of Education, Boston College. International Association for the Evaluation of Educational Achievement.

Nagayama, M., & Gilliard, J. (2005). An investigation of Japanese and American early care and education. *Early Childhood Education Journal, 33*(3), 137–143.

National Center on Education and the Economy. (2014). *Center on International Education Benchmarking: Japan*. Retrieved from http://www.ncee.org/programs-affiliates/center-on-international-education-benchmarking/top-performing-countries/japan-overview/

National Center for Education Statistics. (2014). *Data point: Problem-solving skills of 15-year-olds: Results from PISA 2012*. NCES 2014-203. Retrieved from http://nces.ed.gov/pubs2014/2014103.pdf

National Institute for Educational Policy Research. (2012). *Primary schools in Japan*. Retrieved from http://www.nier.go National Center on Education and the Economy. (2014). *Center on International Education Benchmarking: Japan*. Retrieved from http://www.ncee.org/programs-affiliates/center-on-international-education-benchmarking/top-performing-countries/japan-overview/jp/English/educationjapan/pdf/201109BE.pdf

Organisation for Economic Cooperation and Development. (2009). *Viewing the Japanese school system through the prism of PISA*. Paris, France: OECD. Retrieved from www.oecd.org/japan/46623994.pdf

Organisation for Economic Cooperation and Development. (2010). *Strong performers and successful reformers in education: Lessons from PISA for the United States.* Paris, France: OECD.
Organisation for Economic Cooperation and Development. (2012a). *Policies for a revitalization of Japan.* Paris, France: OECD.
Organization for Economic Cooperation and Development. (2012b). *Quality matters in early childhood education and care: Japan 2012.* Paris, France: OECD.
Organisation for Economic Cooperation and Development. (2013). *Country note: Education at a glance 2013, Japan.* Retrieved from http://www.oecd.org/edu/Japan_EAG2013%20Country%20Note.pdf
Organisation for Economic Cooperation and Development. (2014a). *PISA 2012 results: Creative problem solving.* Retrieved from http://www.oecd.org/pisa/keyfindings/pisa-2012-results-volume-v.htm
Organisation for Economic Cooperation and Development. (2014b). PowerPoint, *ECEC system in Japan.* Retrieved from http://www.oecd.org/dataoecd/16/20/44647895.ppt
Organisation for Economic Cooperation and Development. (2014c). *Programme for international student assessment (PISA) results from PISA 2012.* Retrieved from http://www.oecd.org/pisa/keyfindings/PISA-2012-results-japan.pdf
Pasion, A. (2014, February 16). Prepping for university straight from the crib. *Japan Times.* Retrieved from http://www.japantimes.co.jp/community/2014/02/16/issues/prepping-for-university-straight-from-the-crib/#.VInlrorF9xs
Powell, M. (2014, August 9). A star-powered school sputters. *The New York Times.* Retrieved from http://www.nytimes.com/2014/08/10/sports/prime-prep-academy-founded-by-deion-sanders-comes-under-scrutiny.html?smid=tw-share&_r=0
Schwab, K. (Ed.). (2014). *The global competitiveness report 2014–2015.* Geneva, Switzerland: World Economic Forum.
Shimbun, M. (2013, January 23). Japan considers 6-day school week: Teachers not enthusiastic. *Japan Times.* Retrieved from http://www.japantoday.com/category/lifestyle/view/japan-considers-6-day-school-week-teachers-not-enthusiastic
Takayama, K. (2007). *A Nation at Risk* crosses the Pacific: Transnational borrowing of the U.S. crisis discourse in the debate on education reform in Japan. *Comparative Education Review, 51*(4), 423–446.
Tsuneyoshi, R. (2001). *The Japanese model of schooling.* New York: RoutledgeFalmer.
U.S. Department of State. (1946). *Report of the United States Education Mission to Japan.* Washington, DC: U.S. Government Printing Office. Retrieved from http://babel.hathitrust.org/cgi/pt?id=pur1.32754081234191;view=1up;seq=1
Vasquez Heilig, J., & Jez, S.J. (2014). *Teach For America: A return to the evidence.* Boulder, CO: National Education Policy Center. Retrieved from http://nepc.colorado.edu/publication/teach-for-america-return
Willis, D., Yamamura, S., & Rappleye, J. (2008). Frontiers of education: Japan as "global model" or "nation at risk"? *International Review of Education, 54,* 493–515.
Yoshida, R. (2013, October 13). Required English from third grade eyed. *Japan Times.* Retrieved from http://www.japantimes.co.jp/news/2013/10/23/national/required-english-from-third-grade-eyed/#.VMviRXB4rzE

CHAPTER FIVE

Canada

Education in Canada: Separate but Similar Systems in the Pursuit of Excellence and Equity

JASON D. EDGERTON, LANCE W. ROBERTS, AND VERONIKA ELIASOVA

In Canada there are no national ministries or departments that govern single education systems. Instead, each of ten Canadian provincial and three territorial governments mandate responsibility for the organization and delivery of education programs and the assessment of outcomes in their jurisdiction. Although jurisdictions vary both in terms of governance of education and in outcomes on international standardized tests such as PISA, overall Canada's education systems are more alike than different. These independent systems are, in practice, characterized by a considerable level of legislative and policy harmonization that resembles a de facto national education policy.

Over the first five cycles of PISA, Canada has consistently been one of the top performers both in terms of excellence and equity, although its ranking in math and science has slipped a few spots over successive PISA cycles. Even with generally high achievement on PISA, some segments of the Canadian population do not enjoy the same level of success as their higher-performing compatriots, and Canada faces many of the same challenges to educational equality that confront many OECD countries. Educational disparities related to social background, gender, and region—even if less than in most OECD countries—persist and are of primary concern to Canadian educators and policymakers in all jurisdictions and at all levels.

This chapter will begin with a brief overview of Canada's PISA results, including its relative standing internationally, and the differences between boys and girls across provinces and through time. Next it will consider challenges to the shared goals of excellence and equity in educational opportunity and outcomes, including the impact of socioeconomic and gender differences among students and the plight of the most socially and educationally disadvantaged segment of the Canadian population—Aboriginal Canadians. Then it will focus on teachers and teaching: the status of teaching, public attitudes toward teachers, and teachers' working conditions. It will discuss educational expenditures in Canada; the structure and governance of Canadian educational systems, including efforts to promote inclusiveness and equity; and the impact of large-scale assessment and intergovernmental collaboration on education policy and curricular convergence across the country. The final section will discuss Canadian attitudes toward education and educational issues, including the performance of schools and the importance of assessment, homework, and tutoring.

CANADIAN STUDENTS' PERFORMANCE ON PISA

2012 Results[1]

National

Canadian results compare favorably with other OECD countries in terms of both achievement and equity. The mean scores for 15-year-old Canadians were 518 in math, 523 in reading, and 525 in science—all well above the OECD average. Only 9 of the 65 participating countries—and only 3 of 34 OECD countries—performed better in math than Canada. Similarly, only five countries (3 OECD members) outperformed Canada in reading, while seven (5 OECD members) countries did so in science. In terms of equity, Canadian 15-year-olds in the highest decile scored 231 points higher in math than those in the lower decile, 235 points higher in reading, and 232 points higher in science. Each of these gaps was less than the respective OECD averages of 239 points in both math and science and 242 points in reading. Boys, on average, outperformed girls in math by 10 points in Canada, a gap nearly identical to the OECD average of 11 points. Girls, on average, outperformed boys in reading by 35 points, a gap similar to the OECD average of 38 points.

Provincial

At the provincial level in Canada, statistically significant disparities exist among the 10 provinces in the average scores of 15-year-olds. In math, Quebec performed above the national average; Alberta, British Columbia, and Ontario performed at the national average; and the remaining six provinces performed below the national average. In reading, British Columbia performed above the national average; Quebec, Ontario, and Alberta performed at the national average; and the remaining provinces performed below the Canadian average. In science, Alberta and British Columbia exceeded the national average, Ontario was at the national average, and the remaining provinces were below the Canadian average. All provinces, except Prince Edward Island, performed at or above the OECD average in math, reading, and science.

Over Time

The average PISA mathematics and science scores of Canadian 15-year-olds decreased between 2003 and 2012, while reading scores remained stable. The average math score for Canadian 15-year-olds decreased 14 points since 2003, from 532 to 518. Relative to 2003, proportionally fewer Canadian students attained the benchmark level established by the OECD (Level 2), and fewer attained the highest levels (Levels 5 and 6). Declining math scores are evident in every province except Quebec and Saskatchewan, with the greatest dips occurring in Manitoba, Alberta, Newfoundland, and Labrador. The gender gap in math has remained stable at 10 or 11 points across PISA cycles, while girls' reading advantage has increased from 32 to 35 points since 2000. Canada's average scores in reading and science decreased between 2000 and 2012, from 534 to 523 in reading and from 534 to 525 in science. Although the Canadian average in reading achievement was fairly stable between 2000 and 2012, it decreased in 5 out of 10 provinces. Science scores also decreased in 4 out of 10 provinces. Although Canada continues to perform quite strongly in reading and science, its position relative to other countries has slipped somewhat: the number of countries that outperformed Canada in reading rose from one in 2000 to five in 2012, and in science from two in 2006 to seven in 2012.

CHALLENGES TO EXCELLENCE AND EQUITY IN CANADIAN EDUCATION

Socioeconomic Status

If, according to the OECD (2013a), we consider "the overall relationship between socio-economic background and student performance" to be an indication of "the capacity of education systems to provide equitable learning opportunities" (p. 44), then Canada compares rather well to its fellow OECD member countries. The relationship between educational outcomes and socioeconomic status (SES) is referred to as the socioeconomic gradient. Such gradients can exist at multiple levels—within schools, across schools, and/or across regions and countries (Willms, 2006). High performance on PISA and relatively shallow gradients suggest that

Canada has been fairly successful at mitigating the effects of socioeconomic disparities on educational attainment. In 2012, 9.4% of variance in PISA mathematics scores was attributed to socioeconomic status (SES) in Canada—below the OECD average of 14.8%. The slope of the SES gradient in Canada is also significantly flatter than the OECD average—a one-point difference on the PISA SES index is associated with a 31-point difference in math scores in Canada compared to a 39-point difference across the OECD (OECD, 2013a).[2] Only 18.4% of the total variation in math scores is accounted for by between-school differences in Canada, which is about half the OECD average of 36.9% (OECD, 2013a). Furthermore, a one-point change in school-level SES in Canada is associated with a 41-point difference in school-level average math scores, compared to a 72-point difference across the OECD.

A further measure of equity concerns the strength of the relationship between socioeconomic status and performance. In Canada, only 41.8% of between-school differences in math performance is accounted for by socioeconomic (student-level and school-level) disparities, less than in any OECD country except Finland (38.3%), and well below the OECD average of 62.8%. A student's study program[3] also accounts for a significant proportion of performance differences across schools in many countries—40% across the OECD—but this is not the case in Canada, where it accounts for less than 1%. On average, across the OECD, students' study program and socioeconomic status together account for 71% of the performance difference across students in different schools, compared to only 33.4% in Canada (OECD, 2013a).

Canada's education system also fares well in terms of social and academic inclusion measures of equity. Social inclusion is "the degree to which students with different socio-economic status attend the same school or the degree to which different schools have different socio-economic profiles" (OECD, 2013a, p. 59). Higher social inclusion indicates less socioeconomic segregation and greater educational equity. Canada scored 82.8 on the PISA index of social inclusion,[4] higher than the OECD average of 75.6, and less than only Sweden, Norway, Finland, and Iceland among OECD countries. Academic inclusion is "the degree to which students with different academic abilities and needs share the same school, or the degree to which schools have different average performance levels. It is also a measure of the likelihood that a country or economy's low- and high-achieving students attend the same school" (OECD, 2103a, p. 62, n. 14). Canada's index of academic inclusion score was 80.2, higher than the OECD average of 64.1.

The lack of study program differences in Canada reflects the relative lack of formal tracking or streaming in Canadian education systems. Although it varies somewhat by province, streaming/tracking in Canada occurs to a much lesser degree than in many European countries and does not take place until secondary school (and hence would not be reflected in the PISA scores of tenth-grade students). Even then, most secondary school students encounter the same broad curriculum, and almost all Canadian secondary schools offer the same credential, a high school diploma (Davies & Guppy, 2006). Additionally, socioeconomic segregation of schools and ability grouping appear much less prevalent in Canada than in many OECD countries, at least in relation to the primary and middle school year educational experiences of 15-year-olds tested in PISA.

Private Schools

In Canada, only about 6% of high school students attend private schools (Frenette & Chan, 2015). In some provinces, private schooling systems are partially subsidized by the subnational government, but the majority of the cost is borne by the parents. Canadian students from families with higher socioeconomic status, measured both by family income and parental education, are more likely than lower socioeconomic status students to attend a private school. Students attending private schools score significantly higher on standardized tests and have considerably better educational attainment than their peers in the public school system; however, the majority of this difference disappears once students' socioeconomic status and the socioeconomic composition of the schools are controlled. Only a small portion of the difference is attributable to differing practices and resources available to private schools (Frenette & Chan, 2015).

Immigrants

While data from 2012 PISA show that the average proportion of 15-year-olds with immigrant backgrounds is only 11% across all OECD countries, it is about 30% in Canada. Across OECD countries, a significant performance gap exists between immigrant and non-immigrant students, with immigrant students performing significantly lower. In Canada, this difference is insignificant at the national level; however, differences do exist across provinces, with first-generation immigrant students performing better than non-immigrant students in some provinces (British Columbia, Ontario, and the Atlantic provinces) and worse in others (Quebec). The data suggest that this difference is related to the fact that in some jurisdictions first-generation immigrant students enjoy significantly higher socioeconomic status than their non-immigrant counterparts. Overall, academic performance of first-generation immigrant students is much more sensitive to their socioeconomic background compared to that of non-immigrant and second-generation immigrant students. In the case of second-generation immigrants, socioeconomic status has the smallest explanatory value (CMEC, 2015).

Gender

With every passing decade, Canadians spend more time in school, and women's level of education increases relative to men's. In the past 2 decades, the percentage of women obtaining a university degree more than doubled. Women currently receive more than 60% of university degrees awarded annually in Canada (Hango, 2013). After decades of catching up, there are now more university-educated women than men.

This disparity has led some commentators to declare that Canada has a "boy crisis"[5] in educational achievement similar to that noted in several OECD countries. Canada's national newspaper summarized the situation:

> [D]ata suggests that boys, as a group, rank behind girls by nearly every measure of scholastic achievement. They earn lower grades overall in elementary and high school. They trail in reading and writing, and 30 percent of them land in the bottom quarter of standardized tests, compared with 19 percent of girls. Boys are more likely to be picked out for behavioural problems, more likely to repeat a grade and to drop out of school altogether. (Abraham, 2010, para. 6)

The implications of this situation support a future "crisis." Success in obtaining marketable academic credentials is strongly related to students' overall academic achievement, reading abilities, study habits, and parental expectations (Abraham, 2010). Canadian boys' scores are significantly poorer than girls' on all four of these predictors. Evidence from PISA shows that this is the case for academic achievement, as girls continue to significantly outperform boys in reading, while boys' advantage in math and science continues to diminish.[6] Evidence from Canada's Youth in Transition survey (Looker & Thiessen, 2004) shows that boys spend significantly less time studying and that their parents have lower educational expectations.

The educational advantage of females should not be overestimated, however. Evidence of female participation in postsecondary education still conforms to traditional gender divisions. At the postsecondary level in Canada, more women than men are enrolling in and graduating from universities (Canadian Association of University Teachers [CAUT], 2012). However, even though female representation has been growing in traditionally male-dominated fields, most of the growth in Canada has been in traditionally female fields such as education, nursing, arts, languages, sociology, and psychology. Conversely, men account for about three-quarters of graduates in STEM (science, technology, engineering, mathematics, and computer science) fields (CAUT, 2012).

Canada, like other developed nations, systematically encourages students to pursue studies in STEM fields. Nationally, STEM courses are a strategic focus because these areas directly contribute to economic competitiveness and prosperity.

In a knowledge-based economy, STEM fields are areas rich in high-paying jobs (Knowles, 2013). The ten highest-paying bachelor's degrees are all in STEM fields (Dehaas, 2011). Yet women are participating in STEM fields at less than half the rate of men, concentrating instead in less scientifically oriented, lower-paying areas (Hango, 2013). Even young women with a high level of mathematical ability "are significantly less likely to enter STEM fields than young men, even young men with a lower level of mathematical ability." This suggests that the gender gap in STEM-related programs is due to other factors. "Other possible explanations might include differences in labour market expectations including family and work balance, differences in motivation and interest, and other influences" (Hango, 2013, p. 7).

Gender preferences appear to play a role in understanding the male reading deficit as well. Analysis of Canadian PISA 2009 results for reading found that enjoyment of reading had the strongest association with reading performance (Chuy & Nitulescu, 2013). In addition to reporting greater enjoyment of reading (and reading more diversely), girls were more likely than boys to employ effective reading strategies such as control, "a cognitive strategy focusing on understanding a task's purpose and its main concepts," and summarizing, "a meta-cognitive strategy reflecting an awareness of the most efficient ways to condense information" (Chuy & Nitulescu, 2013, p. 24). The authors suggest that, in addition to nurturing boys' enjoyment of reading, educators would do well to focus on how boys engage with reading, encouraging them to adopt more effective meta-cognition and control strategies.

Aboriginal Canadians[7]

While Canada's aggregate educational performance is impressive, pockets of serious underachievement remain. Aboriginal educational achievement in Canada is particularly problematic. Aboriginal people in Canada are composed of three groups, including Indian (First Nation), Metis, and Inuit peoples, each with a unique culture, heritage, and language.

Aboriginal peoples currently comprise 4% of the population, and this proportion will grow in the coming decades. Aboriginal peoples tend to be younger than other Canadians, with a median age of 26.5 years, compared to the non-Aboriginals' 39.5 years. As the general Canadian population ages, Aboriginal peoples will comprise a growing share of the labor force. For example, by 2020, over half of First Nation people will be under the age of 25 (Canadian Teachers' Federation [CTF], 2013). Yet despite their strategic importance, Aboriginal education outcomes are comparatively weak.

Data on Aboriginal students' performance on PISA is limited and unreliable,[8] but Table 5.1 shows the general trend in Aboriginal educational attainment.

Almost 40% of Aboriginal Canadians do not complete high school. This rate is double that of non-Aboriginals, and the gap has remained constant over time. Among those with some postsecondary education (PSE), Aboriginal peoples have shown improvement, but their rate is still substantially and consistently below the educational achievement of non-Aboriginals. Moreover, Aboriginal people with a university education are seriously underrepresented in the high-demand, high-paying STEM fields (science, technology, engineering, mathematics) (Fong & Gulati, 2013). The best estimates indicate that the educational achievement gap between Aboriginals and others will either remain at current levels or worsen (Gordon & White, 2014).

Table 5.1. Educational Attainment Rates by Aboriginal Identity.

	Aboriginal Peoples			Non-Aboriginal Peoples			Aboriginal Peoples Gap		
	2001	2006	2011	2001	2006	2011	2001	2006	2011
Less than high school	48.0%	43.7%	38.0%	30.8%	23.1%	19.4%	17.2%	20.6%	18.5%
High school only	22.4%	21.8%	23.9%	25.0%	25.7%	25.6%	-2.6%	-3.9%	-1.7%
Apprenticeship & trades	12.1%	11.4%	11.8%	10.8%	10.8%	10.8%	1.3%	0.6%	1.0%
PSE less than bachelor's	13.0%	17.3%	18.9%	17.6%	22.8%	22.8%	-4.6%	-4.6%	-3.9%
Bachelor's and above	4.4%	5.8%	7.4%	15.7%	21.4%	21.4%	-11.3%	-12.7%	-13.9%
Total PSE	29.5%	34.5%	38.1%	44.2%	54.9%	54.9%	-14.6%	-16.7%	-16.9%

Source: Statistics Canada Censuses of Population, National Household Survey

The pattern of low educational achievement among Aboriginal peoples is no coincidence. The systematic operation of social forces over time produced this result (Sengupta, 2013). To begin with, the implementation of Aboriginal treaty rights was routinely ignored or reduced (Mercredi & Turpel, 1993). Since pre-Confederation times (pre-1867), Aboriginal peoples have never been provided the adequate standard of living that was their right and Canada's constitutional obligation. In addition, the enforced assimilationist policies of residential schools (the last of which ended in 1996) produced a legacy of personal and social dysfunction that continues over generations. The goal of these schools—which removed Aboriginal children from their families and communities—was to "take the Indian out of the child," but this misguided effort resulted in many cases of physical, mental, emotional, and sexual abuse (Truth and Reconciliation Commission of Canada, 2012). The history of social mistreatment was compounded in the 1960s when policies permitted over 20,000 Aboriginal children to be adopted or fostered by middle-class White families. These children were consequently separated from their families and cultures, and now, as adults, they are faced with cultural and identity confusion (Sinclair, 2007).

In short, a multi-generational assault on the integrity of Aboriginal cultures has left large numbers of these peoples at the margins of Canadian society, where self-respect is low and personal and social dysfunction are high (Frideres & Gadacz, 2011). Low educational achievement is only one outcome of this social legacy, but given the importance of education for social mobility, it is a crucial path that holds promise for change and improved quality of life for many Aboriginal Canadians. Closing the gap between Aboriginal and non-Aboriginal educational achievement would have positive effects on suicide and incarceration rates, family stability, civic participation, and health outcomes. The economic returns of closing the educational gap alone are estimated at about $500 billion (Sharpe & Arsenault, 2009). For economic and humanistic reasons, the social inequalities of Aboriginal education are important gaps that Canadians must address. To date this challenge has been daunting, but there is growing recognition that increasing Aboriginal educational attainment (i.e., completion of high school and continuation into PSE) will require, among other changes, increased control and self-governance by Aboriginal communities of higher quality and better-funded Aboriginal schools that deliver culturally relevant curriculum complemented by student exposure to successful Aboriginal mentors and role models (Gordon & White, 2014).

TEACHERS AND TEACHING

Status

Despite growing concerns that large-scale assessment and related discourses of accountability (see below) threaten to diminish the autonomy and status of teachers and teaching in general, teaching remains a well-regarded and well-remunerated occupation in Canada. This favorable status renders it a relatively desirable middle-class occupation that attracts a high caliber of talent into teacher-training programs at the university level.

Salaries

Canadian public school teachers, on average, receive higher salaries than teachers in other OECD countries. These professionals have a steeper trajectory of salary increments as measured at 10 and 15 years of teaching experience, and they reach the top of their pay scale sooner (10 years in most provinces/territories) than their OECD counterparts (the average scale top-out occurs at 24 years) (OECD, 2013b). Primary and secondary school teachers in Canada are generally paid on the same salary scales with increments linked to experience, unlike some OECD countries where teacher pay is tied to the level of school taught. Calculated in U.S. dollars, the average starting salary for Canadian teachers in 2011–2012, with the minimum level of teacher training, was $37,145 at the primary and lower secondary education levels, compared to the OECD averages of $29,411 and $30,735 respectively. Add 10 years of experience, and these teachers are paid an average of $55,765 in Canada, compared to OECD averages of $36,846 and $38,419. Add another 5 years of experience, and they are paid an average of $58,494 in Canada, compared to $39,024 and $40,570 on average across OECD countries. The average salary scale maximum for Canadian teachers is $58,494, compared to $46,909 and $48,938 across all OECD countries (CESC, 2015).

> [Data from the 2012 PISA survey] suggest that high performing systems tend to prioritise higher salaries for teachers, especially in high-income countries. Among countries and economies whose per capita GDP is more than USD 20 000, including most OECD countries, systems that pay teachers more (i.e. higher teachers' salaries relative to national income per capita) tend to perform better in mathematics. The correlation between these two factors across 33 high-income countries and economies is 0.30, and the correlation is 0.40 across 32 high-income countries and economies, excluding Qatar. (OECD, 2014, p. 457)

The ratio of teachers' salaries at 15 years to per capita GDP in Canada in 2011 was 1.5, compared to a ratio of 1.24 to 1.29 for OECD. The top of the scale in Canada is right near the OECD average of 1.6 (OECD, 2013b).

Furthermore, in terms of attracting high-caliber candidates, Canadian teachers' salaries are quite competitive relative to other occupations requiring similar levels of education. In 2012, Canadian teachers earned 5% to 6% more "relative to earnings for full-time, full-year workers with tertiary education," while the OECD average was 15% less at the primary level, 12% less at the lower secondary level, and 8% less at the upper secondary level (OECD, 2014, p. 469).

Public Attitudes Toward Teachers

A national survey of public attitudes toward education by the Canadian Education Association found a high degree of consensus across the country in terms of views on education. In general, "Canadians in all regions share a high level of satisfaction with the jobs that teachers are doing in elementary and secondary schools and are consistently more satisfied with teachers' work than the school system in general.... [Overall,] 70 per cent of Canadians agree that teachers are doing a good job" (Dunleavy, 2007, p. 7).

On the 2009 PISA, which focused on reading, Canadian students generally reported that they felt teachers did a good job at stimulating students' interest and engagement in reading, with an average index score of .23, compared to the OECD average centered at 0 (higher values indicated greater teacher involvement in stimulating engagement (Brochu, Gluszynski, & Cartwright, 2011). A more general index of student-teacher relations asked students their degree of agreement with a number of questions about their teachers—whether they got along with the teachers, whether teachers were interested in their personal well-being, whether teachers took the student seriously, whether teachers were a source of support if the student needed extra help, and whether teachers treated the student fairly. Higher scores on this index indicate better teacher-student relations, and the average score in Canada was .32, above the OECD average, which is set at 0 (Brochu et al., 2011).

Teachers' Work

In 2005–2006, Statistics Canada reported that there were over 313,000 full-time equivalent educators working on school boards or in districts across Canada. The term "educators" is used to refer "to all those with recognized teacher qualifications whether they are working as teachers, principals, counsellors or in other professional roles" (CMEC, 2008, p. 25). This broad category of educators was comprised of 291,000 teachers, 15,600 school administrators, and 6,600 pedagogical support staff. "Almost all public school educators have four or five years of postsecondary education and all are licensed by the provincial and territorial departments or ministries of education" (CMEC, 2008, p. 25).

The average number of teaching hours per day in Canada in 2010/11 was 4.4 for primary school teachers and 4.1 for secondary school teachers, compared to OECD averages of 4.3 hours for primary, 3.8 for lower secondary, and 3.6 for higher secondary. Canadian primary school teachers taught an average of 799 hours, compared to an OECD average of 782 hours. Canadian teachers at the secondary level spent substantially more hours teaching than their OECD counterparts. Lower secondary school (grades 7–9) teachers in Canada taught an average of 744 hours, while upper secondary teachers (grades 10–12) taught an average of 747 hours, compared to OECD averages of 694 and 655 hours. The proportion of total working time spent teaching for Canadian teachers is near the OECD average for both primary and secondary school teachers (Canadian Education Statistics Centre [CESC], 2015). The proportion of Canadian teachers' total working time spent teaching was close to the OECD average at both primary (65% in Canada and the OECD) and secondary levels—60% and 61% in Canada at the lower secondary and upper secondary levels, compared to 58% across the OECD for both levels (CESC, 2014).

A 2005 national study by the Canadian Teachers' Federation (CTF) revealed that, compared to 2001, "teachers were working longer hours and the conditions under which they worked were making it increasingly difficult to maintain high quality learning environments for students" (CMEC, 2008, p. 30). More recently, a CTF (2014) survey found that teachers reported high levels of stress related to high workloads (e.g., lack of preparation time and grading/marking time, development and implementation of Individualized Education Programs, administrative paperwork), lack of support (human and material resources, professional development), and increasing demands in general. Over half of teachers surveyed indicated that their professional autonomy had decreased "significantly" (25%) or "somewhat" (28%) over the last 5 years.

EDUCATIONAL EXPENDITURES

Canada's expenditures on schooling are somewhat higher than the OECD average. As a share of GDP, Canada spends about 6.4%, while the OECD mean is 6.1% (Statistics Canada, 2014a). Measured in terms of purchasing power parity, Canada spends about 13% more on primary and secondary education than the OECD average (Statistics Canada, 2013).

School expenditures in Canada are administered by local school boards. Recent estimates indicate that about $60 billion is spent annually on primary and secondary education (Statistics Canada, 2012; Van Pelt & Emes, 2015).

The most appropriate measure for tracking school spending is per-pupil school expenditure, since this indicator adjusts for enrolment changes over time. In the past decade, school enrolments have declined by about 400,000, a decrease of about 6.2% (Statistics Canada, 2014a). During the same period, inflation-adjusted per-student expenditures have increased from $7,250 to $11,835 (Nazareth, 2014). In recent years, while enrolments have declined, expenditures increased by over 60%.

Canadian provinces vary in the amount they spend on education. Within Canada, using a purchasing power parity measure, there is notable variation among provincial expenditures, with several western provinces spending about 13% more than those on the east coast (Statistics Canada, 2013).

The allocation of educational expenditures in Canada is very similar to the OECD average. Canada devotes about 95% of expenditures to core services and 5% to ancillary services such as transportation and meals (Statistics Canada, 2013).

The OECD averages 94% for core services. The principal operating expenditure by Canadian school boards is the salaries of teachers and other school staff. This category accounts for about 70% of spending (Statistics Canada, 2014b). In terms of the last decade's growth in educational expenditures, salary increases for teachers and other staff are somewhat below the curve. They increased by about 50%, compared to the overall increase of 60%. In the last decade, the largest growth in expenditures was related to capital expenditures, which currently account for about 7% of all spending. Capital expenditures increased by over 270% in the last decade (Statistics Canada, 2014b).

SYSTEM STRUCTURE AND GOVERNANCE OF EDUCATION

As stated at the beginning of this chapter, there is no federal system of education in Canada and no overarching governmental body with enforcement power (CMEC, 2008). The legislative responsibility for organization and delivery of education as well as for the assessment of educational outcomes was granted to the 10 provinces by the 1867 Constitution Act of Canada. The three territories have been entrusted with similar rights and responsibilities by the federal government (CMEC, 2012b). The involvement of the federal government in educational governance is, therefore, severely limited, and involves responsibility for education of military personnel and federal inmates, and shared responsibility for education of Aboriginal people, who usually reside on the reserves (CMEC, 2008).

In each jurisdiction, there is either one ministry of education or two education departments if postsecondary education is governed separately. These are headed by a minister—an elected member of the provincial or territorial legislature appointed to the position by the leader of the subnational government. Responsibility for operation of the departments lies with deputy ministers, professionals from the ranks of civil service (CMEC, 2008).

The provincial/territorial ministries define the educational services to be provided, their standards, and the circumstances of their provision; they set the legislative and high-policy framework specifying the organization and delivery of those services and assessment of their outcomes. In other words, the provincial/territorial governments define the greater framework within which the local units of governance and schools operate.

At the local level, power is delegated to school boards or district education councils, which govern in school divisions or school districts. The scope of their authority is established by the provincial government but typically includes operation of schools within the board's geographical division, including administration and management of finances and personnel, implementation of curricula, enrolment of students, and the creation of proposals for major capital expenditures. Within that scope, school boards are charged with development of mid-level policies, which allows them to tailor the wider provincial guidelines to the specific context of the population they serve. For instance, in the province of British Columbia, this involves "determining specific educational programming for students, which could include establishing specialty schools"[9] in order to best address the specific needs and challenges faced by the communities.

The boards also ensure democratic involvement of the public in local governance of education, as the board trustees are publicly elected (Vergari, 2010). This system of representative democracy ensures that the goals and needs of communities are taken into account, while also ensuring that the policies conform to the greater framework set by the subnational government.

PROMOTING INCLUSIVENESS AND EQUITY IN CANADIAN EDUCATION

Despite the generally acceptable performance of Canadian students on large-scale standardized tests such as PISA and the relatively small performance gap between the highest- and lowest-achieving students in comparison with most other OECD countries (Brochu et al., 2013), there is ongoing concern with improving attainment of those at the lower end of the performance curve. In 2008, the Council of Ministers of Education, Canada (CMEC) issued a document called *Learn Canada 2020* in which the ministers expressed their commitment to improving inclusiveness and equity of the Canadian educational system as well as the overall quality of education and educational outcomes. Progress reports are being produced annually by individual jurisdictions in order to increase commitment to the vision and accountability.

CMEC (2008) defines inclusivity as "an approach that looks into how to transform education systems and other learning environments in order to respond to the diversity of learners" (p. 3). To ensure equal access for all, elementary and secondary education in Canada is free of charge for anyone who meets the specific age and residency requirements outlined by each jurisdiction. This includes Canadian citizens, landed immigrants, and persons legally admitted to Canada on a short-term basis, usually between 5 and 18 years of age.

Canadian educational leaders, nevertheless, recognize that ensuring equal access to education is not enough to create a truly inclusive educational system. Subnational governments have therefore been developing programs and policies that help create equality of opportunity for groups that are most at risk of exclusion.

Funding as a Tool for Building Inclusiveness and Equity

One of the tools governments use to promote inclusiveness and equity is funding. Only a very minor portion of public education systems' funding comes from the federal government. The majority of funds are provided either directly by the provincial or territorial government or come as a mix of provincial transfers and local taxes (CMEC, 2008). Nevertheless, in an effort to equalize public service provision across the provinces, the federal government administers a funding adjustment program to provide some degree of wealth redistribution. This enables the six less affluent provinces to provide services more comparable to those in Alberta, British Columbia, Quebec, and Ontario (Vergari, 2010).

On the subnational level, the provincial/territorial governments revise funding regulations on an annual basis to determine the funding budgets for each school board, taking into account factors such as number of students within the board's competence, their needs, and the place-specific challenges of the communities served, such as low socioeconomic status or high proportion of immigrant families. This differential approach to funding is tied to positive discrimination practices at the school level, where students at risk of exclusion are identified. This entails special funding provisions for intervention tools and programs aimed at increasing inclusion and equity of opportunity (CMEC, 2008).

For example, the funding system in Manitoba reflects the special needs of schools and boards based on the specific circumstances they face. Funding is determined on a per-student basis, and the funding formula has two components: (a) the base-support component, which includes the basic financing of curricular material, support for instruction, and other basic necessities, and (b) extra, more targeted, funding that must be applied for by schools, with eligibility determined based on identification of students' special needs, according to an extensive list of criteria and conditions, for example, children with learning disabilities and/or behavioral problems, English as second language education for immigrant students, and academic achievement grants for Aboriginal students (CMEC, 2008).

Pre-elementary Education as Early Intervention

Education leaders in Canada recognize the potential of kindergarten education as an early intervention method to mitigate inequality (CMEC, 2008). A 2012 CMEC report for UNESCO notes the following:

> the children who are most successful in school are those who were nurtured, and stimulated in the early years—whether at home or in early learning and child care settings. Being ready to learn continues to have an impact throughout a child's education, with a strong link to secondary school completion and to future employability, earnings, and life satisfaction. (CMEC, 2012b, p. 15)

Data from the National Longitudinal Survey of Children and Youth (NLSCY) indicate that between 25% and 30% of Canadian children show lack of school readiness at the age of 5. Given the critical nature of this developmental period, formally organized pre-elementary education presents a unique opportunity to help children from vulnerable populations early on, both through involvement in the formal pre-school educational programs, and through engagement of key stakeholders such as parents and adult caregivers, educators, and communities. All Canadian subnational jurisdictions offer a non-compulsory kindergarten education for 5-year-olds, and over 90% of Canadian children attend these programs (CMEC, 2008; 2012b).

EDUCATION POLICY AND CANADIAN EDUCATION SYSTEMS: SEPARATE BUT SIMILAR

Since there is no overarching governmental body with the authority to formally enforce legislation and policies that would promote an integrated national system of education, there are some differences among the individual jurisdictions—especially in the matters of curriculum, assessment, and accountability. Despite some variation, there are a number of direct and indirect influences that lead individual provinces and territories to adopt similar educational policies. Vergari (2010) points out that there are strong efforts among the subnational governments to learn from each other, driven by the economic competitive pressures in a global era of knowledge economies, as well as by the desire to legitimize their educational systems through reference to comparable standards of quality in other provincial/territorial jurisdictions.[10] This leads to a considerable level of legislative and policy harmonization, which contributes to the formation of shared national policy (CMEC, 2008; Hargreaves & Shirley, 2012; Vergari, 2010).

The primary body facilitating cooperation and policy learning among the jurisdictions is the Council of Ministers of Education, Canada (CMEC), which provides a forum for the provincial and territorial ministers to discuss matters of mutual significance, to learn from each other, and to join their efforts in pursuit of shared goals. Comparing the federal structure of Canadian education to that of the United States, Vergari (2010) notes the following:

> CMEC fulfills some functions that are comparable to those of the U.S. Department of Education. For example, CMEC administers the Official Languages Program, manages a pan-Canadian student assessment program, develops and reports on education indicators, partners with Statistics Canada to provide education statistics, provides a clearinghouse to facilitate recognition of foreign educational and occupational credentials, and consults and acts on other issues such as Aboriginal education. (p. 540)

Moreover, the education ministers use CMEC to represent the interests of their jurisdictions in interaction with the federal government as well as with other national and international educational organizations. Other entities facilitating development of national educational policy in Canada include the Canadian Education Association (CEA) and various regional curriculum consortia. Furthermore, the effort to increase cooperation and learning among provinces is also evident in numerous intergovernmental agreements. In 1993, the provinces of Manitoba, Saskatchewan, Alberta, British Columbia, Yukon, and Northwest Territories established the Western and Northern Canadian Protocol for Collaboration in Education, which was later joined by Nunavut, and in 1995, Newfoundland and Labrador, Nova Scotia, New Brunswick, and Prince Edward Island initiated the Atlantic Provinces Education Foundation (Vergari, 2010). All these examples signify efforts to develop coordinated standards of quality education contributing to the development of common education policy across jurisdictions.

Nevertheless, despite the many similarities among the educational systems and collaborative efforts, there is constant tension between the tendencies toward national policy building and the desire to safeguard jurisdictional autonomy (Vergari, 2010). Thus, despite numerous shared goals with respect to educational standards and system performance, many reforms and initiatives serving those ends have been adapted differently across the jurisdictions, reflecting their unique cultural, sociohistorical, and political context (CMEC, 2008).

The "Canadian Way"

Hargreaves and Shirley (2012) argue that understanding the success of the highest-performing educational systems in Canada requires looking past the latest or most-discussed reforms and initiatives adopted by individual provinces and instead examining closely the enduring similarities among these jurisdictions in terms of educational policies and strategies, as well as professional histories. Together these similarities form what they call an embedded, inclusive "Canadian Way" of organizing and managing educational systems.

Drawing on their extensive experience with analysis of Canadian educational systems and policies, Hargreaves and Shirley (2012) conclude that it is nearly impossible to isolate the independent effects of individual policies because of the way in which various policies and strategies mutually interact and become intertwined with the very logic of the system. Moreover, they point out that the impact of these policies is often much broader than their immediate impact on students' performance, so it makes little sense to look at them separately. Even policies that seem to have little or no direct impact on student performance may contribute toward creating fertile ground for other strategies. In the face of such complexity, judging the performance of educational systems exclusively in terms of achievement on large-scale standardized programs provides an overly constrictive view of educational success, one that overlooks other important, often less-quantifiable educational outcomes that are also vital to social well-being in a diverse society such as Canada's (Vergari, 2010). Education systems may contribute to decreasing inequality overall, both in terms of promoting students' performance and educational outcomes, and also through the creation of a more inclusive society. It is therefore the cumulative effect of these initiatives and their synergistic interaction that underlies the success of these high-performing Canadian education systems, not any one policy in isolation (Hargreaves & Shirley, 2012).

Hargreaves and Shirley (2012) identify seven factors associated with long-term high performance of educational systems in Canada which also provide wider social and educational benefits—benefits that go beyond student achievement on standardized tests. First, educational leaders understand the importance of projecting an inspiring vision—a vision that galvanizes people and compels them to change their beliefs in order to change their practices, not the other way around (as is usually the case with externally imposed changes). Second, the local systems of governance provide the opportunity to address the specific context of the communities being served. For instance, in Ontario, many policies are specifically designed to allow for flexible development and implementation of projects that best address specific needs of various communities, depending on whether the communities consist of a high proportion of immigrants, Aboriginals, religious minorities, and so on. Third, there is a balance in these systems between innovation through invention of new strategies and improvement through fine-tuning of existing strategies that have already proven effective. In other words, there is an understanding of the need to capitalize on current developments. Fourth, changes from above are not imposed in a homogenizing way; instead, reforms and high-level policies function as platforms for change that provide the local levels of governance, schools, and teachers with tools for expanding their skills and capacity to "help themselves" and to change systems from within. Fifth, in addition to selecting the highest-achieving teachers in these systems, there is considerable investment in educators' professional capital. In Ontario, teachers are encouraged to become professionals who are actively engaged in their own professional development through continuous inquiry; they explore and keep up with the trends in the field of education and implement their knowledge in practice. Similarly, ongoing training comes less often externally—in the form of workshops or seminars—and more often through job-embedded training where teachers, based on their performance in the classroom, get feedback and assistance from more experienced colleagues. In addition, there is a strong culture of shared responsibility; the success of students and improvement in teaching never rests on the shoulders of a single individual. Finally, these systems encourage intensive communication, which promotes coherence of the system through development of a culture of organic relationships between individuals and institutions. For example, in Ontario, there is ongoing movement of personnel back and forth among various institutions such as the teachers' association and the education ministry, and the province also has special support teams of researchers that engage in various policy-design projects in order to cross-pollinate ideas and facilitate connections among these projects.

In sum, Hargreaves and Shirley (2012) articulate how these high-performing systems have mechanisms built into them that ensure ongoing innovation in a context-sensitive, perhaps even holistic, way that comes from within the system. It is from this perspective that they observe with concern that "[t]his embedded and inclusive Canadian way…is being threatened by the global trend to weaken district involvement and control in favour of more and more centralized direction" (p. 5). Similarly, Vergari (2010) points to a neoliberal trend toward taking control away from the local systems of educational governance, in favor of centralization of power at the provincial level. Hargreaves and Shirley (2012) note that the characteristics that make these high-performing Canadian systems so successful include their ability to respond flexibly and effectively to the diversity of learners and to expand system capacities accordingly. They argue that it is the very strengths of this approach—which lie in not imposing change externally in a homogenizing, constraining way—that are at risk of being undermined by larger centralizing tendencies.

The Homogenizing Effect of Large-Scale Assessment

As with the neoliberal pressures toward centralization of powers on a subnational level, there are pressures toward policy homogenization that are directly and indirectly associated with the global trend of increased engagement in large-scale assessment (LSA) programs (Volante & Jaafar, 2008; Volante, 2013). Indeed, Vergari (2010) observes that in the last 2 decades the number of different kinds of province-wide assessment programs has greatly increased. Further, these programs show marked similarities to the national and international ones, indicating a significant convergence with global trends in LSA policy (Volante & Jaafar, 2008).

Presently all Canadian jurisdictions, with the exception of Nunavut, have some form of province-wide assessment program, and many of them also participate in international LSA programs such as PISA, in addition to a national LSA program—The Pan-Canadian Assessment Program (PCAP)—which has been implemented in all 10 provinces.[11] PCAP is administered every 3 years to test 13-year-olds in literacy, mathematics, and sciences. It is scheduled 2 years before each PISA cycle, which means that the same cohort of students tested on PCAP is then tested on PISA 2 years later.

The problem is, however, that this convergence of LSA policies is not benign. Today, LSA programs are used as a tool for a wide variety of purposes. Volante and

Jaafar (2008) note that "[i]n addition to promoting jurisdictional consistency, standards, and school improvement, the purposes in the Canadian system have expanded to include quality control and accountability" (p. 7). However, because systems' effectiveness is increasingly being framed in terms of performance on these standardized testing programs, so, too, is accountability becoming narrowly associated with the push to utilize and incorporate the feedback information from these programs.

In practice, this feedback is institutionalized through two types of accountability (Volante & Jaafar, 2008). First, there is an ethical-professional mechanism of pressure wherein the principle of accountability is tied to educators' sense of professionalism and pride in one's work. Although there are no direct career consequences (e.g., merit pay, promotion/demotion) to educators, unsatisfactory student performance on LSA can affect not only teachers' sense of professional identity, but also public perceptions of teachers and schools. Moreover, in some jurisdictions LSA results are published in local newspapers and reported via popular media in the form of rank-ordered lists of schools sorted by students' aggregated raw performance scores. The second accountability mechanism is of an economic-bureaucratic character, wherein educational leaders at all levels of governance are expected to interpret the feedback information and its implications and to outline a plan indicating how to address deficiencies through policy and strategy changes.

In effect, this assessment and accountability regime functions as a vehicle for policy homogenization. Volante (2013) examined subnational policy responses to large-scale international testing in Canada and concluded that "[i]nternational comparison testing has had a noticeable impact on curriculum renewal efforts across Canada" (p. 174). More specifically, this has led to intensifying core curriculum efforts in literacy, mathematics, and the sciences—the most frequently tested subjects in standardized testing programs. The concrete strategies assumed by individual provinces and territories vary, depending on their relative standing nationally in comparison with other provinces and internationally in comparison with other OECD (or OECD partner) countries. The high-achieving provinces often use their superior results to justify the course of their educational strategies and to portray themselves as leaders in educational policy whose example is to be emulated by other Canadian and international education systems. In provinces with comparatively lower and/or declining levels of performance on PISA or other international LSAs, critics and commentators point to unsatisfactory results as evidence of the need for educational reform.[12]

Others argue that this competitive pursuit of national and international test score rankings threatens to undermine the very source of our educational success—the inclusive Canadian Way. Volante (2013) warns that framing educational systems' performance predominantly in terms of students' performance on narrowly conceptualized large-scale standardized tests obfuscates the need to improve educational systems in a more holistic way that would lead to more wide-ranging social and economic benefits. These trends toward centralization of powers and policy homogenization on both a national and global scale threaten the inclusivity of Canadian educational systems, which thrive on the ability of local systems of governance to respond to the needs of the communities they serve in a context-sensitive way. Such concerns may be warranted, given, for example, the case of the United States, where LSA-based accountability policies implemented in a more centralized educational system (Vergari, 2010) have failed to improve educational outcomes while siphoning time and resources away from other potentially more beneficial educational reforms and innovations (Darling-Hammond, 2014).

CANADIAN ATTITUDES TOWARD EDUCATION

Schools

The Canadian Council on Learning (CCL) conducted a survey of the Canadian public in 2008 and found that the majority of Canadians were satisfied that elementary and high schools were meeting or exceeding key public educational expectations, such as teaching "the basics" of reading, writing, and arithmetic (62%), teaching computer skills (66%), teaching problem-solving skills (56%), preparing students for further education after high school (60%), teaching students to be good citizens (60%), and teaching students to love learning (53%). Interestingly, Canadians with children at home are generally more satisfied with the performance of Canadian schools than are Canadians without children at home (CCL, 2009).

A 2007 national survey by the Canadian Education Association (CEA) found that 60% of Canadians were satisfied with their local schools and school systems (an increase from previous CEA surveys), but were less confident in public schools (45%) than in previous CEA surveys (Dunleavy, 2007). Dunleavy (2007) says that this "upward trend in satisfaction and downward trend in confidence suggests that Canadians generally believe school systems are improving, but are largely unsure about the sustainability of improvements over time" (p. 10). Consistent with this finding, few (19%) Canadians expressed confidence in their provincial governments in relation to education policy. Furthermore, 60% of Canadians feel they have "too little" say in local education decisions about how schools are run, and 72% feel that provincial governments should increase funding for public schools, with 56% willing to pay more taxes to increase funding. Conversely—and consistent with strong support for public education—only 38% support public funding of private schools (Dunleavy, 2007). In terms of improvements in schools, 34% of the 2007 CEA survey respondents felt that the quality of education received by elementary students had improved a little (26%) or a lot (8%) in the previous 10 years, 27% felt it was unchanged, and 31% felt it had declined. Similarly, 28% felt the quality of education received at the secondary level had improved in the previous 10 years, while 30% felt it was unchanged, and 29% felt it had declined. When it comes to educational changes, 46% of CEA survey respondents believed that moderate changes were required to fix problems with education systems in their province, while 21% supported minor changes, and 27% wanted major changes (Dunleavy, 2007).

Assessment

Public support for large-scale assessments was strong in both CEA and CCL national surveys. The CEA survey found strong public support (77%) nationally for province-wide high school graduation exams (Dunleavy, 2007). CCL data indicate strong support for large-scale provincial, national, and international achievement tests, with 75% of Canadians agreeing that achievement tests "measure vital aspects of learning and help schools to provide better instruction" and 66% agreeing that tests "are a good tool to hold schools accountable for their performance" (CCL, 2006, p. 3). CCL data indicated that 60% of Canadians felt that large-scale assessments were superior to teacher-assigned grades, but CEA results suggest that the majority (60%) of Canadians prefer teacher assessments as the primary means of deciding high school grades. Taken together, these results suggest support for the maintenance of "parallel provincial and classroom-based student assessment systems" (Dunleavy, 2007, p. 8).

Homework

Canadians highly value homework, with over 80% believing it "enhances learning" and "develops good work habits," although they express less certainty about the appropriate amount of homework (CCL, 2007b). Canadian teenagers do an average of 9.2 hours of homework per week, with girls doing more (10.3 hours) than boys (8.1 hours) (Marshall, 2007). This gender difference was not evident for children of immigrant parents. The probability of doing homework, and of doing more of it, also increased for teens in two-parent families (compared to single-parent families) and for those whose parents had university education (compared to those with less-educated parents) (Marshall, 2007). A number of studies suggest that it is the style (i.e., active learning) of and effort invested in homework that are more important than the amount of time spent doing it (CCL, 2009). But given the perceived connection between homework and academic achievement, finding the right balance appears to be a source of considerable stress for many Canadian families (CCL, 2007b).

Tutoring

According to the CCL survey, in 2007, one-third of Canadian parents with children aged 5–24 years reported that they had "hired a private tutor or a tutoring company to assist their child with reading and/or writing, math, science, or other subjects" (CCL, 2007b, p. 18). The number of tutoring businesses in major Canadian cities grew substantially (with gains of 200% to 500% in various cities) over the 1990s, as did the diversity of services they offer (Davies, 2004). Concomitant with this growth has been a change in the perception of tutoring, which is no longer viewed primarily as remedial intervention for low-achieving students but rather as a supplementary learning enhancement to improve academic performance. In fact, "the majority of tutors are hired by parents of children whose academic performance is average to high achieving" (CCL, 2007b, p. 19). Tutoring serves as a more affordable form of school choice for middle-class parents who want more control over their children's education and are concerned with maintaining their children's competitive advantage within demanding education and labor markets (Davies, 2004). Higher-earning, more educated parents who are dissatisfied with their children's schools and/or the amount of time they spend helping with homework are more likely to hire tutors (CCL, 2007b).

CONCLUSION

This chapter has provided a brief overview of Canada's performance on PISA, showing that Canada is still one of the highest-performing countries, but that its scores and relative ranking have slipped some across cycles. Certain Canadian provinces (British Columbia, Alberta, Ontario, and Quebec) have consistently scored significantly above OECD averages on PISA, and while the remaining provinces have scored at or above OECD averages, some have experienced notable declines in recent cycles, sparking concerns in some quarters about the effectiveness of schools in these provinces.

Gender differences across cycles have remained fairly stable nationally, with boys outperforming girls in math, although the difference has disappeared in a number of provinces and is substantially less than the advantage enjoyed by girls in reading. Despite no significant gender differences in science scores, as well as the lack of a significant math gap in a number of jurisdictions, girls remain far less likely to pursue higher education and careers in STEM fields, an apparent indication that the traditional gendered occupational preferences still retain substantial traction in Canada.

The socioeconomic gradient in PISA performance in Canada is much shallower than in most OECD countries, indicating a comparatively high degree of inclusivity and equity in Canadian education systems. However, there is still much room for improvement, and Canadian educators and policymakers continue to work toward increasing equality of educational opportunity and outcomes across all segments of the Canadian population. Further (although not adequately captured by PISA data), the enduring educational disadvantage of Aboriginal Canadians represents a significant unresolved social problem in Canada, from both the economic and social justice perspectives.

Although each province and territory is responsible for its own education system, there is, despite important variation, a substantial degree of similarity in education policy and curricula across jurisdictions. The phrase "the Canadian Way" has been used by some authors (Hargreaves & Shirley, 2012) to refer to the unique balance that exists in Canada, one that manages a high level of coordination and collaboration among provincial/territorial education ministries, while still preserving the autonomy and local context-sensitive responsiveness of individual education systems. This convergence and homogenization is encouraged by participation in large-scale standardized tests both at the inter-provincial (PCAP) and inter-national (PISA, TIMMS, PIRLS) levels, as less successful jurisdictions, confronted by discourses of accountability and competitiveness, feel pressure to emulate more successful ones.

Survey evidence and OECD-leading rates of PSE attainment suggest that Canadians place a high value on the importance of learning and education and are mostly satisfied with their public schools and, especially, with their teachers. Teaching remains a well-regarded middle-class occupation that attracts capable and qualified personnel (almost all teachers have 4 years of university education). Despite general satisfaction with their education systems, the majority of Canadians believe that large-scale standardized testing has a role to play in keeping educators accountable for school performance. Some voices call for strengthening regimes of large-scale assessment and accountability to promote educational excellence and high international standing, while others—pointing to the dubious effects of programs like *No Child Left Behind* and *Race to the Top* in the United States—worry that such a narrow focus on test performance will undermine the very strengths of the Canadian Way and its effective—though at times imperfect—capacity to promote a relatively high degree of educational inclusiveness and equity (compared to other OECD countries) while still performing near the top. It seems more likely than not that these tensions will continue to grow as governments continue to be pressed by fiscal constraints, structural inequalities, and the exigencies of international economic competition.

NOTES

1. This summary of Canadian PISA results is adapted from Brochu, Deussing, Houme, & Chuy (2013).
2. The 2012 PISA results for reading and science were very similar, with 8.1% of variation in reading scores and 7.8% in science accounted for by SES in Canada—significantly below the OECD averages of 13.1% and 14%. The slopes of the SES gradient in Canada were also significantly flatter than the OECD average—a one-point difference on the PISA SES index is associated with differences of 30 and 29 points in reading and science scores in Canada, compared to 38-point differences in each across the OECD.
3. "The program is identified by education level (e.g. upper or lower secondary), orientation of the curriculum (e.g. general or vocational), and intent (e.g. providing general access to other education levels or direct access to the labour market)" (OECD, 2013a, p. 46).
4. Values on both the social inclusion and academic inclusion indices range from 0 to 100, with higher scores indicating greater inclusion.
5. Other observers take issue with framing girls' increasing academic success as a "crisis" for boys, arguing that such an antagonistic approach is overly simplistic and ultimately unhelpful in increasing educational opportunity and equality (e.g., Ringrose, 2009).
6. There is no significant gender difference for Canadian science scores in PISA 2012, and while at a national level there is a significant gender difference in math scores, it is much smaller than the reading gap (10 points versus 35 points). At the provincial level there were no significant gender differences in math in 6 out of 10 provinces (Brochu et al., 2013).
7. This section is adapted from Brym, R., Roberts, L., Strohschein, L., and Lie, J. (2015).
8. "The usefulness of PISA...in tracking achievement among Aboriginal students is limited both by unavailability of Aboriginal identifiers in some early PISA cohorts and by limited accuracy due to small sample size" (CMEC, 2012a; p. 11). Aboriginal students performed dramatically lower than non-Aboriginal students in PISA 2000 (CCL, 2007a). Additionally, the PISA sample never covered on-reserve Aboriginal students, who tend to be more educationally disadvantaged than off-reserve Aboriginal students (Gordon & White, 2014).
9. http://www2.gov.bc.ca/gov/topic.page?id=CA395D52F68844529BAFB97CFDEECA51
10. Four provinces—Alberta, British Columbia, Ontario, and Quebec—have consistently performed well above the OECD average on PISA and other international standardized tests.
11. CMEC website, http://www.cmec.ca/511/Programs-and-initiatives/Assessment/Pan-Canadian-Assessment-Program-(PCAP)/PCAP-2013/Overview/index.html)
12. Right-wing public policy think tanks such as the Fraser Institute, the Frontier Centre for Public Policy, and the Atlantic Institute for Market Studies are at the forefront of such reform advocacy.

REFERENCES

Abraham, C. (2010, October 15). Part 1: Failing boys and the powder keg of sexual politics. *Globe and Mail*. Accessed May 2, 2015, from http://www.theglobeandmail.com/news/national/time-to-lead/part-1-failing-boys-and-the-powder-keg-of-sexual-politics/article4081751/?page=1

Brochu, P., Deussing, M-A., Houme, K., & Chuy, M. (2013). *Measuring up: Canadian results of the OECD PISA Study 2012. First results for Canadians aged 15*. Toronto: Council of Ministers of Education, Canada.

Brochu, P., Gluszynski, T., & Cartwright, F. (2011). *Second report from the 2009 Programme for International Student Assessment*. Toronto: CMEC.

Brym, R., Roberts, L., Strohschein, L., & Lie, J. (2015). *Sociology: Your compass for a new world*. Toronto: Nelson.

Canadian Association of University Teachers [CAUT]. (2012). *CAUT almanac of post-secondary education in Canada 2011–12*. Ottawa: CAUT.

Canadian Council on Learning [CCL]. (2006). *Survey of Canadian attitudes toward Learning: Elementary, secondary and post-secondary structured learning*. Ottawa: CCL. Accessed May 8, 2015, from http://www.ccl-cca.ca/pdfs/SCAL/2006/FactSheetStructureENGmtg.pdf

Canadian Council on Learning [CCL]. (2007a). *The cultural divide in science education for Aboriginal learners*. Retrieved from http://www.ccl-cca.ca/pdfs/LessonsInLearning/Feb-01–07-The-cultural-divide-in-science.pdf

Canadian Council on Learning [CCL]. (2007b). *2007 survey of Canadian attitudes toward learning: Results for elementary and secondary school learning*. Ottawa: CCL.

Canadian Council on Learning [CCL]. (2009). *2008 survey of Canadian attitudes toward learning: Results for learning throughout the lifespan*. Ottawa: CCL.

Canadian Education Statistics Council [CESC]. (2014). *Education indicators in Canada: An international perspective 2013*. Toronto: Canadian Education Statistics Council.

Canadian Education Statistics Council [CESC]. (2015). *Education indicators in Canada: An international perspective 2014*. Toronto: Canadian Education Statistics Council.

Canadian Teachers' Federation [CTF]. (2013). First Nation, Inuit, and Metis. Retrieved May 2, 2015, from www.ctf-fce.ca/Research-Library/BGHillDay2013_FNMI.pdf

Canadian Teacher's Federation [CTF]. (2014). Highlights of CTF survey on the quest for teacher work-life balance. Retrieved April 30, 2015, from http://www.ctf-fce.ca/Research-Library/Work-Life-Balance-Survey-DW-CAPTO.pdf

Chuy, M., & Nitulescu, R. (2013). *PISA 2009: Explaining the gender gap in reading through reading engagement and approaches to learning*. Toronto: Council of Ministers of Education, Canada (CMEC) and Human Resources and Skills Development Canada (HRSDC).

Council of Ministers of Education, Canada [CMEC].(2008). *The development of education: Reports for Canada. Report one: The education systems in Canada—Facing the challenges of the twenty-first century. Report two: Inclusive education in Canada—The way of the future*. Retrieved from http://www.cmec.ca/Publications/Lists/Publications/Attachments/122/ICE2008-reports-canada.en.pdf

Council of Ministers of Education, Canada [CMEC]. (2012a). *Key policy issues in Aboriginal education: An evidence-based approach*. Retrieved from http://www.cmec.ca/Publications/Lists/Publications/Attachments/295/Key-Policy-Issues-in-Aboriginal-Education_EN.pdf

Council of Ministers of Education, Canada [CMEC]. (2012b). *Promoting equality of educational opportunity. Canada report for the UNESCO eighth consultation of member states on the implementation of the convention and recommendation against discrimination in education*. Retrieved from http://www.cmec.ca/Publications/Lists/Publications/Attachments/289/2012.11_Promoting_Equality_of_Educational_Opportunity_EN.pdf

Council of Ministers of Education, Canada [CMEC]. (2015). Immigrants in Canada: Does socioeconomic background matter? *Assessment Matters!, 9*. Retrieved from http://www.cmec.ca/Publications/Lists/Publications/Attachments/343/AMatters_No9_EN.pdf

Darling-Hammond, L. (2014). What can PISA tell us about U.S. education policy? *New England Journal of Public Policy, 26*(1), article 4.

Davies, S. (2004). School choice by default? Understanding the demand for private tutoring in Canada. *American Journal of Education, 110*, 233–255.

Davies, S., & Guppy, N. (2006). *The schooled society: An introduction to the sociology of education.* Toronto: Oxford University Press Canada.

Dehass, J. (2011, November 7). Students are fleeing STEM degrees: And why they may want to reconsider. *Maclean's on Campus.* Retrieved May 1, 2015, from http://www.macleans.ca/work/jobs/students-are-fleeing-stem-degrees/

Dunleavy, J. (2007). *Public education in Canada: Facts, trends and attitudes.* Toronto: Canadian Education Association (CEA).

Fong, F., & Gulati, S. (2013). *Employment and education among Aboriginal peoples.* Special Report TD Economics. Retrieved May, 2015, from http://www.td.com/document/PDF/economics/special/EmploymentAndEducationAmongAboriginalPeoples.pdf

Frenette, M., & Chan, P.C.W. (2015). *Why are academic prospects brighter for private high school students?* Statistics Canada. Catalogue no. 11-626-X—No. 044. Ottawa: Statistics Canada. Retrieved from http://www.statcan.gc.ca/pub/11-626-x/11-626-x2015044-eng.htm

Frideres, J., & Gadacz, R. (2011). *Aboriginal peoples of Canada* (9th ed.). Toronto: Pearson Education Canada.

Gordon, C.E., & White, J.P. (2014). Indigenous educational attainment in Canada. *International Indigenous Policy Journal, 5*(3). Retrieved from http://ir.lib.uwo.ca/iipj/vol5/iss3/6

Hango, D. (2013). *Gender differences in science, technology, engineering, mathematics and computer science (STEM) programs at university.* Statistics Canada. Catalogue no. 75-006-X. Retrieved May 1, 2015, from www.statcan.gc.ca/pub/75-006-x/2013001/article/11874-eng.pdf

Hargreaves, A., & Shirley, D. (2012). The international quest for educational excellence: Understanding Canada's high performance. *Education Canada Magazine, 52*(4). Retrieved from http://www.cea-ace.ca/education-canada/article/international-quest-educational-excellence-understanding-canadas-high-perfo

Knowles, A. (2013, October 17). Growing STEM: Careers abound in science, technology, engineering and mathematics. *Industry Trends.* Retrieved May 1, 2015, from https://www.eco.ca/community/blog/growing-stem-careers-abound-in-science-technology-engineering-and-mathematics/81945/

Looker, D., & Thiessen, V. (2004). *Aspirations of Canadian youth for higher education: Final report.* Gatineau, Quebec: Human Resources and Skills Development Canada Publicentre. Retrieved from http://www.pisa.gc.ca/eng/pdf/SP-600-05-04E.pdf

Marshall, K. (2007). The busy lives of teens. *Perspectives, 8*(5), 5–15. Ottawa: Statistics Canada.

Mercredi, O., & Turpel, M. (1993). *In the rapids: Navigating the future of First Nations.* Toronto: Viking Canada.

Nazareth, L. (2014, January 24). Canada's education spending: Going up, but is it going to the right places? *Globe and Mail.* Retrieved April 30, 2015, from http://www.theglobeandmail.com/report-on-business/economy/economy-lab/canadas-education-spending-going-up-but-is-it-going-to-the-right-places/article16458671/

OECD. (2013a). *PISA 2012 results: Excellence through equity: Giving every student the chance to succeed* (Vol. II). PISA, OECD Publishing.

OECD. (2013b). *PISA 2012 results: What makes schools successful?* (Vol. IV: *Resources, policies and practices*). PISA, OECD Publishing.

OECD. (2014). *Education at a glance 2014: OECD indicators*. OECD Publishing.

Ringrose, J. (2009). "The future is female": The post-feminist panic over failing boys. In C. Levine-Rasky (Ed.), *Canadian perspectives on the sociology of education* (pp. 213–232). Don Mills, Ontario: Oxford Press.

Sengupta, U. (2013). *The war on Canada's Aboriginal youth*. McMaster Centre for Scholarship in the Public Interest. Retrieved May 1, 2015, from http://mcspi.ca/summer-institute/2013-the-war-on-youth/student-projects/ushnish-sengupta/

Sharpe, A., & Arsenault, J. (2009). *Investing in Aboriginal education in Canada: An economic perspective*. Ottawa, Canada: Canadian Policy Research Networks.

Sinclair, R. (2007). Identity lost and found: Lessons from the sixties scoop. *First Peoples Child and Family Review*, *3*(1), 65–82.

Statistics Canada. (2012). *Summary of elementary and secondary school indicators for Canada, the provinces, and territories*. Culture, Tourism, and Centre for Educational Statistics. Catalogue No. 81–595-M No. 099.

Statistics Canada. (2013). *Education indicators in Canada: An international perspective*. Tourism and the Centre for Education Statistics Division.

Statistics Canada. (2014a, December 15). *Education indicators in Canada: An international perspective*. Retrieved May 1, 2015, from http://www.statcan.gc.ca/pub/81–604-x/2014001/intro-eng.htm.

Statistics Canada. (2014b). *Table 477–0025, Enrolments in regular programs for youth in public elementary and secondary schools, by grade and sex, Canada, provinces and territories*.

Truth and Reconciliation Commission of Canada. (2012). *Truth and Reconciliation Commission of Canada: Interim report*. Retrieved May 1, 2015, from http://www.trc.ca/websites/trcinstitution/index.php?p=9

Van Pelt, D., & Emes, J. (2015). *Education in Canada: What is actually happening?* Vancouver: The Fraser Institute.

Vergari, S. (2010). Safeguarding federalism in education policy in Canada and the United States. *Publius: The Journal of Federalism*, *40*(3), 534–557.

Volante, L. (2013). Canadian policy responses to international comparison testing. *Interchange*, *44*, 169–178.

Volante, L., & Jaafar, S.B. (2008). Educational assessment in Canada. *Assessment in Education: Principles, Policy & Practice*, *15*(2), 201–210.

Willms, J.D. (2006). *Learning divides: Ten policy questions about the performance and equity of schools and schooling systems*. Report prepared for UNESCO Institute for Statistics.

CHAPTER SIX

South Korea

South Korea's Education: A National Obsession

MICHAEL J. SETH

South Korea is among the highest-ranking countries in most comparative assessments of education. Enrollment and graduate rates at all levels are extremely high, and South Korean students score at or near the top in most international comparative tests. This country has made rapid progress in creating educational opportunities for all citizens: in 2000, South Korea experienced a literacy rate of almost 100% (Kim-Renaud, 2005). In 2010, 98% of all 25–34-year-olds had completed upper-secondary education, the highest percentage of the 30 members of the Organisation for Economic Co-operation and Development (OECD), which represents the developed, industrialized nations (Organisation for Economic Co-operation and Development [OECD], 2012). Of this age group, 63% have completed some form of tertiary education, also the highest of any OECD country. A remarkable 80% of all high school graduates go on to an institution of higher education. South Korea was also on top in the total percentage of the population enrolled in tertiary education, regardless of age (Clark & Park, 2013).

On the 2012 Program for International Scholastic Achievement (PISA) tests, South Korean students achieved some of the highest scores in math, reading, and science, scoring in the top 10 among all participating countries (OECD, 2014). On all recent PISA tests, South Korean students have consistently ranked at or near the top in all categories. On the 2011 Trends in International Mathematics and Science Study tests, South Korea's fourth graders ranked second behind Singapore in math, and its eighth graders achieved the highest scores of any of the 63 participating countries (International Association for the Evaluation of

Educational Achievement, 2012). Pearson, an educational service, ranked South Korea's education output in 2013 as second in the world in overall cognitive skill and academic attainment, using data from the *Economist Intelligence Unit*, and revised this rating to first place in 2014 (Pearson, 2014).

PRIMARY AND SECONDARY EDUCATION

Created after 1945, the South Korean educational system has a structure modeled on that of the United States, with 1 year of kindergarten (*yuch'iwon*), 6 years of primary school (*ch'odŭng hakkyo*—called *kungmin hakkyo* or "citizen's schools" until 1996), 3 years of middle school (*chung hakkyo*), and 3 years of upper-secondary school or high school (*kodng hakkyo*). This experience is followed by 4 years of college (*taehakkyo*). Although education is only compulsory through middle school, almost all students complete 12 years. South Korean students attend classes 220 days a year, a higher-than-average number. The school year begins in early March and ends in December.

Almost all South Korean children attend kindergarten. As of 2014, 412,000 attended the nation's 3,861 private kindergartens, and 126,000 attended the 4,498 public kindergartens. Of South Korea's 5,855 primary schools, all but 77 are public. Primary education is mandatory and tuition-free. Children attend 850 hours of classes a week during their first 2 years, 986 hours during their 3rd and 4th years, and 1,088 hours the last 2 years. Primary education consists of algebra, geometry, Korean history, art, music, and physical education. Students also take English starting in the third grade. There are 3,144 middle schools; 658 are private and the rest are public. Public middle schools are tuition-free, and private school fees are strictly regulated. The country's 2,313 high schools are divided into general/academic schools and vocational schools. A total of 75% of the students are enrolled in academic institutions, and the rest (about 25%) are enrolled in vocational schools. About 30% of high schools (959) are private (Ministry of Education, 2014). Although continuation is not compulsory, about 99% of middle school students go on to high school, and almost all graduate. While many children attend their local primary and middle schools, students in large metropolitan areas, where the majority of Koreans live, are assigned to an academic public or private high school by lottery in their district.

About 10% of those enrolled in academic high schools attend special-purpose foreign language, science, and art schools. Vocational high schools follow the same curriculum as academic schools during the first year and then offer specialized courses in industry, technology, agriculture, fisheries, and home economics. They are not necessarily terminal, as students take the college entrance exam at almost the same rate as students from academic high schools. In recent years, nearly one-fourth of those completing vocational high schools attended a university upon graduation, and a larger number enrolled in 2-year colleges.

Historically, vocational high schools have been less popular with families, because attending these schools was perceived to decrease opportunities for their sons and daughters to enter a good tertiary school. In 2007, the government tried to make them more appealing by changing their name to "professional schools." It has also pioneered a Meister School program to train highly skilled workers. But in comparison to academic schools, fewer students enroll. In the past, most secondary schools were same-sex. In recent years, however, some have become coeducational. Parents tend to prefer non-mixed schools, feeling they offer less distraction. Group solidarity is emphasized in secondary schools, with each class electing a class leader. High school graduates form strong bonds, and members of the same graduating class often maintain those ties throughout their lives.

In the past, the educational system was highly centralized under the Ministry of Education (MOE). The ministry has undergone a number of name changes: it was first called the Ministry of Education and Culture; in 2001, the Ministry of Education and Human Resources; and from 2008 to 2013, the Ministry of Education, Science, and Technology. Its administrative duties have largely remained the same. The MOE sets the curriculum, credentials teachers, and issues detailed regulations. Schools are allowed to select textbooks from a list approved by the MOE. In recent years, more leeway has been granted to provincial and city school authorities, but the system remains centralized. Since 1955, all primary and secondary schools have followed the national curriculum, which has been periodically revised. The current Seventh Curriculum was drawn up in 1998 and revised in 2009 and again in 2012. Up to and including the first year of high school, all schools require the same subjects. During the last 2 years of high school, students have some options regarding social science, art, or other subjects. Academic performance determines promotion from one grade to another, but almost all students earn promotion.

TEACHER PREPARATION

South Korean teachers are highly trained; almost all have a 4-year degree from teacher education programs closely supervised by the MOE. In-service training programs for teachers have long been a major feature of teacher education. Teachers in South Korea are also well paid, receiving some of the highest salaries offered among industrialized countries. A lower-secondary teacher earns an average mid-career salary of about $52,699, approximately $10,000 higher than the OECD average (National Center on Education and the Economy, 2015).

Entrance to teacher training programs is very competitive. Only those with well-above-average grades are admitted. In recent years, entrance to elementary teacher programs has generally been restricted to the top 5% of the academic high school cohort. Most primary school teachers are women, but about two-thirds of secondary school teachers are men. About half of Korean educators belong to the Korean Federation of Teachers' Associations (KFTA), but 20% belong to the politically leftist Korean Teachers Union (Chŏnkyojo).

In addition to the formal education system, a "shadow" system of private institutions (*hagwŏn*) offers after-school instruction. Mostly small, they are a ubiquitous presence in South Korea. A large majority of secondary students and an increasingly large number of primary and even pre-school children attend these as well. Many private study halls for students are also available. Most families devote considerable financial resources to sending their sons and daughters to these institutions. Private tutoring, often provided by college students, is also common.

HIGHER EDUCATION IN SOUTH KOREA

While policymakers have striven to make primary and secondary schools uniform in standards, universities are ranked in a hierarchy of prestige. What are popularly called "SKY"—Seoul National University, Korea (Koryŏ) University, and Yonsei University—are at the apex of the prestige rankings, along with the more specialized Korea Advanced Institute of Science and Technology (KAIST) and Pohang University of Science and Technology (POSTECH). These rankings are informal but universally recognized. Admission to a university has chiefly been determined by scores on highly competitive college entrance exams, although there have been many attempts to tinker with this system by using high school grades and other methods of selection. The current exam is called the College Scholastic Ability Test (CSAT), known popularly as the *sunŭng*, and is administered by the Korea Institute for Curriculum and Evaluation. It is given each year in November. The 8-hour exam covers math, science, history, the Korean language, and English. The exam day marks a major event during which restrictions on traffic, construction, and noise are imposed. In recent years, in order to reduce the pressure placed on students preparing for the exams, the admission process has also considered school grades, attendance, and participation in extracurricular and service activities. However, the entrance exam remains the main factor in determining college admission.

Unlike primary and secondary education, higher education is generally private. Of the 149 two-year colleges, 140 are private, and of the 222 four-year colleges and universities, 180 are private. Nearly 80% of all university students attend private institutions. All higher education institutions charge tuition, with the government providing about 23% of the funding for colleges and universities. Tuition at private schools is regulated and kept within range of that at public institutions. The MOE regulates the establishment of institutions of higher education and their academic departments, curriculum, degree requirements, and student quotas. The Korea Council for University Education accredits institutions, whereas specialized agencies regulate individual programs. About 20% of those enrolled in higher education attend junior colleges. These institutions mostly offer a technical or commercial-oriented curriculum but allow students to transfer to a 4-year university upon completion (Ministry of Education, 2014).

A bachelor's degree (*haksa*) generally requires 4 years of study, but there are some 5-year specialized and some 3-year accelerated programs. A master's degree (*sŏksa*) requires two more years of study. Students with a master's can study for a doctoral degree (*paksa*), which usually requires 2 more years of study plus completion of a dissertation or project. As of 2014, 3.3 million students were enrolled in the 371 institutions of higher education (Ministry of Education, 2014). Until the 1990s, most university students were men, but in recent years the gender gap has been closing. In 2009, women made up 49% of all bachelor's degrees, 49% of all master's degrees, and 31% of all doctorates. The percentage of women in graduate school rose from 25% to 39% from 2000 to 2012 (Ahn, 2014).

HISTORICAL BACKGROUND

South Korea has not always been a top-ranked nation in education—far from it. At the time of its 1945 liberation from 35 years of Japanese occupation, it was a nation of illiterate or semi-literate peasants. Primary school education had recently been expanded, but still only 40% of school-age students were enrolled in grades one through six. Only 5% of the population had a secondary school education. There was only one university in the country, founded in 1925. The Japanese created this institution for their residents in the country, and only one-third of the students were Korean. Most of the teachers were Japanese and were repatriated immediately after the Second World War (Seth, 2002b).

Korean students lacked suitable textbooks or materials in their native language. Factors that threatened progress included a flood of refugees from the North and elsewhere and a highly destructive civil war that lasted from 1950 to 1953, followed by years of political turmoil ending with a military coup in 1961. South Korea was a very poor country with a per capita income in 1960 similar to that of Haiti. Prospects for economic development appeared dim to most observers. Most foreign experts had low expectations for its educational development (Seth, 2002b).

RAPID PROGRESS IN EDUCATIONAL DEVELOPMENT

Educational development proceeded rapidly despite these problems. From 1945 to 1960, enrollment in primary schools rose threefold, in secondary schools more than eightfold, and in higher education tenfold. By 1960, 96% of all children of primary school age were attending school. Enrollment continued to grow, and by the 1970s almost all students were attending middle school. By the early 1990s, the high school graduation rate reached 90%. Successful adult literacy programs sharply reduced illiteracy. Primary education had become almost universal by the time the nation's economic takeoff began in the early 1960s (Seth, 2002b).

Furthermore, educational development, as measured in enrollment levels and teacher training, continued to keep pace with South Korea's much-praised economic growth. In fact, at every point in its development from the 1950s through the late 1990s, when it attained developed status, South Korea's education system was at the extreme end among developing countries—that is, South Korea had higher levels of school enrollment than any other developing nation in its per capita GNP range (Seth, 2002b). Current statistics indicate how recently this expansion occurred: by 2012, among 25–34-year-olds, 98% had completed high school, and 63% had some tertiary education. However, among 55–64-year-olds, less than 48% had completed high school, and only 14% had some tertiary education, the greatest generational difference among the OECD member states (OECD, 2014).

THE EVOLUTION OF THE SCHOOL SYSTEM

Several features marked the evolution of South Korea's school system. One was its sequential nature of educational development. The state first focused on schooling for younger children. Until the 1960s, state resources gave priority to primary education. Private foundations accounted for much of the secondary and most of the tertiary schooling. As a result, up to the early 1960s, the majority of upper-secondary school students attended private schools. With universal primary education accomplished, government investment in secondary education expanded in the 1960s and 1970s. Greater priority was initially given to middle schools, then to high schools. Government policy encouraged universal secondary education but sought to prevent an oversupply of college graduates by curbing the number of university students in the 1960s and again in the early 1980s, with only limited success (Seth, 2002b).

The state also attempted to impose uniform standards and promoted equal access to education. "Uniformity of Education" became a watchword for educational development after 1945. In addition to establishing a uniform curriculum, the state invested in rural schools. Teacher standards were uniform. To avoid concentrations of the best teachers in a few areas, in the 1950s, a policy of rotating teachers among schools every 5 years was implemented (Seth, 2002b). While schools in the major cities—especially Seoul—were regarded as better, the disparity in school standards as judged by test scores and internal efficiency between urban and rural areas and within school districts was generally lower than in most developing and even many wealthier nations (Seth, 2002b).

A commitment to uniformity of education was linked with equal access. For post-1945 South Korea, uniformity in education meant, at the very least, that the entrance examination system ought to be fair. This official policy was often termed the "equalization of education." At the time of the debates over the Education Law in 1949–1951, the idea of early tracking was rejected. Only by making no level of education terminal could access to upper tiers of schooling be assured (Seth, 2002a). As a result, even vocational high schools offered college preparatory courses. In a further effort to impose uniform standards, the MOE abolished the middle school entrance exam in 1968 to avoid early tracking. In 1973, it passed the High School Equalization Act, which abolished high school entrance exams. In both cases students were assigned to secondary schools within a district by lottery in an effort to avoid disparities in school standards and to provide equality of opportunity. Since school districts tended to be large, this meant that students often took long bus rides to reach schools (Seth, 2002b).

Another feature included the high standards of teacher training. South Korea suffered from a severe shortage of teachers in the late 1940s and from the 1950s into the 1960s. But rather than quickly training new teachers, the country made teacher education programs highly selective and invested in intensive training. As a result, South Korea had one of the largest numbers of highly trained educators for a country at its income level, but their numbers fell far short of what was needed. Consequently, classroom sizes were often huge. In fact, it was not uncommon for primary and secondary school teachers to teach 100 pupils in two or even three shifts. Before 1970, South Korea had one of the highest teacher-to-student ratios in the world. Through the 1990s, it continued to have one of the highest ratios for any country of its income and education level (Seth, 2002b). Only in recent years, with enrollment falling due to a low birth rate and to the gradual expansion in the numbers of teachers, have classroom sizes become smaller, although they are still higher than average when compared to other developed countries. From 1967, in-service training became systematized into a routine feature of the teaching profession to improve levels of subject knowledge and competency. Teacher training programs set high standards and admitted only top academic achievers. Entrance into teacher education programs has remained highly competitive (Seth, 2002b).

Another feature of South Korean educational development was the transfer of much of the economic burden onto the students and their families. Although technically free, primary education involved various fees, including "voluntary" gifts to teachers, payment for exam question papers, and so on. School fees were a major expense for families at all levels in the decades after 1945. Secondary school expansion relied on private foundations for funding. State support for education gradually increased starting in the 1960s. However, higher education has remained largely funded by tuition. As incomes rose, the costs of the formal education system became less of a burden, but families still had to pay for the cost of private after-school classes (Seth, 2002b).

CULTURAL ATTITUDE TOWARD EDUCATION

A key factor in South Korea's educational transformation, one that still shapes the nature of education today, is the broad-based public demand for schooling—what Koreans often refer to as their "education fever" (*kyoyukyŏl*). Most Koreans attribute this zeal for education, or more precisely for prestigious degrees, to the nation's "Confucian" cultural heritage; however, the origins of education fever are complex (Kim, S., 2005). Education in traditional Korea was valued as both a means of personal self-cultivation and a way of achieving status and power.

While education was recognized as an end in itself, in practice it was generally seen as a means of social mobility and status selection. Under the Chosŏn Dynasty (1392–1910), a series of highly competitive examinations served as the means of selection for prestigious government positions. Confined for the most part to the aristocratic *yangban* class, the examination system acted as the main selection device for the limited number of government posts. Consequently, formal education was largely organized around preparation for the exams. Elite families, at least, devoted a great deal of energy and expense to education and examination preparation. In this way they behaved much like modern South Korean families (Seth, 2002b).

THE IMPACT OF JAPANESE RULE AND THEREAFTER

Four decades of Japanese rule also shaped South Korea's social demand for education. The colonial regime developed a modern educational system that was sequential in nature, with a concentration on basic education followed by a slow growth in secondary and tertiary levels of schooling. The Japanese emphasis on education and meritocracy helped to reinforce traditional Korean attitudes. However, colonial officials limited the access of Koreans to upper levels of schooling and assigned them to inferior schools. Japanese wartime policies after 1938 further limited the number of schools of higher education and redirected the curriculum away from literary to less prestigious technical education and vocational training.

These educational restrictions greatly frustrated families of the emerging middle class because they limited economic advancement and because they equated education with rank and status. This unmet demand for educational advancement is a key factor in explaining the "education fever" of South Korea since the end of the Second World War (Seth, 2002b).

The desire for schooling was not limited just to the few. The wartime mobilization of society in the 1930s, World War II, the postwar chaos, the collapse of the colonial regime, and the Korean War uprooted millions of Koreans, broke down the old *yangban*-dominated social order, and removed the barriers that had limited higher education to a hereditary elite. Millions of ordinary Koreans saw the possibility of improving their lives through their children's education. Meanwhile, American progressive education reinforced and influenced traditional beliefs in the transformational value of schooling, and American and socialist ideas of egalitarianism and democracy contributed to the growth of educational aspirations among Korean families of all backgrounds (Seth, 2002b).

The result was a general population impatient with any restrictions placed on the pursuit of degrees. After liberation from Japan in 1945, the pent-up demand for education was immediately felt. Hundreds of new schools at all levels were opened, yet they were unable to accommodate the sudden increase in enrollment. Parents, even poor ones, were willing to make enormous personal sacrifices to put their children through school. The broad-based nature of the public demand for schooling led the state to pursue its goals of establishing a universal basic education, alleviating the problems of school dropouts, and lessening regional disparities in education development (Seth, 2002b).

Public policymakers also contributed to the education fever in two crucial ways just after liberation. One way involved the decision to end the strict tracking system created by the Japanese. While secondary schools were divided into academic and vocational, both types of institutions could lead to higher education. There was no structural winnowing of students; all could—and most did—seek to advance to higher levels, resulting in fierce competition. The state committed itself to a second policy to establish universal and uniform basic education. This effort eliminated the sharp disparities between regions and social classes that often characterized developing nations. Although this policy contributed to social cohesion and provided a literate workforce with the skills needed for a newly industrializing economy, it also created strains between the demand for higher levels of education and the state's efforts to prevent an oversupply of advanced degree holders. And it made competition for the restricted entry into higher educational tiers fiercer, adding to the intensity of South Korea's "education fever" (Seth, 2002b).

The social demand for schooling, the highly competitive examination system, the willingness of families to devote resources to improving the life chances of their children through education, and the government's commitment to teacher training and open access to higher levels of schooling all contributed to the rapid transformation of South Korea into a well-schooled nation, but it also contributed to the creation of many problems in its educational system.

PROBLEMS AND CHALLENGES TODAY

Despite their country's achievements in schooling, many South Koreans are highly critical of their education system. A recent study of parents' feelings about schooling, for example, found that only 37.6% of parents in or near Seoul were satisfied with the education that schools provided (Lee, 2010). Talk of the "collapse of education" and the "failure of the schools" dominates public discourse. In fact, the difference between the high praise that South Korea's education system receives abroad and the general dissatisfaction it has earned at home is striking. For example, a comparative study undertaken by the Korean Educational Development Institute found that the public in Finland was, in general, "optimistic" over its schools' ability to meet their nation's challenges, while the majority of the Korean public expressed pessimism (Lee, 2010).

There are doubts about whether the South Korean educational system, which has served the nation well in the past, can meet current and future needs (Lee, Kim, & Byun, 2012). Public criticism centers on many problems: the high degree of pressure on students, the financial burden on families, and the heavy emphasis on gaining prestigious degrees. Other concerns include the perception that higher education has not set the lofty standards needed for a technologically advanced society and that educational reforms will undermine equal opportunity.

Financial Burden

The enormous financial burden that education places on families is a serious problem. While the 5% of South Korea's GDP that is devoted to public expenditures on schooling is about average for a developed nation, millions of families spend considerable portions of their income on private tutoring and on cram schools—or *hagwŏns*, as they are called—in seeking a competitive advantage in gaining access to prestigious universities. The same social demand for education that enabled the state to develop education with modest expenditures by placing much of the financial burden on families and that led to such high rates of enrollment has created a large private market for supplementary schooling.

Even in the 1950s and 1960s, the public decried the cost of tutoring, but over the years, expenditures have escalated as private lessons have become virtually universal and are seen by most families as a necessary part of schooling. While the actual cost in private spending is difficult to measure, since families often underreport it, it is clearly considerable. Since the mid-1990s, studies have indicated that Korean families spend a larger percentage of their income on schooling than almost any other nation. In early 1995, the Korean Educational Development Institute estimated that families paid 17 trillion won (U.S. $21 billion) on direct educational expenditures such as tuition, mandatory fees, extracurricular activities sponsored by schools, transportation, and textbooks. By contrast, total government public expenditures on education in 1994 amounted to 16.7 trillion won (Seth, 2005). This means that the public paid 51% of the total direct cost of education.

Since then, public spending on education has increased considerably, and so has private spending. The financial crisis of 1997–1998 may have slowed spending a bit, but after 2000, spending on private tutoring and cram schools increased again. When the 2008 economic recession slowed spending among Koreans, only private educational expenditures rose. In 2009, South Koreans spent $19 billion on private tutoring, more than half of what they paid for public education (Chandler, 2011). According to the OECD, when private spending is factored in, South Korea devoted 8% of its GDP to education in 2011. This expenditure was the third-highest of any developed nation and well above the 6.1% average among OECD members, even though the public expenditures of 5% were about average.

Other studies have shown that total spending was much higher. In 2013, a McKinsey report estimated the amount of private spending on schooling and found that more than 9% of the GDP was devoted to education. This report confirmed the findings of other studies indicating that education cost was continuing to increase faster than household income. Only housing was a greater financial burden (McKinsey Global Institute, 2013).

Private lessons contribute greatly to rising costs. Many South Koreans believe that the formal educational system is inadequate for preparing their students for entry into a good college. The result is the vast shadow school system of *hagwŏns* (Byun, 2014). High school students have long taken private lessons, but with the opening of a number of special high schools with competitive entry requirements and with greater emphasis on getting an early start on the competition for college entry, many primary students attend cram schools. At the beginning of the twenty-first century, the Korean Educational Development Institute conducted a survey that found that approximately 83.1% of elementary students were using the services of private tutors (Park, 2003).

Parents have sought options other than expensive private schools and sometimes use home schooling as an alternative. These approaches are based on the idea that full-time tutoring and supervised studying at home and at cram schools is a more effective use of time than attending public schools. The effort to find the best method to educate students has ramifications: the nearly full-time role of the mother in selecting the right cram schools or tutors and supervising the study of students contributes to the low percentage of married women in the workforce and those pursuing professional careers. It is often considered a major factor in the country's extremely low fertility rate, since the cost of education makes having more than one child difficult.

Higher Education: Problems and Limitations

Koreans spend about 2.6% of their GDP on higher education, second only to the United States, which spends 2.8%. This proportion is well above the OECD average of 1.6% (OECD, 2013a). However, that expenditure has not translated into the quality one would expect. Student-teacher ratios are the highest among industrialized countries. Although the quality of higher education has improved in recent years, university standards are below those of the most modern developed states. A major portion of the financial burden for higher education falls on students and their families. Government support accounts for one-quarter of the costs. Three out of four students attend private college, and universities typically derive 70%–80% of their financial support from tuition and fees. Institutes of higher education, dependent on tuition, cannot afford to fail students, and few do; graduation is almost automatic. While too much pressure is placed on secondary students, often too little is placed on students at the university level. A shortage of funds hampers research.

Lacking the great financial endowments of many American universities, and lacking the traditions and tax codes that encourage generous alumni giving, Korean universities have less money to invest in research. Public expenditures on higher education that could improve its quality have been modest. Practices at universities such as awarding grants to faculty according to their seniority rather than through true competition have also contributed to the modest research output of even the best universities. As a result, Korean universities lag behind their foreign counterparts, and the large investment by families in higher education does not pay the dividends it should. Many students still feel the need to go abroad for better educational opportunities, while foreign students who come to Korea are modest in number.

Few Korean universities do well in international rankings. The Times Higher Education World University Rankings listed only four Korean universities in the top 200, with Seoul National ranked 50th, the Korean Advanced Institute of Science and Technology 52nd, and Pohang University of Science and Technology 66th (Times Higher Education, 2014). In addition, universities face declining enrollment, since the nation's low birth rate means a smaller number of high school graduates. The government has sought to merge departments at institutions to deal with this problem.

Exodus Overseas

The competition to enter prestigious universities has led many South Koreans to travel overseas for schooling. A foreign degree is viewed as more prestigious than one from a second- or third-tier domestic university. South Koreans generally believe that the best postgraduate programs are in the United States and other developed nations. Additionally, the learning of a foreign language, especially English, provides a competitive advantage for graduates. In 2012, the Fulbright Commission in Seoul estimated that 30.7% of Koreans studied in the United States, 26.3% in China, 8.6% in Canada, 8.4% in Japan, and 7.2% in Australia (Rubin, 2014). South Korean students are disproportionately represented in universities in many countries. Increasingly, students are going to China and to other nearby countries.

A growing number of students going abroad are attending high schools or even primary schools, leading to the *"kirogi"* (wild goose) phenomenon of families separated by the Pacific Ocean. Their parents send them abroad to live with relatives or with non-relatives to whom they pay monthly support, allowing them to learn English by attending American or sometimes Canadian, Australian, or other foreign schools. Since English is a valuable skill, it gives the students an edge that may enable them to attend a top university in the United States or another nation (Kim, 2009). A few wealthy parents began sending children abroad when the restrictions on overseas travel eased after the 1988 Seoul Olympics, but the number of these students became significant only after 2000. In 1995, just over 2,000 pre-college students left to study abroad, but in 2006 that number increased to nearly 30,000, according to the Korean Educational Development Institute (Zagier, 2012).

This trend resulted in financial hardships, separated families, and sharply rising divorce rates. An easier solution was for the family to move abroad, particularly if it could not afford the high cost of a place with a host family or in a boarding school. While acquiring English language skills is a major reason for sending students abroad, surveys find *kirogi* parents to be critical of the Korean educational system, including its Confucian conformity, which is believed to stifle creativity, and the attention devoted to top students at the expense of the less academically gifted. Parents also are attracted to the opportunities for extracurricular activities that they believe foster students' social skills.

Pressure on Students

South Korean parents and educators often express concern about the pressure the Korean education system places on children. In fact, South Korea's highly competitive system has achieved some notoriety, with one popular book on education calling it "the pressure cooker" (Ripley, 2013). Comparative studies suggest that the country's young people, driven by competition to get into a good university, put in more time studying than their counterparts elsewhere. By some measures, secondary school students spend an average of 13 to 14 hours a day taking some sort of class or studying. Other estimates place the figure as high as 15 hours, especially for upper-level secondary students cramming for the college entrance exam.

Most students spend their waking hours in classrooms, at cram schools, in study halls, or at home, where they also study. These long hours take a physical and psychological toll on youth. The suicide rate among 13- to 24-year-olds has risen to one of the highest in the world. By 2010, it had become the leading cause of death in that age group, outstripping traffic accidents, the main cause of death for that demographic in most developed countries. Anecdotal evidence attributes the pressure to succeed academically as a leading cause of this high suicide rate. A recent article reported that among South Koreans who mentioned having suicidal thoughts in 2010, 53% attributed these feelings to inadequate academic performance (Koo, 2014). A recent survey of 6,791 elementary, middle, and high school students indicated that these students had the lowest happiness level when compared with the OECD average (Suh-young, 2012). The pressure to succeed academically may be robbing young people of their youth, leaving them with little time to freely explore, play, and interact socially.

Student scores on comparative tests cannot justify these long hours, which are far more prevalent in South Korea than in many other OECD countries. Children in Finland, for example, spend considerably fewer hours on studying and attend class 30 fewer days a year, but achieve nearly the same results. According to a PISA criterion known as "study effectiveness," which is the number of hours attending class or studying and the outcomes as measured by comparative tests of educational attainment, South Korea ranks only 24th of 30 developed nations (OECD, 2013b). Efforts by local and national governments to reduce the burden on students who are studying too much by limiting cram school and study hall hours have been unsuccessful (Ripley, 2013).

Problems Involving Inequality and Creativity

Another issue of central concern to many Koreans has been the move away from egalitarian policies on education. The commitment by the state to bring all students up to the same basic level of instruction and to provide equal opportunity to all children came under criticism in the 1990s (Park, 2010). The lack of differentiation between schools, and within them, was feared to be an impediment to more gifted students.

Neoliberal ideas led educational reformers to focus on producing highly competent talent in an increasingly competitive global economy and to develop creative skills for what was called a "creative economy" based on innovation rather than adapting existing technologies (Kim, K., 2005). Ability grouping was introduced in some primary and middle schools around 2000, and by the end of the decade, a majority of schools had special classes for advanced students in mathematics and English (Park, 2013). This practice had long been resisted because it was feared that it would lead to a form of elitist education and inequality. In 2002, the Gifted Education Law allowed for the creation of special schools of science and foreign languages. These institutions differed from regular schools in that students were not assigned at random but competed for admission on an examination.

In another experiment, students in some districts were allowed to present their two or three choices among the high schools they wished to attend, although this approach was not adopted in Seoul and other places. Schools have also been allowed some freedom to develop differentiated curricula to make learning more flexible and to better provide for higher-performing students (Park, 2013). The uniformity of Korean education has also been challenged by the growing ethnic diversity among the population. Although by international standards South Korea is a very homogeneous society, the number of children from non-Korean ethnic backgrounds has increased considerably in recent years (Choi, 2010). This increase has led to calls for a more multicultural approach to education that allows for teaching according to students' backgrounds.

The move toward educational reform is closely tied to politics and ideology. Advocates for moving away from a uniform education and the highly centralized and standardized educational system often argue for an education that is more humanizing, one that cultivates individuality, creativity, and flexibility. Their emphasis is on a pedagogy that will liberate the talented students and turn education into a dynamic marketplace of competing ideas and methods. For these reformers, the consequences of promoting socioeconomic inequality are of less concern than promoting a liberal, creative society that can compete internationally in the new knowledge-based global economy. Opponents of these reforms are more committed to the egalitarian ideals that underpinned much Korean educational development. They fear a long-term threat to a democratic society and the replication of the rigid hierarchical society based on the inherited inequality that had characterized Korea until the twentieth century (Oh, 2011).

These opponents believe that private tutoring and cram schools, with their escalating costs, already promote inequality and give wealthier families an advantage in the pursuit of prestigious degrees. However, studies have suggested that they may not give wealthier families the advantage they are believed to offer (Park, 2013). When school location and socioeconomic background are taken into consideration, the gain in college entry test scores they provide is modest. Studies have also found that although some school districts—such as Seoul's Eighth—have far higher college entrance test scores than others, this difference can be attributed to the concentration of wealthier, better-educated families, not to variations in school standards, which are still relatively minor (Kim & Byun, 2014).

Additionally, critics of the system point to its emphasis on rote memorization and repetitive drills. Educators and the public have unfavorably contrasted Korean schools with the more creative ones found in the United States and, to a lesser extent, in Europe. In fact, critics have argued that the cram schools offer more innovative and effective learning experiences and also attract some of the best teachers, who are freed from the tight restrictions on the methods imposed on formal schools by the MOE. Indeed, some cram school teachers have become "superstars," earning much more money than any public school teachers.

The Korean public has been critical of schoolteachers. Despite their high standard of training and the traditional esteem for teachers, they have become less respected. In a 2013 survey, South Korean parents ranked them the third-lowest among 21 countries in providing a good education (Dolton & Marcenaro-Gutierrez, 2013). Surveys also reveal low morale among teachers, even though South Korea's schoolteachers are well paid. Teachers have strongly resisted attempts to introduce student and parent evaluations to assess their performance, as well as a government effort to send poorly performing teachers back for retraining. However, many still find it an attractive career, and competition to enter teacher programs remains high.

Education experts such as Hyunjoon Park, whose own studies found that standardized education, memorization, drills, and test preparation did not stifle creativity, have challenged some of these criticisms (Park, 2013). A careful analysis of comparative educational data suggests that South Korean students are no less creative than their American or European counterparts. In 2003, PISA problem-solving tests indicated that Korean students scored near the top, just behind students from Finland and Japan (OECD, 2003). Further, since Korean students in the top 10 percentiles do as well as or better than their counterparts in almost every other country, including in problem solving, the belief that the most gifted young people are not well served by the education system is questionable.

Some educators have suggested that criticisms of Korean pedagogy are unfair because the actual instructional methods employed by teachers focus more on creativity and problem solving than critics believe (Park, 2013). Skeptics, it has been suggested, underestimate the skill and resourcefulness of the country's well-trained public teachers and exaggerate the effectiveness of cram schools. Moreover, vigorous criticism over education is not new; the South Korean public has always seen the country's schools as falling short of its expectations.

CONCLUSION

South Koreans often view their focus on education as a national obsession or "fever." This concern for educational attainment has contributed to the development of one of the world's most competitive school systems. Overall, it has been a major factor in the nation's "economic miracle" and a source of great pride. Its ability to produce a highly educated citizenry deserves admiration and even emulation. Yet for all the admiration it has achieved abroad, there is a growing consensus among educators and the public in South Korea that the education system has some basic underlying problems that need to be addressed, including the financial burden it places on families, the excessive competition to enter elite universities, the long hours and pressure on the youth, the threats to equality of opportunity, and the use of an outmoded pedagogy. However, despite public awareness of these issues, little progress has been made in addressing them. South Korea's education is likely to remain intensely competitive and expensive, and the "educational arms race" will probably continue unabated in the near future.

REFERENCES

Ahn, J. (2014). Analysis of women doctorates entering the labor market in Republic of Korea. In Y. Park & K. Kim (Eds.), *Korean education in changing economic and demographic contexts* (pp. 59–76). New York: Springer.

Byun, S. (2014). Shadow education and academic success in Republic of Korea. In Y. Park & K. Kim (Eds.), *Korean education in changing economic and demographic contexts* (pp. 39–58). New York: Springer.

Chandler, M. (2011, April 3). S. Korea tries to wrest control from booming private tutoring industry. *The Washington Post*. Retrieved from http://www.washingtonpost.com

Choi, J. (2010). Educating citizens in a multicultural society: The case of South Korea. *Social Studies, 101*(4), 174–178.

Clark, N., & Park, H. (2013, June 1). Education in South Korea. *World Education News & Reviews*. Retrieved from http://wenr.wes.org/2013/06/wenr-june-2013-an-overview-of-education-in-south-korea/

Dolton, P., & Marcenaro-Gutierrez, O. (2013). *2013 global teacher status index*. London: Varkey GEMS Foundation.

International Association for the Evaluation of Educational Achievement. (2012). *TIMSS 2011 international results in mathematics*. Retrieved from http://timss.bc.edu/timss2011/downloads/T11_IR_Mathematics_FullBook.pdf

Kim, K. (2005). Globalization, statist political economy, and unsuccessful education reform in South Korea, 1993–2003. *Education Policy Analysis Archives, 13*(12), 1–24.

Kim, K., & Byun, S. (2014). Determinants of academic achievement in Republic of Korea. In Y. Park & K. Kim (Eds.), *Korean education in changing economic and demographic contexts* (pp. 23–37). New York: Springer.

Kim, S. (2005). *Korean pattern of education growth and development.* Unpublished Paper. Seoul National University.

Kim, S. (2009, October 16). *Kirogi families in the U.S.: Transnational migration and education.* Unpublished paper, Harvard University.

Kim-Renaud, Y. (2005). Introduction. In Y. Kim-Renaud, R.R. Grinker, & K.W. Larsen (Eds.), *The Sigur Center Asia Papers: Korean education* (pp. v–vii). Washington, DC: The George Washington University.

Koo, S. (2014, August 1). An assault upon our children: South Korea's education system hurts students. *The New York Times.* Retrieved from http://www.nytimes.com/ 2014/08/02/opinion/sunday/south-koreas-education-system-hurts-students.html?_r=1

Lee, C., Kim, Y., & Byun, S. (2012). The rise of Korean education from the ashes of the Korean War. *Prospects, 42*(3), 308–318.

Lee, Y. (2010). Views on education and achievement: Finland's story of success and South Korea's story of decline. *KEDI Journal of Educational Policy, 7*(2), 379–401.

McKinsey Global Institute. (2013). *Beyond Korean style: Shaping a new growth formula.* Retrieved from http://www.mckinsey.com/insights/asia-pacific/beyond_korean_style

Ministry of Education. (2014). *Republic of Korea.* Retrieved from http://english.moe.go.kr/web/1721/site/contents/en/en_0219.jsp

National Center on Education and the Economy. (2015). *Center on International Education Benchmarking: South Korea.* Retrieved from http://www.ncee.org/programs-affiliates/center-on-international-education-benchmarking/top-performing-countries/south-korea-overview/south-korea-teacher-and-principal-quality/

Oh, J. (2011). High school diversification against education equalization: A critical analysis of neoliberal educational reform in South Korea. *Asia Pacific Education Review, 12*(3), 381–392.

Organisation for Economic Co-operation and Development. (2003). *Problem solving for tomorrow's world: First measure of cross-curricular competencies from PISA 2003.* Paris: Organisation of Economic Cooperation and Development.

Organisation for Economic Co-operation and Development. (2012). *Education at a glance 2012: Highlights.* Paris: Organisation of Economic Cooperation and Development.

Organisation for Economic Co-operation and Development. (2013a). *Education at a glance 2013: OECD indicators.* Paris: Organisation of Economic Cooperation and Development.

Organisation for Economic Co-operation and Development. (2013b). *2012 PISA results.* Paris: Organisation of Economic Cooperation and Development.

Organisation for Economic Co-operation and Development. (2014). *Education at a glance 2014: OECD indicators.* Paris: Organisation of Economic Cooperation and Development.

Park, H. (2013). *Re-evaluating education in Japan and Korea: Demystifying stereotypes.* New York: Routledge.

Park, J. (2003, November 19). Tutoring costs back to pre-crash levels. *The Chosun Ilbo.* Retrieved from http://english.chosun.com

Park, S. (2010). Crafting and dismantling the egalitarian social contract: The changing state-society relations in globalizing Korea. *Pacific Review, 23*(5), 579–601.

Pearson. (2014). *Index of cognitive skills and educational attainment.* Retrieved from http://thelearningcurve.pearson.com/index/index-ranking

Ripley, A. (2013). *The smartest kids in the world: And how they got that way.* New York: Simon & Schuster.

Rubin, K. (2014). The changing tide of South Korean student flows. *International Educator, 32*(2), 28–34.

Seth, M.J. (2002a). Creating a Korean educational system, 1945–1951. In *The Korean Academy of Korean Studies, Proceedings of the 1st World Congress of Korean Studies: Embracing the other: The interaction of Korean and foreign cultures* (pp. 866–877). Seoul: Academy of Korean Studies.

Seth, M.J. (2002b). *Education fever: Politics, society and the pursuit of schooling in South Korea.* Honolulu: University of Hawaii Press.

Seth, M.J. (2005). Korean education: A philosophical and historical perspective. In Y. Kim-Renaud, R.R. Grinker, & K.W. Larsen (Eds.), *The Sigur Center Asia Papers: Korean education* (pp. 3–16). Washington, DC: The George Washington University.

Suh-young, Y. (2012). Korean children least happy among OECD states. *Korea Times.* Retrieved from http://www.koreatimes.co.kr/www/news/nation /2012/05/113_110307.html

Times Higher Education. (2014). *World university rankings 2014–2015.* Retrieved from http://www.timeshighereducation.co.uk/world-university-rankings

Zagier, A. (2012, April 2). Early study abroad for U.S. education means split families in South Korea. *Huffington Post.* Retrieved from http://www.huffingtonpost.com

CHAPTER SEVEN

Singapore

Success in Singapore: A Model for Excellence in Education

VIVIEN GENESER AND HSIAO-PING WU

The success of the educational system in Singapore, a tiny island city-state that has only been in existence as a nation since 1965, has generated interest among educators from all over the world. Indeed, a look at the test results from the Program for International Scholastic Achievement (PISA) reveals that students in Singapore consistently rank near the top in all academic content areas in comparison to the other 64 nations and territories that participate in this triennial global assessment survey (Hogan, 2014; Lee, 2014; Organisation for Economic Co-operation and Development [OECD], 2012; Ripley, 2013). To comprehend the complexities of these impressive scholastic accomplishments as demonstrated by international rankings of test scores, secondary school graduation rates, and the percentage of students accepted into universities abroad, it is necessary to examine all of the variables that have coalesced to support such a high rate of student academic success.

LOCATION AND DEMOGRAPHICS

The 5.3 million residents of Singapore share approximately 637.5 square kilometers (247 square miles), and because of the thriving economy, the population has increased rapidly for several decades. In fact, in 2010, Singapore was listed for the second successive year as the leading immigration hot spot in Asia (*The Straits Times*, 2010). However, the numbers have stabilized in recent years. The population is diverse, yet it is mostly comprised of three major ethnicities. The Chinese represent the dominant ethnicity with approximately 74.3% of the population; 13.3% of the citizens claim a Malaysian identity; 9.1% self-identify as Indian; and 3.3% are listed as "other" in the annual report from Singapore Population Trends (Department of Statistics Singapore, 2014).

SCHOLASTIC ACHIEVEMENT DATA

Scholastic achievement is of paramount importance to the citizens of Singapore, and many factors contribute to students' consistent success on the PISA. One of the objectives of this assessment is to rank student scores from various educational systems around the world to evaluate their effectiveness. In addition, the scores can be used as indicators of the students' abilities to use their expertise to meet real-life challenges.

The following graph shows that the students of Singapore scored extremely well on the 2012 PISA assessment and reflects their superior standing as academic achievers from a global perspective.

Table 7.1. Mean PISA scores 2012 (from OECD.org).

Subject	Mathematics	Reading	Science	Problem solving
OECD average	494	496	501	500
Shanghai-China	613	570	580	536
Singapore	573	542	551	562
Hong Kong-China	561	545	555	540
Chinese Taipei	560	523	523	534
Korea	554	536	538	561
Macao-China	538	509	521	540
Japan	536	538	547	552
Finland	519	524	545	523

In addition to their high rankings in the academic content areas, students from Singapore also achieved exemplary scores in problem-solving skills. Problem-solving competency is defined as "an individual's capacity to engage in cognitive processing to understand and resolve problem situations where a method of solution is not immediately obvious. It includes the willingness to engage with such situations in order to achieve one's potential as a constructive and reflective citizen" (OECD, 2014, p. 30).

A remarkable 29% of Singaporean students achieved high scores on the problem-solving component of the exam, compared with the OECD average of

11% on a recent PISA test. In 2012, results from the PISA exam confirmed that Singaporean students were capable of exploring complex problem scenarios and devising multi-step solutions at a rate higher than students from the other countries participating in the assessment (OECD, 2014).

CULTURAL PERSPECTIVE

To develop an understanding of the educational system in Singapore, it is important to investigate the influence of the region and its culture. Singapore is a small country, approximately the size of New York City, located on the southern tip of the Malay Peninsula in Southeast Asia, between the Indian Ocean and the South China Sea (Eveland, 2011). Although it is highly developed in the areas of technology, tourism, and manufacturing, Singapore lacks an abundance of natural resources. As a result, the citizens of Singapore consider human resources to be its most valuable commodity. Furthermore, they recognize that building a strong workforce requires a solid education and thus acknowledge the vital role that effective teaching plays in the development of citizens (Ministry of Education Singapore [MOE], 2015).

The culture of Singapore embodies respect on the part of Singaporeans for each other, for property, and for their country. Due to the national policy of an open acceptance of the multicultural and multilingual component of their citizenry, the people unite as a population despite their diverse heritages. Visitors are impressed by the cleanliness and beauty of Singapore. In this atmosphere of respect for the environment, even chewing gum is forbidden because of its potential for harming the ecosystem (Eveland, 2011).

Similarly, in this culture that emphasizes reverence for all aspects of life, teachers are treated with dignity. They are held in high esteem and duly recognized for their influence on young minds. Additionally, the majority of these Confucian-heritage students demonstrate a strong work ethic toward school assignments. They are committed to excelling in their studies and performing well on summative assessments (Lee, 2014).

HISTORICAL PERSPECTIVE OF EDUCATION IN SINGAPORE

The people of Singapore refer to their country as a "tiny red dot" on the map, yet this nation that occupies such a diminutive geographical area has consistently outperformed larger, more prominent countries on all of the benchmarks for student assessment for the past decade (Hogan, 2014). Despite the fact that their educational system was developed over a period of less than 50 years, or roughly the span of one generation, the Republic of Singapore has emerged as a global model for academic and economic success. The remarkable transformation of this tiny nation from an area marked by abject poverty and high rates of illiteracy to one of prosperity and high rates of educational attainment in such a short period reflects the power of a shared vision by the heads of state who recognized that, in a country with limited natural resources, they would need to emphasize the development of a skilled workforce (Huff, 1995). The ideologies that propelled the initial leaders to promote a cohesive culture with an emphasis on national identity have prevailed throughout the administrations of subsequent leaders. One of these ideologies involved the link between schools and the well-being of the nation.

SURVIVAL-DRIVEN PHASE

Under British rule since 1819, Singapore was established as a seaport and served as a harbor for trade to the neighboring countries of India and China for over a century. During this era, people migrated mostly from China, India, and the Malay archipelago. Following its separation from Britain in 1959 and the subsequent departure from the rule of Malaysia in 1965, Singapore became an independent nation. Early on, the newly formed republic suffered from poverty, illiteracy, unemployment, and tension among the diverse factions. Education under British rule had been reserved for the elite class, so the vast majority of the population in the early 1960s was undereducated, resulting in a largely unskilled workforce (Adams, 1970).

In 1965, the leaders of this new nation were faced with the daunting task of unifying the people in order to create a national identity and an educational system to serve their multi-racial and multi-ethnic society in an era that the Ministry of Education has deemed the "survival-driven phase." Singapore's first Prime Minister, Lee Kuan Yew, recognized the power of an effective national educational program to achieve these lofty goals and implemented a plan to promote the new country's motto of *One united people, regardless of race, language, or religion*, which became the rallying cry of speakers for many years to come (MOE, 2015; Yew, 1998).

With the intention of promoting prosperity and in an effort to unite the citizenry, Lee Kuan Yew and his advisors proposed the implementation of a public school system that would provide education for all children while also fostering pride in their national identity. By instilling in children from the youngest age the spirit of nationalism, the leaders hoped to unify the diverse population. Soon a new tradition of allegiance to Singapore emerged along with a curriculum promoting nationalistic pride in honor of their new country. As an expression of this pride, the teachers and students in Singapore began to recite the national pledge and sing the national anthem each morning, and to study the history of their fledgling country (MOE, 2015).

During the survival-driven phase, government administrators recognized the benefits of adopting a shared language for all of the citizenry, and they chose English for practical reasons. From a fiscal point of view, speaking English would help to promote an East-West perspective among the citizens of Singapore and thus facilitate economic transactions with Western nations. From a cultural standpoint, students who developed a high level of proficiency in English would have more opportunities for careers and scholarly pursuits in the global arena. Furthermore, the government administrators believed that the practice of speaking a common language throughout the country would serve as a unifying social element among the diverse factions (Goh, 1979; MOE, 2015).

Along with the mandate to develop national pride, students in Singapore were encouraged to retain a connection to their original culture by speaking their mother tongue. Prime Minister Yew believed that the citizens should retain their native languages for the sake of honoring their heritage. Although the Singapore educational system had designated English as the official language, the schools were expected to also offer instruction to students in their native tongue. Thus a curriculum for bilingual education was created, and bilingualism continues to be a national educational policy of Singapore (Goh, 1979; MOE, 2015).

Despite earnest efforts during the survival-driven phase to expand the availability of education and to improve the quality of the system, achievement scores remained low, and high dropout rates persisted throughout the late 1960s and early 1970s. Studies revealed that fewer than 60% of the children who had entered grade school during that period had advanced to secondary school by the mid-1970s, so the Ministry of Education continued to reform the educational system (Goh, 1979).

EFFICIENCY-DRIVEN PHASE

As government officials sought solutions to this educational dilemma, the country's infrastructure was also shifting from an economic system that relied on labor-intensive industry to a greater reliance on technological skills. To address the changing needs of the global economy, the government identified a need to reform the entire educational system. Members of the Ministry of Education were called to create an entity to monitor curriculum on a national level, which resulted in the formation of the Curriculum Planning and Development Institute in 1980.

During the efficiency-driven phase, the national standardized curriculum was modified from one that utilized a universal approach to educational practice to one that focused on individualized plans. In this new curriculum, students were offered more choices based on their abilities and interests. Additionally, by recognizing that not all students achieve at the same rate, the revisions provided new options in the form of multiple pathways or streams of instruction to accommodate a wide range of talents and abilities. The plan was implemented in the hope of providing a partial solution to the problem of the school dropout rate (MOE, 2015).

The actions that were taken during the efficiency-driven phase effectively shifted the focus in education from a one-size-fits-all perspective to a pedagogy that was designed to accommodate the individual needs of the students. Concurrently, the government sought to destigmatize the trades for the purpose of supplying the demand for skilled workers in these professions. The new program was deemed a success when, in 1986, studies showed that the dropout rate for secondary pupils had decreased to less than 6% of the high school population. Additionally, by 1995, Singapore had achieved academic prominence, leading the world in scores on the Trends in International Mathematics and Science Studies (TIMSS) exam (MOE, 2015).

As the reputation of this fledgling nation-state flourished during the latter part of the twentieth century, Singapore was celebrated on the global stage for the astounding success of its education system. For a country to demonstrate such impressive gains in a relatively brief period of time was unprecedented. As a result of the attention Singapore received following the publication of international test scores, representatives from numerous educational professions around the world visited the country in the hope of deciphering its blueprint for success. Replication of the Singaporean educational system has been difficult, however, due to the unusual mix of factors that contributes to its success. A broad range of cultural components support an instructional regime that consists of didactic methods, a heavy reliance on textbooks, and an emphasis on teaching to the test, all elements that are considered to be less than optimal in many Western systems (Hogan, 2014).

ABILITY-BASED, ASPIRATION-DRIVEN PHASE

The Ministry of Education labeled the next historical segment, which spanned the years 1997–2011, as the ability-based, aspiration-driven phase. To commemorate this era, the Prime Minister, Goh Chok Tong, coined the motto: "Thinking Schools, Learning Nation" in 1997. In an address to the nation, he stated the following:

> We cannot assume that what has worked well in the past will work for the future. The old formulae for success are unlikely to prepare our young for the new circumstances and new problems they will face.... Singapore's vision for meeting this challenge for the future is encapsulated in these four words: THINKING SCHOOLS, LEARNING NATION. It is a vision for a total learning environment, including students, teachers, parents, workers, companies, community organizations and government. (MOE, 2004, para. 16–17)

With the advent of the Program for International Student Assessment (PISA) in the year 2000, the students of Singapore continued to demonstrate superior academic achievement. In the interest of promoting the vision of a school system to facilitate the development of creative thinking skills, national pride, and learning skills, the "Thinking Schools, Learning Nation" agenda promoted a broad array of subjects for students at the lower levels, as well as additional offerings for extracurricular activities. To promote the philosophy of this phase, Prime Minister Loong stated that educators must follow the mandate of "Teach Less, Learn More" as a way to communicate the need for students to engage deeply in learning. In this new phase, students were able to participate in a variety of activities that served to facilitate the development of problem-solving skills. The subsequent PISA scores from 2012 reflect the success of this effort (MOE, 2015).

In addition to the enhancement of arts and creative pursuits, an increased emphasis was placed on moral education at this time. Indeed, for the National Rally Day Speech in 2004, Prime Minister Lee Hsien Loong stated the following:

> The most important gift that we can give to our young and to prepare for their future is education. It's not just preparing them for a job, but learning to live a life, learning to deal with the world, learning to be a full person, what in Chinese, they say, "xue zhuo ren" (学做人) and in schools, there are plenty of opportunities to learn to be a person. (Singapore Government Media Release, 2004, para. 102)

As global connections continue to expand at an ever-increasing rate, the need for educational systems to keep pace with rigorous teaching requirements escalated. However, the focus in Singapore evolved into a concentrated effort to prepare global citizens instilled with a moral fiber that will enable them to enjoy a high quality of life. The Ministry of Education adopted holistic assessment methods as a way to provide pupils with a broad and solid foundation for lifelong learning. With this approach, students are expected not only to learn knowledge and skills, but also to develop the ability to apply these skills in real-life situations (MOE, 2015).

Student-Centric, Values-Driven Phase

For the current period, the Singapore Ministry of Education website identifies its motto for education as "Student-Centric, Values-Driven" and emphasizes the goal of helping students to discover their unique talents, potential, and passions in the hope that they will continue to develop the skills to be lifelong learners (MOE, 2015).

On that website, the Minister of Education, Heng Swee Keat, elaborates on this theme by describing the "Values in Action Program" that was formed by the Character and Citizenship Education Branch. Mr. Keat supports the development of character and promotes a spirit of volunteerism by expressing a desire to develop the values in students that will enable them to succeed in their lives and to care for each other (MOE, 2015).

STRUCTURE OF SINGAPORE'S EDUCATIONAL SYSTEM

Singapore has advanced tremendously from the days when large portions of the population lacked access to educational opportunities and were thus confined to low-level jobs throughout their lives. Public education is available to all of the young citizens of Singapore, and systemic support for academic success prevails throughout the schools.

Ministry of Education

One of the foremost strengths of the educational system in Singapore lies in the alliance between the entities that make decisions for the schools. The office of the Minister of Education values the concerns of the teachers and provides the school with the power to make decisions (Tan & Dimmock, 2014). Moreover, the Ministry of Education in Singapore actively supports teachers in their mutual goal of developing future citizens who will lead the country. A statement on the Ministry of Education website declares that one of the goals is to create in every child a confident person, a concerned citizen, a self-directed learner, and an active contributor (MOE, 2015).

Within each category, the factors that facilitate the desired outcomes are also itemized. For example, a confident person is one who is able to think independently, communicate effectively, and maintain good interpersonal skills. The concerned citizen is someone who is well informed about local and world affairs, is able to empathize and respect others, and is willing to actively participate in the community. The self-directed learner is one who takes responsibility for his or her own learning, consistently asks thoughtful questions, uses technology skillfully, and develops the quality of perseverance. In the last category, the active contributor is a citizen who encompasses the quality of adaptability, possesses the ability to take the initiative, engages in risk-taking, functions in a resilient and innovative manner, and aspires to high standards (MOE, 2015).

National Institute of Education

The National Institute of Education, which was constructed on a grand scale in the heart of the city within the confines of the Yunnan Gardens, is the heart of teacher education services in Singapore. Located in central Singapore on 16 hectares and adjacent to the Nanyang Technological University, it is a magnificent campus that features extensive landscaping, modern facilities, and large classrooms. Inside the buildings, the students have access to state-of-the-art technological amenities, vast libraries, and comfortable areas well suited for study or meetings (National Institute of Education [NIE], 2015).

Although the physical site is impressive, the real benefits that students derive from attending lies in the superb quality of the NIE teacher preparation programs. The institute offers educational research and methodology courses for undergraduate education students, as well as in-service training and leadership classes for current teachers. Additionally, students have access to professional development programs, webinars, and classes that are available through a wide variety of online courses (NIE, 2015).

The NIE is made up of four major divisions: teacher preparation programs, graduate programs and research, academic computing and information services, and corporate planning and development. The framework for each program is rigorous and multidisciplinary, and strikes a balance between pedagogy and content. Students are able to obtain their teaching credentials through the courses offered by their chosen program, which are endorsed by the national accreditation system (NIE, 2015).

Curriculum Development Division

The Ministry of Education created the Curriculum Development Institute of Singapore in 1980 to craft and monitor a curriculum for all schools. Now known as the Curriculum Development Division, the organization has designed two broad phases to guide the development of curriculum in Singapore. In the first phase, administrators review, design, and develop the national curriculum that will be utilized throughout the country. The professional development sessions are designed to ensure that teachers understand the curricular objectives of the new material, as well as the tools for successful implementation. In the second phase, the curriculum objectives and goals are implemented in the classrooms. Instructors from NIE utilize assessment instruments to gauge the effectiveness of the curriculum and instruction (MOE, 2015).

The design of the curriculum is guided by the goals of the Ministry of Education, which reflect the values and aspirations of Singaporean society to produce citizens of good character. An effective curriculum will have a broad-based design that emphasizes current knowledge, skills, and competencies, and will also encompass a vision for the future. Effective implementation of the national curriculum is key to the success of the educational program, so it is necessary to consider professional development as an essential component whenever a new curriculum agenda is proposed for the system (MOE, 2015).

Bilingual Program

The Singapore government has implemented a strong bilingual education program to support multiculturalism. The population of Singapore is predominantly Chinese, but it also includes a significant number of people who speak English, which is also taught in all of the schools. Graduates of the school system are expected to converse fluently in English, so it is taught at all grade levels.

Nevertheless, the mother tongue language (MTL) policy requires all students to study their official mother tongue (Chinese, Malay, Mandarin, and Tamil) in addition to English. The government of Singapore respects languages such as Bengali, Gujarati, Hindi, Punjabi, and Urdu, but does not provide instruction in those dialects. Citizens of European heritage may speak French, German, or Italian in addition to English. A small segment of the population speaks Japanese (Silver, 2002).

The ultimate goal of the language policy is to unify the people by mandating a common language that fosters their ability to communicate with all members of the Singapore community. Additionally, the Ministry of Education has sought to strengthen the bonds of East-West communication for the sake of promoting commerce, since English is the dominant language of the Western world. However, by also retaining their mother tongue, Singaporeans sustain a link to their history and heritage. Therefore, all citizens are encouraged to maintain their ethnic identities by speaking their mother tongue (Tan, 2010).

Collaborating for Effectiveness

One of the strengths of the Singaporean educational system is the close relationship that has recently developed between the entities that create policy, those that design curriculum, and the educators who teach in the schools. For example, over the past 2 decades, the Ministry of Education has devolved some of the decisions it previously made to the schools, decisions such as using non-academic criteria to select students and allowing advanced students to take examinations earlier than other students (Tan & Dimmock, 2014).

By actively striving for alignment with each component of educational policy, members of the school system affected by each decision have a share in the process. The ongoing collaboration among the Ministry of Education, the National Institute of Education, and the teachers and administrators in the decision-making process contributes to Singapore's success in education.

Policy decisions are carefully considered by all of the stakeholders. After much deliberation and careful examination of recent studies by the numerous researchers at the National Institute of Education, the Ministry of Education issues new educational policy decisions. Such a successful alignment of policy coherence and implementation consistency is made possible by the routine, open discussions among professors at NIE who participate in the Ministry meetings, resulting in a high level of mutual accountability for everyone involved. Furthermore, the government of Singapore consistently supports academic innovation by providing the funds to implement new policies.

Teacher Recruitment

Administrators fully acknowledge the role of the teacher in a successful educational system; thus, recruiting qualified teacher candidates is a high priority. One of the factors that has undoubtedly contributed to the development of Singapore's elite educational system is the ability to recruit and retain highly qualified professionals. Students who rank in the top one-third of their high school graduating class in Singapore are recruited to enter the teaching profession. It is an honor to be selected as a student at the National Institute of Education. Indeed, for each opening for a new education student, seven candidates will apply. Once students are admitted as undergraduates to the National Institute of Education (NIE) at Nanyang Technological University, they will be granted not only a full scholarship for tuition and books, but also a monthly stipend funded by the government of Singapore. Graduation and job security go hand in hand, because each student who completes the program is guaranteed a position in Singapore's public schools. The graduates can expect to be paid a competitive salary that is comparable to other professions that require a university degree. Singapore also offers bonuses based on a system that evaluates teachers in 16 areas on an annual basis, increasing teachers' salaries significantly throughout their careers (National Center on Education and the Economy, 2015).

Teacher Preparation

The National Institute of Training provides both intensive training on the Singapore national curriculum and courses in pedagogical content to all of the pre-service teachers. The teacher candidates are expertly guided throughout their coursework and training. Members of the NIE faculty continue to provide mentoring services long after the student has graduated and entered the profession.

From the beginning, the goal of the program is to develop the emerging educators' pedagogical skills. Mastery of the content is vital, of course, but the professors begin by emphasizing the importance of an effective delivery. Additionally, since all of the pre-service teachers study the same national curriculum, there is greater consistency in the quality of preparation among the emerging educators. Not surprisingly, the teaching profession in Singapore has a low attrition rate in comparison to other countries, further evidence that they have successfully implemented an exemplary training program for their teachers (Stewart, 2015).

Teaching as a Profession

The teaching profession is held in high esteem in Singapore. To illuminate the contrast between the American perception of teachers and the Singaporean view of education as a career choice, Dan Rather compared the two perspectives in a special program, "Take a Lesson from Singapore," that was produced for a television series on global education. Following the publication of Singapore's impressive PISA scores in 2012, Rather traveled to Singapore to glean insights about the multitude of factors that contribute to the success of its public school system.

During the program, Rather discussed many of the characteristics of the Singaporean educational system that are relevant to its students' remarkable achievement scores. He also shared the results of a recent survey conducted by the company CareerCast.com in the United States. In this study, American adolescents ranked education 127th out of 200 possible choices as an occupational preference. In a similar study in Singapore, the first choice for a career of the adolescent participants was teaching (Rather, 2012). The distinct contrast between the surveys illustrates the disparity of cultural perspectives on the education profession between the United States and Singapore. Whereas in Singapore the teaching profession is fully credited for its vital role in shaping the culture, the results of the survey reflect the lack of respect that American students have for teachers and their role in society. The fact that the teaching profession is revered for its pivotal role in shaping citizens in Singapore is clearly an instrumental factor in the success of its educational system.

Professional Development

The availability of ongoing professional development opportunities is another factor that contributes to educational effectiveness. In Singapore, teachers continue their education throughout their careers through professional development sessions that are conducted in their respective schools or at NIE at regular intervals. The Singapore government provides 100 hours of training per year for teachers, a practice that provides a continuous feedback loop throughout their careers. The NIE also offers a database of books and journals to help teachers stay abreast of current trends and research findings that are pertinent to their educational practices (MOE, 2015).

In some cases, the NIE professional development sessions will address specific problems to support an individual teacher, or they will design training for a group of teachers who work together on a campus. The training sessions may be pedagogical in nature and address an academic content area, or they may provide guidance for teachers facing challenges pertaining to diverse needs (MOE, 2015).

Teachers who wish to diversify their vocational experience are encouraged to take a sabbatical from their classroom positions. During their time away from the classroom, they have the option of working in another environment, such as a hospital, of playing an active role in shaping educational policy with the National Institute of Education, or of pursuing an administrative position within the government. When teachers decide to use this time to return to school, they may choose to attend NIE, or to study abroad. The teachers benefit from knowing that they are allowed to resume their teaching duties upon their return, and the system benefits from providing options that prevent the phenomenon of teacher burnout (MOE, 2015).

Teacher Dispositions, Parental Expectations, and Student Achievement

Teachers in Singapore are encouraged to provide support for learning in an emotionally safe environment and to show respect for the emotional domain. The emphasis on positive reinforcement is evident throughout the literature on teaching in Singapore, as well as in the videos that portray classroom teachers in action. Overall, the structure of a classroom in Singapore is conducive to learning, and teachers are successful in motivating students to learn skills and acquire knowledge in an environment based on collaboration and trust (American Federation of Teachers, 2012).

Teachers are committed to providing interesting lessons to stimulate the cognitive domain and to nurture students for the sake of addressing their emotional domain. They build bridges for achievement and strive to create a learning community in which every student is valued and encouraged to succeed. Teachers bolster confidence in order to bring out the potential of each student (American Federation of Teachers, 2012).

Parents play a vital role in the success of each student. In most homes, they take great pains to create opportunities for their children to succeed academically. They do this by providing books, assessment materials, and tutors. More affluent families involve their children in enrichment activities such as piano and swimming lessons. Children in Singapore participate in these paid classes at an early age (Garces-Bacsal, 2013).

In response to the high expectations for academic achievement, classrooms in Singapore are orderly, and the students are generally compliant. Students strive to do well and feel pressured to excel. In fact, although many American educators favor the Singaporean system, there are those who argue that the high level of stress placed on students to succeed harms them (Hong, 2014).

Early Childhood Education

One of Singapore's national priorities in the recent past has been to improve the preschool sector. New research indicating that high-quality preschool programs make an important difference in children's developmental outcomes contributed to Singapore's efforts to enhance preschool education (Ang, 2014). Beginning in the 1980s, new policies involved intervention programs, subsidies for disadvantaged children, and other incentives for improving the workforce. Singapore's renewed interest in preschool education led to an increase in the number of childcare programs. For example, centers providing childcare increased from 785 in 2009 to 982 in 2012. Although the country is making an effort to improve in this area, a recent report evaluating 45 countries conducted by the Economic Intelligence Unit indicated that Singapore ranked 29th on various aspects of preschool services such as affordability, availability, and quality of services (Ang, 2014).

Primary Schools

Children in the primary grades follow a common curriculum for 4 years that encompasses the English language, their native language, and mathematics. As they progress, students take classes in science, art, music, social studies, and health. All students have access to physical education and take part in classes that emphasize civics and moral education. In this climate of respect for the teacher's role, students are less disruptive and more cooperative during class sessions, so teachers are able to invest more energy into the content rather than deal with challenges involving classroom logistics. Despite the larger class sizes of as many as 40 students, behavioral issues are the exception rather than the norm. In this environment of respect, in which teachers do the talking, students seldom interrupt the lesson (Hogan, 2014).

Secondary Schools

Following their 6-year course of study during the primary years, students in Singapore are expected to pursue a secondary education. To advance through the system, they must take exams that define their curricular paths. Results from each examination provide information about their skills and abilities and thus determine their placement for the next level. Approximately 60% of the student body qualifies for the express path, which is an accelerated option for high-achieving students. Another 25% will continue on a normal academic path through high school and then attend an institute of higher education. The remaining 15% will be placed in a technical course stream for their secondary school experience (OECD, 2011).

The students who are accepted into the accelerated or express route participate in a 4-year program that culminates in an O-level exam, which then leads to a general certificate of education (GCE). Afterwards these students typically enroll in a local institute of higher education such as the National Institute of Education.

The students who are streamed into the normal academic course of study continue on a less challenging path for the duration of their secondary school experience. They have an opportunity to take the O-level exam after their fifth year of study. As soon as they pass the O-level exam, they are eligible to apply to a university.

The remaining 15% of the students participating in the technical program complete a curriculum that focuses on general skills. The students taking this route, which culminates in the General Certificate of Education, N-Level (GCE-N), may enter positions that provide on-the-job training. Some students will apply to the Institute of Technical Education to pursue specialization as skilled trade workers. Post-secondary education in Singapore is available to qualified students in the form of junior colleges, polytechnic schools, and universities.

Gifted Education

Initiated by the Ministry of Education, the gifted education program was first used in Singapore in 1984 (MOE, 2015). This program addresses the needs of intellectually gifted students at the primary and secondary levels. Initially, the gifted program was founded in response to a new emphasis on the individualized approach during the efficiency-driven phase in 1984. Educators and parents called for a set of curricular guidelines to provide an optimal environment for students whose test scores indicated that they were in the highest-performing rank of intelligence.

In the beginning, the parameters for acceptance into the gifted program required evidence that the prospective student was in the top 0.5% of the population in intellectual ability. The student would be tested on his or her verbal, mathematical, and spatial abilities prior to admittance. Over time, the requirements were modified, so that now the gifted segment comprises 1% of the population. Due to the belief that their needs will be better served in some of the older establishments such as Oxford in London, or Harvard in the United States, many academically gifted students in higher education are encouraged to study abroad (MOE, 2015).

Higher Education

The government of Singapore recognizes that education is vital to success at all levels, so it supports innovative efforts to enhance learning throughout the system. The Singaporean institutes of higher education use the Agency for Science, Technology, and Research (A*Star), a government agency, to further their research and educational goals. The A*Star agency provides abundant resources for the National University of Singapore and Nanyang Technological University in the form of funding and research partnerships with other universities around the world. Additionally, A*Star invites foreign nationals to serve as visiting professors at the institutions of higher education in Singapore (MOE, 2015).

CONCLUSION

From a tiny island struggling with a high rate of illiteracy and a flailing economy in 1965, to a country with the world's seventh-largest gross domestic product (GDP) per capita as well as one of the highest-ranking educational systems in the world, the story of Singapore is one of remarkable success and triumph over adversity. Because of this phenomenal rise from pervasive hardship among the general population to a country that reports one of the highest rates of educational attainment and per-capita income, Singapore has attracted the attention of educators from all over the world.

In addition to these impressive statistics, the quality of life for citizens at all levels appears to be improving. The dropout rate for secondary school students since 2010 has been calculated at less than 1% (MOE, 2015), the crime rate is one of the lowest in the world (BBC, 2013), and the national unemployment rate in 2014 was approximately 2% (Ministry of Manpower, 2015). Clearly, the combined efforts of the government and Ministry of Education to create a proactive economic and educational system have had far-reaching effects on the quality of life in Singapore.

The success of the school system of Singapore is a testament to the efforts of the members of the National Institute of Education as well as the government of Singapore. Together their collaborative efforts to plan, implement, and monitor educational practices have resulted in impressive scholastic gains, as evidenced by the scores on global assessments such as PISA. The noteworthy achievements of this nation-state have generated considerable interest among foreign educators who seek insight into components that have contributed to the success of this educational system. Though this system has impressed experts from around the world, it would be difficult to emulate its model of excellence due to the unique combination of elements that are inherent in the culture of Singapore.

The superior PISA scores students from Singapore achieve reflect cultural factors that have combined to generate academic success, yet this unique set of components may limit the ability of admirers to transfer the methods to another country. Educators who aspire to emulate this formula must acknowledge the deep respect that Singaporeans have for the teaching profession. Ultimately the people of Singapore believe that achievement can be attained through an efficacious synergy between students and teachers and that teaching is a crucial component of any successful educational program.

REFERENCES

Adams, D. (1970). *Education and modernization in Asia*. Reading, MA: Addison-Wesley.
American Federation of Teachers. (2012, March 16). *Why education in Singapore works*. Retrieved from https://www.youtube.com/watch?v=sEn6OKsVoMs
Ang, L. (2014). Vital voices for vital years in Singapore: One country's advocacy for change in the early years sector. *International Journal of Early Years Education, 22*(3), 329–341. doi:10.1080/09669760.2014.911695
BBC. (2013). *Why does Singapore top so many tables?* Retrieved from http://www.bbc.com/news/world-asia-24428567
Department of Statistics Singapore. (2014). *Singapore in figures: 2014*. Retrieved from http://www.singstat.gov.sg/docs/default-source/default-document-library/publications/publications_and_papers/reference/sif2014.pdf
Eveland, J. (2011). *Frommer's Singapore and Malaysia* (3rd ed.). New York: Wiley.
Garces-Bacsal, R. (2013). Perceived family influences in talent development among artistically talented teenagers in Singapore. *Roeper Review: A Journal on Gifted Education, 35*(1), 7–17.
Goh, K. (1979). *Report on the Ministry of Education 1978*. Singapore: Singapore National Printers.
Hogan, D. (2014). *The conversation: Why is Singapore's school system so successful, and is it a model for the West?* Retrieved from http://theconversation.com/why-is-singapores-school-system-so-successful-and-is-it-a-model-for-the-west-22917
Hong, B. (2014). Why schools in America should not be like schools in Singapore. *AASA Journal of Scholarship & Practice, 10*(4), 43–50.
Huff, W. (1995). *The economic growth of Singapore: Trade and development in the twentieth century*. Cambridge, UK: Cambridge University Press.
Lee, J. (2014). Universal factors of student achievement in high-performing Eastern and Western countries. *Journal of Educational Psychology, 106*(2), 364–374.
Ministry of Education. (2004). *Shaping our schools: Thinking schools, learning nation*. Retrieved from http://www.moe.gov.sg/media/speeches/1997/020697.htm
Ministry of Education. (2015). *Singapore*. Retrieved from http://www.moe.gov.sg/
Ministry of Manpower. (2015). *Unemployment*. Retrieved from http://stats.mom.gov.sg/Pages/Unemployment-Summary-Table.aspx

National Center on Education and the Economy. (2015). *Center on International Education Benchmarking: Singapore*. Retrieved from http://www.ncee.org/programs-affiliates/center-on-international-education-benchmarking/top-performing-countries/singapore-overview/singapore-teacher-and-principal-quality/

National Institute of Education. (2015). *Singapore*. Retrieved from http://www.nie.edu.sg/

Organisation for Economic Co-operation and Development. (2011). *Strong performers and successful reformers in education: Lessons from PISA for the United States*. Paris: OECD Publishing.

Organisation for Economic Co-operation and Development. (2012). *PISA 2012 results in focus: What 15-year-olds know and what they can do with what they know*. Retrieved from http://www.oecd.org/pisa/keyfindings/pisa-2012-results-overview.pdf

Organisation for Economic Co-operation and Development. (2014). *PISA 2012 results: Creative problem solving (Vol. V): Students' skills in tackling real-life problems*. Paris: OECD Publishing. Retrieved from http://dx.doi.org/10.1787/978926420870-en

Rather, D. (2012, July 19). *Dan Rather reports: Singapore education*. Retrieved from https://www.youtube.com/watch?v=RHSR5Niv4jU

Ripley, A. (2013). *The smartest kids in the world*. New York: Simon & Schuster.

Silver, R.E. (2002). Policies on English language education and economic development. In R.E. Silver, G. Hu, & M. Iino (Eds.), *English language education in China, Japan, and Singapore* (pp. 100–169). Singapore: Nanyang Technological University.

Singapore Government Media Release. (2004). *Our future of opportunity and promise*. Retrieved from http://www.nas.gov.sg/archivesonline/speeches/view-html?filename=2004083101.htm

Stewart, V. (2015). *How Singapore developed a high-quality teacher workforce*. Retrieved from http://asiasociety.org/how-singapore-developed-high-quality-teacher-workforce

The Straits Times. (2010, August 22). Singapore most desired by migrants: Gallup poll. Retrieved from http://news.asiaone.com/News/AsiaOne+News/Singapore/Story/A1Story20100822-233240.html

Tan, C., & Dimmock, C. (2014). How a "top-performing" Asian school system formulates and implements policy: The case of Singapore. *Educational Management Administration and Leadership*, 42(5) 743–763.

Tan, E. (2010, May 5). *Mother tongue: A hot button issue*. Retrieved from http://www.smu.edu.sg/sites/default/files/smu/news_room/smu_in_the_news/2010/sources/TODAY_20100505_1.pdf

Yew, L.K. (1998). *The Singapore story: Memoirs of Lee Kuan Yew*. Singapore: Straits Times Editions.

CHAPTER EIGHT

New Zealand

Education in New Zealand: Maintaining Quality in an Era of Change

MICHAEL FORRET AND LOGAN MOSS

INTRODUCTION

In the twenty-first century, New Zealand has outperformed many nations in international testing. On the 2009 PISA test, for example, the Organisation for Economic Co-operation and Development's executive summary report mentioned that it performed very well in reading literacy and scored significantly higher than the OECD average in mathematics and science (Organisation for Economic Co-operation and Development [OECD], 2010). To understand how New Zealand's education system has developed into what it is today, it is necessary to understand its history in relation to education. To this end, we have organized our chapter into several parts. We begin with some general information about New Zealand to provide a background for the reader lacking familiarity with this country. We then focus on education in particular and provide an account of the history and development of education in New Zealand up to the beginning of this century to offer a more accurate understanding of this nation's current situation. Then, we describe key features of today's education system. In this section, we cover key elements that characterize the current system. Read in conjunction with the earlier historical account, we hope to provide a thorough picture of the influences and decisions that have shaped education in New Zealand. In the final section, we provide a summary and discussion of some of the crucial issues at play in New Zealand's contemporary education system.

ABOUT NEW ZEALAND

New Zealand, or Aotearoa in Māori, is an island country in the southwestern Pacific Ocean and consists of two main landmasses—the North Island, or Tika-a-Māui, and the South Island, or Te Waipounamu—and numerous smaller islands. It is situated some 1,500 kilometres (900 miles) east of Australia across the Tasman Sea and roughly 1,000 kilometres (600 miles) south of New Caledonia, Fiji, and Tonga. Because of its remoteness, New Zealand was one of the last lands to be settled by humans.

Polynesians settled New Zealand in the period from 1250 to 1300 and developed a distinctive Māori culture. In 1642, Abel Tasman, a Dutch explorer, became the first European to sight New Zealand; however, Europeans did not return until 1769, when British explorer James Cook mapped the entire coastline, marking the beginning of British interest. During the early nineteenth century, ongoing conflict occurred between the Māori and the British, but in 1840, representatives of the British Crown and Māori chiefs signed the Treaty of Waitangi, making New Zealand a British colony. This resulted in many more immigrants and contributed to more conflict (primarily about land ownership), leading to the New Zealand Wars that lasted from 1845 to 1872 (Sinclair, 2001). Disputes continue but are now fought in the courtroom and by negotiation.

Today the majority of New Zealand's population of 4.5 million is of European descent, and indigenous Māori are the largest minority. In the 2013 census, 74% of New Zealand residents identified themselves as European, and 14.9% as Māori. Other major ethnic groups include Asian (11.8%) and Pacific peoples (7.4%) (Statistics New Zealand, 2015). Reflecting this history, New Zealand's culture is mainly derived from Māori and early British settlers, with recent diversification arising from increased immigration. The official languages are English, Māori, and New Zealand sign language, with English the predominant language. The export of wool has historically dominated the country's economy, but exports of dairy products, meat, and wine, along with tourism contribute more today. This nation is a constitutional monarchy under England, and while the Queen is the head of state, New Zealand effectively governs itself through its parliamentary system. The public votes every 3 years, and changes in government frequently result.

HISTORY AND DEVELOPMENT OF NEW ZEALAND EDUCATION

Administrative Structure

In 1877, New Zealand's first national education act was passed. This act would effectively remain the basis of the New Zealand education system right up until

1990. The principal features of the act included the establishment of a national education system that would be free, secular, and compulsory, and any parent or resident within two miles of a school would be obliged to send any child between 7 and 13 years of age to school (Education Act, 1877). A three-tiered administrative structure was established, consisting of a national department of education, twelve regional education boards, and a school committee for each school. While this act included some provision for secondary education, it focused principally on elementary or primary schools.

Initially, the department of education, under a minister of education, would distribute funding to the education boards, make regulations governing for administrative procedures, and prescribe a national school syllabus. The education boards would be responsible for defining school districts as well as setting up and maintaining schools within boundaries as determined by the act. They were also responsible for training and appointing teachers to individual schools, as well as for establishing a system for inspecting teachers and enforcing the school syllabus.

School committees would be responsible for managing the schools, making recommendations to their boards concerning the appointment, suspension, or dismissal of teachers, and making any decisions concerning the enforcement of compulsory attendance within the school's district. The committees, to be elected by a ballot of local householders, would also be responsible for electing the members of the education board for their region (Butchers, 1930).

Under this system, the central government would be responsible for the cost of education, but control of the actual provision of education, including control of the school inspectors, was in the hands of the local education authorities, the education boards, and school committees. The initial expectation, at least among those responsible for the legislation, was that power would be shared, with perhaps the greater amount held by the school committees. For example, it was thought that the right of school committees to elect board members would enable them to control the policies of boards.

However, this did not occur, and education boards soon came to exercise almost unlimited control over schools in their districts. The boards imposed limitations by allowing school committees to manage only a single school, and poor communication prevented them from acting together in developing policies. With their powers severely curtailed, their activities became largely confined to the day-to-day management of their schools (McLaren, 1974).

The way the system operated limited the powers of the central department of education. While the distribution of funding to the boards was the responsibility of the department, it was up to the boards to decide how that money would be spent in their region. Similarly, although the act empowered the department to prescribe the school syllabus, it depended on officers employed by the boards for its enforcement (Ewing, 1970).

This tripartite system remained central to the organization of education in New Zealand up until 1990, and tensions among the department of education, the education boards, and the school committees continued to characterize the system, often making the initiation of reform and change difficult. However, the power of the department slowly grew, and by the middle of the twentieth century, the education system was highly centralised.

While the transfer of the inspectors from board to department control following the 1914 Education Act contributed significantly to centralization, a more important factor over the years involved the department's ultimate control over the provision of funding (Education Act, 1914). This meant it had the ability to initiate reforms and implement special programs with which the boards had to comply with if they wished to receive the funding available for those programs.

The Curriculum

From the outset, the New Zealand school curriculum was set centrally, and the subjects were specified in the education act. The need for a centralized curriculum was justified, in part, by the high rates of internal migration that had characterized the first decades of the colony.

The department of education set up the first syllabus for schools based on the subjects specified in the act in 1878. This syllabus was mandatory for all state primary schools, and one of the tasks of the school inspectors would be to ensure schools' compliance with it (Ewing, 1970). This created a trend for centralized control of the curriculum, which has continued to the present day.

The examination system reinforced the centralized curriculum. The exams were implemented for the purpose of assessing pupil achievement and their progress in school. The syllabus prescriptions were divided into six standards. A pass on each standard was required for a pupil to progress through school, with the sixth standard, also known as the proficiency examination, marking the satisfactory completion of primary schooling. Pupils entering school at age 7 would follow the syllabus for the first standard, and if they passed the examination for that standard, they would then progress to the syllabus for the second standard, continuing on until the sixth standard or until proficiency was reached. Pupils who failed to pass a standard would remain at that syllabus level until they passed.

These examinations influenced schools to the extent that the term "standard" would become the nomenclature by which classes were specified. Those studying for the first standard were said to be in standard one, those working on the second standard, in standard two, and so on through standard six. Indeed, this procedure was pervasive (Mason, 1945) to the extent that despite the elimination of the system of standards examinations in 1936, another 60 years would pass before the nomenclature of standards disappeared from schools.

Over time, a continual movement toward freeing the curriculum and allowing teachers a greater say over its implementation emerged. This change can be seen in the movement away from a prescribed syllabus, with teachers increasingly encouraged to adapt the syllabus based on the needs of children. This was evident in the revisions of 1914, 1919 (New Zealand Government, 1919), and 1929 (New Zealand Department of Education, 1929), and became more pronounced during 1930s and 1940s with the introduction of the notion of "rolling revisions" of the syllabus (Ewing, 1970). By the 1960s, a more practical curriculum replaced the prescribed syllabus, though the broad outlines would still be determined centrally.

Secondary Education

To this point we have focused mainly on primary or elementary education because the education act made little provision for secondary education. District high schools were effectively primary schools with a secondary department attached. They were intended to provide post-primary education, particularly in rural areas, where demand was likely to be low and the cost of establishing a separate secondary school difficult to justify. Initially, the demand for such schools was low, and only 13 had been established by 1900. However, as the demand for secondary schooling increased during the first half of the twentieth century, so did the number of district high schools, and by 1945, there were 100 of these around the country (Dakin, 1973). With the advent of compulsory secondary schooling, most would eventually become full high schools, with the better part of the remainder becoming today's area schools.

The education act's lack of attention to secondary education does not, however, mean that New Zealand made no provision for post-primary education. By the end of the nineteenth century, secondary schools had been established in all of the major cities and in most of the large regional towns. However, unlike the primary schools, each was established under its own act of parliament. Generally, the establishing legislation would vest governance of the school in a local "board of governors," thus leaving them relatively independent of both central government and the regional education boards. There was, however, provision for inspection by the department, but lack of staff meant that inspection would rarely occur.

While the role of the primary school in New Zealand was generally accepted as the provision of a basic general education, secondary schools were seen rather differently. Their function was to prepare pupils for entry to a university, the professions, or the senior levels of the civil service. As a consequence, their curriculum tended to be highly academic, with little concern for general education. This tended to keep demand low, a situation undoubtedly exacerbated by the fact that secondary education was not free (McLaren, 1987).

Despite this situation, the number of students attending secondary schools slowly increased, and with this increase came a growing demand for the elimination of fees. As a result, in 1903, the Secondary Schools Act allowed any child earning a passing score on the proficiency examination to have a free place in a secondary school (Secondary Schools Act, 1903). In addition to the academically oriented secondary schools, technical high schools, which catered to those wishing to gain an apprenticeship in a trade, were established in 1905.

Following these changes, demand for secondary schooling steadily increased, with attendance roughly doubling each decade. In 1880, there were only 1,986 pupils in New Zealand's secondary schools. By 1900, this number had increased to a little over 3,000, and by the time the proficiency examination was abolished in 1938, it had reached 45,000 (Murdoch, 1943). However, the abolition of the proficiency examination posed a major problem, because it removed the basis for a free system in secondary schools and consequently required a revised form of secondary education. This occurred during the middle years of the Second World War and resulted both in raising the school graduation age to 15 and revising the secondary school curriculum. This change created greater emphasis on the general education of pupils and less focus on purely academic studies, though focus on academics by no means was eliminated (Consultative Committee on the Post-Primary Curriculum, 1944).

The department of education prescribed the new curriculum, as it did with primary schools. However, secondary schools would continue to be administered by their own boards, largely independent of the regional education boards responsible for primary schools. As the now-abandoned proficiency and standards examinations had done for the primary school curriculum, the introduction of an examination at the end of the third year of secondary school—to be known as school certificate—would provide a means for maintaining central control of the curriculum (Consultative Committee, 1944). All students throughout the country would take the same examination at the end of 3 years of secondary schooling, and schools would be forced to adhere relatively closely to the set syllabus.

Thus, by the middle of the twentieth century, New Zealand had in place both a primary school system that was effectively universal for all children and a secondary school system that involved virtually all children for at least several years after leaving primary school. Today, all that has changed substantially is the name and nature of the examination, but as the annual reports of the department of education (and, after 1990, the ministry of education) show, the numbers of students remaining into the later stages of secondary school have steadily increased. Some aspects of the initial differences between primary and secondary education remain today, but there are ongoing efforts to achieve greater integration between the two parts of the system.

The Training of Teachers

Teachers have always been expected to have the qualifications needed to teach. However, in many areas of the country, the demand for teachers exceeded the supply of trained teachers. Thus, many schools had no alternative other than to employ unqualified staff, and it would be the late 1990s before formal teacher training became a mandatory requirement for employment as a teacher (Education Amendment Act, 1996).

The Education Act of 1877 had placed the responsibility for training teachers in the hands of education boards, resulting in the establishment of teacher training colleges within the regions of four of the boards: Dunedin (1877, though this college had existed prior to this, having been established in 1871), Christchurch (1877), Wellington (1880), and Auckland (1881) (Harte, 1972). Other training colleges were subsequently established in Palmerston North, Hamilton, Ardmore, and North Shore, the latter two both being within the Auckland education board's region.

Initially, the colleges were concerned only with the preparation of primary school teachers; for secondary teaching, all that was needed was a degree or a similar tertiary educational qualification. However, with the advent of compulsory secondary education in the 1940s, there was a growing call for specialized training for secondary teachers (Commission on Education in New Zealand, 1962). Consequently, the Auckland and Christchurch colleges created departments for this purpose. During the 1970s and 1980s, small secondary teacher programs began in several of the other colleges.

Changes to the education act in 1989 involving, among other things, the abolition of both the education department and the education boards and hence the controlling authorities of the training colleges meant that new arrangements for the provision (or, more specifically, control of the provision) of teacher education became necessary (Education Act, 1989). The possibility of merging the colleges into existing universities, long regarded as desirable by many but resisted by both department and boards, was actively pursued, and the following 15 years would see all existing colleges merged with universities, beginning with our own University, Waikato, in 1991. Thus, today, apart from a small number of private institutions, all teacher training in New Zealand is in the hands of universities.

Provision for Students with Special Needs and the Disadvantaged

Provision for students with special needs has been part of the New Zealand system since the outset. As early as 1880, a school for the deaf was established in Christchurch, and special schools for children with intellectual disabilities were established shortly after, followed in 1917 by special classes in larger schools for these children. The 1920s and 1930s saw a further extension of such services, especially for the welfare needs of children (National Commission for UNESCO, 1972).

During the 1950s, the position of officer for special education was established within the department of education. This official was responsible for special schools and classes, as well as for the psychological service, a service established by the department in 1949. By the 1980s, the psychological service had a staff of several hundred trained psychologists (Dakin, 1973). However, the tendency in New Zealand has been to focus more on the perceived disadvantages shared by groups within the population rather than those of individuals. For instance, the effect of rural isolation on education has been at the forefront of policy from the beginning.

During the 1920s, small, single-teacher schools were of particular concern. Such schools were seen as limiting the opportunities of children due to the wide age range with which a single teacher had to teach. As a result, the consolidation of small schools to larger, more central ones to which pupils would be taken by bus became a significant aspect of policy during the 1920s and 1930s. As a result, many hundreds of single-teacher schools closed, and their pupils moved to larger schools (Moss, 2006).

The New Zealand Correspondence School, established in 1922, had its origins in addressing similar concerns, but in this case, it focused on how to cater to children living too far away from any school for it to be feasible for them to attend (Butchers, 1930). These children would, instead, receive lessons by mail, supplemented by other media as these became available.

New Zealand has a long history of policies aimed at redressing restricted opportunities for Māori and Polynesian children in schools. In part, this commitment lies behind what is currently the most significant policy (and probably the most contentious) aimed at addressing educational underachievement—the system of decile funding of schools. Introduced in 1995, this scheme provides additional funding for schools to enable them to overcome the barriers to learning faced by students from low socioeconomic communities. A school receives additional funding based on predictions of the number of such students they will have to deal with. The money received is intended to allow a school to buy additional resources and hire the staff needed to cater to those children and their needs (Ministry of Education, 2015b).

However, while this policy was partly prompted by the need to address the perceived disadvantages of specific groups in the community, an equally important impetus involved the results of international surveys such as TIMMS that began to appear during the 1990s. While these showed that the majority of New Zealand children were performing well, there was also clear evidence of a long tail of underachievement, leading to strong pressure to address this issue (Ministry of Education, 1994; Education and Science Select Committee, 1995).

The Educational Reforms of the 1990s

By the late 1980s, New Zealand's education system was well established, and those working within it, while critical of some of its aspects, generally considered that minor reforms would lead to continued improvement in participation rates and in general outcomes. However, they would not have the opportunity to discover if those views were well founded, because in 1990, the system, which had been in place for over 110 years in its fundamental form, was replaced.

No longer would education boards administer schools; rather, each would have its own board of trustees to govern it. Elected by parents, each board would negotiate directly with the central authorities and would replace the department of education. In place of the department would be a ministry of education, responsible for setting overall educational policy, including financing. But it would be joined by other state agencies that would assume responsibility for various aspects of the department's functions (New Zealand Department of Education, 1989).

The reasons for such changes have been widely discussed and debated (Thrupp, 1999). They were initially justified by the government of the day as providing greater choice for parents who, through the mechanism of the board of trustees, would now have a greater say over the running of the schools their children would attend. However, many have seen these changes as an incursion of neoliberal policies—an incursion that has increased with the passage of time. But whatever the ultimate motivation for those changes may have been, for the last quarter century, change and transformation have dominated New Zealand's education system. It is against that background that the newly emerging system must be viewed. While New Zealand's old system no longer exists, its impact has not disappeared completely.

Having examined the key elements of the history and development of New Zealand's education system up to the end of the last century, we will now describe the outcome of this development as it is currently implemented.

THE NEW ZEALAND EDUCATION SYSTEM TODAY

General Organization

The school years are made up of 13-year levels. Primary school education generally starts at year 1 and continues until year 8. Years 7 and 8 may be offered either at a primary school or at a separate intermediate school or composite school. New Zealand education can be divided into four areas:

- Early childhood education (from birth to age 5);
- Years 1–8 or primary/intermediate school (ages 5–13);

- Years 9–13 or secondary school (ages 13+);
- Tertiary education (not compulsory—ages 16+).

Types of Schools

While most students in New Zealand attend state-funded schools, there is a range of school types. Most schools instruct students using the English language, but some schools teach in Māori. Most state schools are secular (non-religious). Below we describe the main types of schools.

- **State Schools**
  Most New Zealand schools are state schools and receive government funding. State schools can be primary, intermediate, middle, secondary, or area/composite. Generally, they accept both boys and girls at primary, intermediate, and secondary levels, although some secondary schools offer single-sex education. Lessons are based on the New Zealand curriculum.

- **State Integrated Schools**
  These schools were private but have become part of the state system. They teach the New Zealand curriculum, but keep their own special character (usually a philosophical or religious belief) as part of their school program. State integrated schools receive the same government funding for each student as other state schools, but their buildings and land are privately owned. They usually charge compulsory fees called "attendance dues" to meet property costs.

- **Designated Character Schools**
  These are state schools that teach the New Zealand curriculum but have developed their own sets of aims, purposes, and objectives to reflect particular values (e.g., religious beliefs or culture).

- **Independent or Private Schools**
  These are schools that charge fees but also receive some funding from the government. They are governed by their own independent boards and must meet certain standards to be registered with the ministry of education. They do not have to follow the New Zealand curriculum but must follow a learning program of at least the same quality.

- **Primary Schools**
  Primary schools generally cater to students in years 1–8, although some only go up to year 6.

- **Intermediate Schools**
  These schools provide education for students from years 7 and 8.

- **Middle Schools**
  Middle schools accept students from years 7 to 10.

- **Secondary Schools**
  Although most secondary schools accept students from years 9 to 13, some cater to years 7 to 13.

- **Area Schools**
  Area schools accept students from years 1 to 13. These schools are often located in rural areas.

- **Composite Schools**
  A composite school is similar to an area school and provides both primary and secondary education. Depending on its classification, it may not provide the full range of levels to year 13.

- **Bilingual Schools**
  At these schools, teachers and children teach and learn in both English and another language (most often English and Māori) for up to 20 hours a week.

- **Te Kura Kaupapa Māori**
  These are state schools where the teaching is in Māori and is based on Māori culture and values. These schools follow the curriculum for Māori-medium teaching, learning, and assessment. One key goal is to produce students who are equally skilled in communicating in both Māori and English. Kura Kaupapa Māori schools generally provide education for students from years 1 to 8, but some go up to year 13.

- **Wharekura**
  These are schools that cater to students above year 8. Some of these schools cater to years 1 to 10, some are for years 1 to 13, and some are for years 9 to 13.

- **Correspondence Schools or Te Aho o Te Kura Pounamu**
  This type of school provides distance education from early childhood to year 13. Learning advisors, teachers, and in-region staff work with students and communities and also support schools to deliver a broad curriculum and specialist support to students in their community (Te Kura, 2015).

- **Regional Health Schools**
  These schools are for students with significant health difficulties who cannot attend their local school because they are in a hospital, at home recovering, or in transition, gradually returning to school. Teachers work with students both in a hospital and at home. New Zealand's three regional health schools jointly cover the whole country and are based in Auckland, Wellington, and Christchurch.

- **Special Schools**
  These schools provide education for children with particular needs arising from special talents and learning or behavioral issues. They use the New Zealand curriculum.

- **Teen Parent Units**
  Teen parent units are attached to some secondary schools and cater to students who are pregnant or raising a child and cannot practically attend a mainstream school.

Five-year-olds starting school begin in year 1 and progress to year 13. Most children in years 1–8 are between 5 and 12 years old. Students enrolled in a primary school can attend either a contributing primary school (for students in years 1–6) or a full primary school (for students in years 1–8). Students attending a contributing primary school will generally move on to an intermediate school (years 7–8). There are also schools known as middle schools (or junior high schools/junior colleges) that cater to years 7–10.

Table 8.1. Shows how year levels, school types, and students' ages fit together.

Year								Age
13	Year 7-13 Schools	Year 9-13 Schools		Composite/Area Schools	Wharekura		Correspondence School	17
12								16
11								15
10								14
9								13
8		Intermediate Schools	Full Primary Schools			Special Schools		12
7								11
6	Contributing Schools				Kura Kaupapa Maori			10
5								9
4								8
3								7
2								6
1								5
Early Childhood Education	Kindergarten, Playcentres, Childcare Home based, Childcare, Te Kohanga Reo, Pacific Island Language Groups, Playgroups							

How Schools Are Managed

Every state school and state integrated school in New Zealand has a board of trustees (Ministry of Education, 2015a). School boards usually consist of the following personnel:

- Three to seven elected parent representatives;
- The principal as the board's chief executive, professional advisor, and educational leader;
- An elected staff representative;
- An elected student representative (in schools with students above year 9);
- Co-opted trustees (optional);
- A state integrated school proprietor/s who may appoint up to four trustees.

The boards of trustees are accountable for their actions and performance to parents and caregivers, their local communities, the minister of education and the ministry of education, other government agencies, and the public. The board is the employer of all the school's staff and is responsible for the following duties:

- Setting the school's strategic and policy direction in consultation with parents, staff, and students;
- Ensuring that the school provides a safe environment and quality education for all its students;
- Overseeing the management of curriculum, staff, property, finance, and administration;
- Continuously monitoring and reviewing progress against targets to inform future planning.

The board must have a charter that sets out long-term goals and annual targets determining the school's priorities and must monitor and report annually to its community and the ministry of education on progress toward those goals and targets.

Boards typically meet once a month between February and December. Meetings are open to the public except when the board is discussing confidential matters. Elections are held every 3 years, and voters do not need to have a child at the school, to be a parent, or to be a trustee. Sections 103 and 103A of the Education Act 1989 (New Zealand Parliamentary Counsel Office, 2015) list the categories of people who are not eligible to be elected, appointed, or co-opted as trustees.

The board employs the principal to manage the school's day-to-day activities within the policies that it has set. Principals manage teaching and learning programs and monitor staff performance. The principal and teaching staff develop learning programs based on the New Zealand curriculum. Teachers manage what goes on in their classrooms, what is taught, and how it is taught. School administration staff (e.g., the school secretary or office administrator) assist the principal and teachers in the administration of the school. Schools also have staff employed to look after the maintenance of the grounds and buildings.

School Decile Ratings

Each school has a decile rating that determines the way the ministry of education allocates additional funding to schools with students from low socioeconomic households (Ministry of Education, 2015b). There are ten deciles, and approximately 10% of schools are in each decile. A school's decile rating indicates the extent to which it draws its students from low socioeconomic communities.

Decile 1 schools are the 10% of schools with the highest proportion of students from low socioeconomic communities, whereas decile 10 schools are the 10% of schools with the lowest proportion of these students. The socioeconomic level of a community is determined using data from the national 5-year census conducted by the government's statistical office.

The lower a school's decile rating, the more decile-based funding it gets. The decile-based extra funding is given to lower-decile schools to support their students' learning needs. A decile does not indicate the overall socioeconomic mix of students attending a school or measure the standard of education offered at a school.

Terms

The New Zealand school year is divided into four terms as follows:

- Term 1—Early February to mid-April;
- Term 2—Late April to the beginning of July;
- Term 3—Mid-July to late September;
- Term 4—Mid-October to mid-December.

The exact dates change from year to year. Students have a 6-week summer holiday break and three 2-week breaks between each of the four terms. Most schools follow the same term dates, but there is some flexibility for schools to work around local events. During term-time, schools will also close for statutory holidays, teacher-only days, and regional anniversary days.

Attendance

ENROL is an electronic student register used by all schools in New Zealand (Ministry of Education, 2015c). When children enroll at a school for the first time, details such as their name, address, and date of birth are recorded in the ENROL system. During their time at that school, the register is used to record student attendance, results of hearing and vision tests, and other appropriate information. School staff will update ENROL when a child changes schools or leaves the school system.

In New Zealand, parents are legally required to make sure their child goes to school every day. Under Education Act 1989 (New Zealand Parliamentary Counsel Office, 2015), parents and caregivers of children between the ages of 6 and 16 can be prosecuted if their child is away from school without a good reason. If a child needs to be away from school because of sickness, or for other valid reasons, parents or caregivers are asked to telephone in advance to inform the school of the absence and the length of time the child will be away. They then write and sign a note for the school confirming the reason for and length of the absence.

Parents or caregivers can expect to hear from the school if the child is absent without a note. The district truancy services help schools with students who regularly play truant (Ministry of Education, 2015d). Truancy officers determine the reason a child is not going to school and inform the school. The school then works with the parents and the child to get the child back into the classroom.

If a child is away for more than 20 days and no contact has been made with the school, the non-enrollment truancy service will help out (Ministry of Education, 2015d). The service can work with the school and the family to help get a child back to school. Children who miss many days of school because of serious illness may be able to get help from a regional health school. Regional health schools have programs for children who suffer from illnesses not allowing them to attend school regularly.

Fees and Donations

Although the government of New Zealand regulates and subsidizes early childhood education, most centers charge a fee, the amount of which depends on the type of service and the age of the child. For example, three- and four-year-olds in teacher-led ECE centers are eligible for up to 20 hours per week of subsidized education.

School donations and fees vary depending on the type of school. There is no charge for primary and secondary education at state and state integrated schools for children aged 5–19 years who are New Zealand citizens or permanent residents, but state integrated schools can charge "attendance dues" for property costs or building maintenance. Independent and private schools receive limited funding from the government and therefore charge a set fee per term or per year.

Schools may ask for donations to help run the school. All schools require parents to provide stationery (e.g., exercise books, folders, pens, pencils, etc.). Some primary schools and most intermediate and secondary schools have a policy requiring all enrolled students to wear a school uniform. Schools may also charge fees for take-home items and for activities or events that support but are not essential for teaching the curriculum. Schools often arrange opportunities for students to experience learning outside the classroom and may ask for money to pay for school trips.

Class Sizes

Most primary and secondary school classes in New Zealand contain 20–30 students, although this can vary considerably. Senior secondary (years 11–13) classes are generally smaller (15–20 students), but this, too, can vary between subjects and schools (Podmore, 1999; Post Primary Teachers Association, 2015).

The School Day

For years 1–8 students, the school day generally goes from 9 a.m. to 3 p.m. Students have a morning recess of about 30 minutes and a lunchtime break of about an hour. Children in years 1–8 are usually based in one classroom and have one main classroom teacher for the whole school day. Most classrooms are individual spaces but include flexible break-out teaching areas that are often shared with other classes. Classrooms can also consist of an open plan arrangement shared by two or more teachers.

Most secondary schools have a longer school day than primary/intermediate schools. Students often start at 8:40 a.m. and end at 3:20 p.m. The day normally starts with a home class that includes a roll call and daily notices. Students then break into subject classes, moving to different classrooms and different teachers for each subject. In larger schools, teachers teach only their specialty subject(s) and instruct hundreds of students each week. Lessons (called periods) can last 50 minutes to an hour, and during an average day, students will have five or six periods. Each school has a different timetable system. Schools change their timetable each term, and some schools have several different timetables that they rotate weekly throughout the year.

Curriculum

The New Zealand curriculum and Te Marautanga o Aotearoa form the national curriculum, and these determine what is taught and learned in New Zealand (Ministry of Education, 2007; Ministry of Education, 2015e). The curriculum applies to all English-medium state schools (including integrated schools). The New Zealand curriculum consists of eight learning areas: English, the arts, health and physical education, learning languages, mathematics and statistics, science, social sciences, and technology. The key competencies taught in tandem with these areas are designed to encourage enjoyment of learning, the ability to think critically, manage oneself, set goals, overcome obstacles, and get along with others. Within each curriculum area, students progress through eight levels. Each level represents a learning stage in that subject. Most year 1–8 students will be learning between levels 1 and 5.

Te Marautanga o Aotearoa applies to Māori-medium state schools. There are nine learning areas in Te Maurautanga o Aotearoa: pāngarau (mathematics), putaio (science), hangarau (technology), tikanga-a-iwi (social sciences), nga toi (the arts), hauora (health and well-being), te reo Māori (Māori language and literature), te reo Pākehā (English language), and ngā reo (learning languages).

The level at which each child is learning will vary by age and curriculum subject. Until year 10, all students in English-medium schools work within the New Zealand curriculum in all learning areas. In years 11 to 13, students can choose which subjects they want to study for the National Certificate of Educational Achievement (NCEA). In addition to the traditional subject areas, many schools offer courses that lead to trades or vocations such as travel, tourism, engineering, and hospitality. These courses may be assessed by unit standards and credited to the NCEA.

Assessment

In 2010, English-medium schools with year 1–8 students began using the national standards to assess and report on each child's progress and achievement in reading, writing, and mathematics (Ministry of Education, 2015f). Progress and achievement in relation to national standards are assessed in a number of ways, including what teachers see in the classroom and how they rate their own progress, as well as results from formal assessments.

In recent years, the overall approach to assessing progress and achievement has changed (Ministry of Education, 2015g). Assessment for learning is currently based on the following general process:

- Planning—the teacher plans and sets learning goals;
- Sharing learning goals and setting criteria for success—the teacher shares the learning goals with the students and asks them to help set criteria;
- Self-evaluation—teachers and students discuss progress toward those goals;
- Feedback—in addition to marking a student's work with a score or grade, the teacher also provides feedback relating directly to the learning goal.

The NCEA (National Certificate of Educational Achievement), introduced between 2002 and 2004, is the main secondary school qualification for students in years 11–13 (New Zealand Qualifications Authority [NZQA], 2015a). It can be gained at three levels—usually level 1 in year 11, level 2 in year 12, and level 3 in year 13. In the past, secondary school qualifications relied heavily on external exams. This meant that students' performance throughout the school year often could not be taken into account. Another limitation was that exam marks were scaled so that only a certain number of students could pass.

Within the NCEA system, any student who demonstrates the required skills and knowledge to the level of a particular standard achieves NCEA credits. Students receive a school results summary that presents all standards taken throughout their school years and the results for each.

Achievement and Unit Standards

There are two types of standards that contribute to NCEA: achievement standards and unit standards. Every school has its own curriculum that outlines its teaching and learning program. The school's curriculum is based on the national curriculum and aligns with achievement standards. Achievement standards can be earned through achievement, merit, or excellence, depending on how well the student performs.

Unit standards are not usually related directly to the curriculum and tend to be used more in workplace-related subjects such as hospitality, tourism, and engineering. Most unit standards are assessed as either achieved or not achieved.

Scholarships

Scholarships are determined by an external exam or assessment top-performing secondary students take in year 13, their last year of school. Scholarship exams are based on level-3 standards relating to areas of the curriculum or Te Marautanga o Aotearoa (the curriculum for Maori-medium schools) studied in year 13. A scholarship does not count toward NCEA credits. However, the fact that a student has gained a scholarship appears on the student's record of achievement.

Teacher Preparation

Initial teacher education in New Zealand is available through more than a dozen registered institutions, but the majority of teachers train within the six main universities (New Zealand Teachers Council, 2015a). Entry requirements to teaching qualifications vary between tertiary providers, but all providers consider academic performance, personal qualities, communication skills, and background experiences. The New Zealand Teachers Council also requires that candidates demonstrate that they are of sound character and fit to be teachers (New Zealand Teachers Council, 2015b). To attend a university, New Zealand requires a minimum of 42 credits at NCEA level 3 gained in approved subjects that focus mainly on literacy and numeracy.

Primary student teachers usually complete either a 3-year Bachelor of Teaching or a Bachelor of Education degree, depending on the institution they attend. Programs of study include papers on educational topics, professional practicum, and curriculum studies within the range of subjects specified in the New Zealand curriculum.

In each of their 3 years of study, students spend several weeks "on practicum" within a local school. During this time they spend each day in a particular school and classroom working with an associate teacher and his or her pupils. In their first year, students are mainly observing, getting to know how schools and classrooms operate, and becoming progressively more involved with the teaching and managing of the class. In subsequent years, students go on practicum at other schools and work in classes at different levels. In each successive year, students take on more of the planning and teaching of the class, and in their final year, they are expected to take full control of the class (planning and teaching) for an extended period of time (at least 1 week).

Most universities also offer a graduate diploma in teaching that is available to students already holding a relevant degree. The graduate diploma in teaching is usually a 1-year program that is a compressed version of the Bachelor of Teaching/Education degree and also includes periods of time in schools.

Secondary student teachers are required to have already completed a subject-based degree with a mix of subjects relevant to their chosen teaching subjects and need to enroll in a graduate teaching program. Some tertiary providers also offer conjoint teaching degrees, allowing students to study their subject-based degree alongside their teaching qualification. Prospective students whose degrees are not subject-based can often complete a 1-year graduate diploma in order to gain the requisite number of subject credits to have a major and a minor secondary school curriculum subject to teach.

SUMMARY AND DISCUSSION

Over the last 20 to 30 years, New Zealand's education system has undergone some of the most profound and far-reaching changes in its history. Since the major reforms of 1990, regional education boards no longer administer schools; an elected board of trustees that reports to the ministry of education now governs each school. Boards of trustees, principals, and teachers are now responsible for both the management of their school and the design and implementation of learning programs to meet the aims and intentions of the New Zealand curriculum introduced in the late 1990s.

Prior to the revisions in the 1990s, the curriculum was specified through more than a dozen syllabi and guidelines. The documents were of different vintages (spanning 1961–1986) and year levels. The total revision of the New Zealand school curriculum began in 1991, in both English and Māori, and the new New Zealand curriculum was introduced over a 2-year period from 1997 to 1999.

The New Zealand curriculum and Te Marautanga o Aotearoa now form the national curriculum and set the direction for teaching and learning in New Zealand. These documents are not, except in general terms, a syllabus or prescription but rather define the overarching educational aims and achievement objectives for the country. Each school works toward achieving these objectives by designing and implementing its own curriculum to meet the learning needs of its students. For some educators, this flexibility is seen as an opportunity for teachers to develop creative ways to respond to the needs of their students and community, while others remain concerned about a lack of consistency between schools and seek more direction and support from the ministry.

An important influence on New Zealand's education has been the long-standing recognition of the restricted opportunities for Māori and Polynesian children in schools. Attempts to redress this concern included the establishment of bilingual and Kura Kaupapa Māori schools. While the contentious 1995 introduction of decile funding was also, in part, prompted by the need to address the perceived disadvantages of specific groups in the community, other important drivers were the results of PISA, TIMMS, and similar international surveys. While the majority of New Zealand children performed well in these surveys, there was also clear evidence of a long "tail" of underachievement, and addressing this "tail" became a key goal of the ministry of education (Clark, 2013).

To address this goal, the ministry placed significant emphasis on literacy and numeracy, to the extent that primary schooling is now dominated by these elements of the curriculum. Much of this emphasis has come from the introduction, in 2010, of national standards, requiring primary schools to regularly assess and report to the ministry of education each child's progress and achievement in reading, writing, and mathematics. At the time of the standards' introduction, there was considerable nationwide resistance from teachers and principals who questioned the need for this level of formal reporting, the time it would take to do it, and the associated reduction in time for other core curriculum areas. Nevertheless, the ministry remained determined, and the national standards are now being implemented.

As a consequence, in most primary schools today, the entire morning of every day is devoted to the teaching of literacy and numeracy, with other subjects occupying whatever time is left in the afternoon. To what extent this heavy emphasis will improve overall achievement and reduce the underachieving "tail" remains to be seen, but many educators are concerned about the lack of attention the other curriculum areas are receiving and the long-term implications this approach has for success in these subjects (Thrupp, 2013).

At the secondary level, the introduction in 2002 of the NCEA (National Certificate of Educational Achievement) replaced the long-standing national external examinations of school certificate, university entrance, sixth form certificate, and university bursary. The introduction of NCEA was also accompanied by the introduction of new sets of standards used to assess students and to allow them to earn NCEA credits. While some standards are externally assessed either by exam or the submission of a portfolio, many are internally assessed. Adding to the complexity of the NCEA system is the fact that there are two sets of standards that students can work toward: achievement standards that align with the New Zealand curriculum and unit standards usually not directly related to the curriculum and often workplace related (New Zealand Qualifications Authority, 2015b).

The introduction of NCEA was, and still is, the source of much debate and concern. Many educators were concerned about the additional teacher workload associated with the move to a predominantly internally assessed system, while others were more concerned about consistency and comparability of NCEA credits between schools (Lyons, 2012). Concerns with NCEA's ability to genuinely reflect students' achievement has caused a number of schools across the country to offer their students the choice of Cambridge International Examinations or the International Baccalaureate alongside NCEA (Education Review, 2013).

Some schools have focused on achievement standards, while others feel that the more practically oriented unit standards are more suitable for their students. Some of these decisions may relate to the resources—both physical and human—available within a school, and there are debates about the relative merits of a general academic education versus vocational preparation.

All changes to an educational system inevitably cause a degree of stress and concern, and it takes time for schools, teachers, and communities to adapt. Doubt exists about whether the numerous, rapid, and profound changes over the last 25 years have caused considerable stress and strain within New Zealand's education system. Despite the relatively short time in which many of these changes have occurred, New Zealand's schools and teachers have responded remarkably well and continue to provide high-quality education that is well regarded internationally. How these changes will play out over time and what effect they will have on New Zealand's future remains to be seen.

REFERENCES

Butchers, A.G. (1930). *Education in New Zealand*. Dunedin, New Zealand: Coulls Somerville Wilkie.
Clark, J. (2013). Inequality of school achievement: Why the events of 2012 will not fix the problem. *Education Review*. Retrieved from http://www.educationreview.co.nz/magazine/january-2013/inequality-of-school-achievement-why-the-events-of-2012-will-not-fix-the-problem/#.VV7IuaZL6yg
Commission on Education in New Zealand. (1962). *Report of the Commission on Education in New Zealand*. Wellington, New Zealand: Government Printer.
Consultative Committee on the Post-Primary Curriculum. (1944). *The post-primary curriculum*. Wellington, New Zealand: Government Printer.
Dakin, J. (1973). *Education in New Zealand*. Auckland, New Zealand: Fullerton.
Education Act. (1877). *Statutes of New Zealand*, 1877. Wellington, New Zealand: Government Printer.
Education Act. (1914). *Statutes of New Zealand*, 1914. Wellington, New Zealand: Government Printer.
Education Act. (1989). *Statutes of New Zealand*, 1989. Wellington, New Zealand: Government Printer.
Education Amendment Act. (1996). *Statutes of New Zealand*, 1996. Wellington, New Zealand: Government Printer.
Education and Science Select Committee. (1995). *Inquiry into children in education at risk through truancy and behavioural problems*. Wellington, New Zealand: New Zealand House of Representatives.
Education Review. (2013). *NCEA vs other systems: The downside of picking sides*. Retrieved from http://www.educationreview.co.nz/magazine/january-2013/ncea-vs-other-systems-the-downside-of-picking-sides/#.VV7MOqZL6yg
Ewing, J. (1970). *Development of the New Zealand primary school curriculum 1877–1970*. Wellington, New Zealand: New Zealand Council for Educational Research.
Harte, A.H.W. (1972). *The training of teachers in New Zealand from its origins until 1948*. Christchurch, New Zealand: Simpson & Williams.
Lyons, P. (2012, November 8). Robust debate key to fixing NCEA problems. *New Zealand Herald*. Retrieved from http://www.nzherald.co.nz/nz/news/article.cfm?c_id=1&objectid=10845832
Mason, H.G.R. (1945). *Education today & tomorrow*. Wellington, New Zealand: Government Printer.
McLaren, I.A. (1974). *Education in a small democracy: New Zealand*. London, UK: Routledge & Kegan Paul.
McLaren, I.A. (1987). The politics of secondary education in New Zealand. In R. Openshaw & D. McKenzie (Eds.), *Reinterpreting the educational past: Essays in the history of New Zealand* (pp. 64–81) Wellington: NZCER.
Ministry of Education. (1994). *Annual report (E1) for the year ended 30 June 1994*. Wellington, New Zealand: Government Printer.
Ministry of Education. (2007). *The New Zealand curriculum*. Wellington, New Zealand: Learning Media.
Ministry of Education. (2015a). *Boards of trustees*. Retrieved from http://www.legislation.govt.nz/act/public/1989/0080/latest/DLM175959.html
Ministry of Education. (2015b). *School decile ratings*. Retrieved from http://www.minedu.govt.nz/Parents/AllAges/EducationInNZ/SchoolsInNewZealand/SchoolDecileRatings.aspx

Ministry of Education. (2015c). *ENROL and enrolment*. Retrieved from http://www.minedu.govt.nz/NZEducation/EducationPolicies/Schools/SchoolOperations/ENROLAndEnrolment.aspx

Ministry of Education. (2015d). *Attendance services*. Retrieved from http://www.minedu.govt.nz/NZEducation/EducationPolicies/Schools/Attendance/ForBoardsAndPrincipals/AttendanceServices.aspx

Ministry of Education. (2015e). *Te Marautanga o Aotearoa*. Retrieved from http://www.tmoa.tki.org.nz/Te-Marautanga-o-Aotearoa

Ministry of Education. (2015f). *National standards*. Retrieved from http://nzcurriculum.tki.org.nz/National-Standards

Ministry of Education. (2015g). *Assessment for learning*. Retrieved from http://nzcurriculum.tki.org.nz/National-Standards/Key-information/Fact-sheets/Assessment-for-learning

Moss, L. (2006). Boarding the school bus. *New Zealand Journal of History, 40*(1), 57–74.

Murdoch, J.H. (1943). *The high schools of New Zealand*. Wellington, New Zealand: New Zealand Council for Educational Research.

National Commission for UNESCO. (1972). *Compulsory education in New Zealand* (2nd rev. ed.). Paris, France: UNESCO.

New Zealand Department of Education. (1929). *Syllabus of instruction for public schools*. Wellington, New Zealand: Government Printer.

New Zealand Department of Education. (1989). *Tomorrow's schools: The reform of education administration in New Zealand*. Wellington, New Zealand: Department of Education.

New Zealand Government. (1919). Regulations for the organization, examination and inspection of public schools and the syllabus of instruction. *New Zealand Gazette*. Wellington, New Zealand: Government Printer.

New Zealand Parliamentary Counsel Office. (2015). *Education Act 1989*. Retrieved from http://www.legislation.govt.nz/act/public/1989/0080/latest/DLM175959.html

New Zealand Qualifications Authority. (2015a). *NCEA*. Retrieved from http://www.nzqa.govt.nz/qualifications-standards/qualifications/ncea/

New Zealand Qualifications Authority. (2015b). *Standards*. Retrieved from http://www.nzqa.govt.nz/qualifications-standards/qualifications/ncea/understanding-ncea/how-ncea-works/standards/

New Zealand Teachers Council. (2015a). *Initial teacher education providers*. Retrieved from https://www.teacherscouncil.govt.nz/content/initial-teacher-education-providers

New Zealand Teachers Council. (2015b). *Supporting resources—Registered teacher criteria*. Retrieved from http://www.teacherscouncil.govt.nz/content/supporting-resources-registered-teacher-criteria

Organisation for Economic Co-operation and Development. (2010). *PISA 2009 results: Executive summary*. Paris: Organisation of Economic Cooperation and Development.

Podmore, V.M. (1999). *Class size in the first years at school*. Retrieved from http://www.nzcer.org.nz/research/publications/class-size-first-years-school

Post Primary Teachers Association. (2015). *Class size matters*. Retrieved from http://www.ppta.org.nz/issues/class-size?showall=1&limitstart=

Secondary Schools Act. (1903). *Statutes of New Zealand*, 1903. Wellington, New Zealand: Government Printer.

Sinclair, K. (2001). *A history of New Zealand*. London: Penguin.

Statistics New Zealand. (2015). *Census 2013*. Retrieved from http://www.stats.govt.nz/Census/2013-census.aspx

Te Kura. (2015). *Te Aho o Te Kura Pounamu—The correspondence school*. Retrieved from http://www.tekura.school.nz/.

Thrupp, M. (Ed.). (1999). *A decade of reform in New Zealand education: Where to now?* Hamilton, New Zealand: University of Waikato.

Thrupp, M. (2013). National standards for student achievement: Is New Zealand's idiosyncratic approach any better? *Australian Journal of Language and Literacy, 36*(2), 99–110.

CHAPTER NINE

China

Reconciling Fairness with Efficiency: Reforming the Chinese Examination System

ANDREAS SCHLEICHER AND YAN WANG

Examination, an essential form of learning assessment, is central to education in China. Historically, the word "education" was used interchangeably with reading books for examination preparation. In spite of a range of attempts to broaden the approaches to student learning assessment, examination remains the dominant method of assessing student-learning outcomes, and high-stakes examinations have a significant impact on students' prospects in life. This chapter reviews the origins of students' learning assessments in China and the ways in which policymakers use these assessments in the current education system. It also discusses reform efforts underway to change policies and practices.

THE ORIGINS OF STUDENT ASSESSMENTS IN CHINA

Education has been highly valued throughout China's 4,000-year history. In ancient times, those who held positions in government administration enjoyed a higher status than farmers, craftsmen, or merchants. Thus Confucius's statement "Excellence in education leads to officialdom" was widely viewed as wise counsel for improving one's position in society, especially because there were few ways of climbing up the ranks of the social hierarchy apart from education. Success in royal court examinations led to an appointment as an official, changing not only the life of the individual but also that of his entire family. The high-stakes college entrance examinations conducted in China today are the most recent manifestation of these types of assessments.

To the Chinese, education benefits—and reflects well on—not only the individual but also the entire family. Parents never spare any effort or expense to see that their children succeed in school and in the college entrance examination (*gaokao*) to "bring glory to their ancestors and the family." As a result of the "single child policy" adopted in China in the early 1980s, parents' high expectations for their children have put further pressure on students to pass the college entrance examinations. It is believed that only by winning one of the limited places in universities and colleges will students be eligible for high-status, high-wage jobs later on (Liu, 2010; Cheng, 2013).

THE ROLE OF EXAMINATIONS IN CHINA'S EDUCATION SYSTEM

Assessment in China serves three purposes: diagnosis, accreditation, and selection. Selection is further divided into school choice and college/university entrance.

Assessment for Diagnosis

In primary and secondary schools, tests are conducted weekly; toward the end of the semester, they may be given daily. These tests help teachers to monitor students' acquisition of knowledge. When students encounter difficulties in learning, teachers intervene accordingly. There are four main types of tests: module-based tests, mid-term tests, end-of-term tests, and quality assurance tests. Although these tests are developed and administered by institutions at various levels of the education system, all four types of tests serve the same purpose: to ensure that no student is left behind.

- **Module tests** are developed by district pedagogical research institutions and administered by the subject teachers. The teachers analyze the results and give advice to students and parents based on the results.
- **Mid-term tests** are developed and administered by individual schools only at the secondary level. The director for instruction at each school analyzes the results and gives advice to teachers on how they can improve their teaching.
- **End-of-term tests** are developed by district pedagogical research institutions. Results are analyzed at both school and district levels. District-level institutions offer advice on school improvement to individual schools, whereas schools offer advice to teachers on how to improve their teaching.

- **Quality assurance tests** are developed by municipal pedagogical research institutions to be conducted at specific stages in education, such as the second term of primary grade 5. The tests are used to compare performance among different schools and to evaluate and improve pedagogical practice (H. Fu, personal communication, December 31, 2014; X. Shen, personal communication, December 31, 2014).

Moreover, teachers develop many additional tests simply for consolidating students' knowledge and preparing them for the aforementioned tests, which are linked implicitly with teachers' appraisal. In the past, teachers wrote questions on the blackboard for students to copy and answer in their exercise books. Today, the advancement of technology has made it possible to produce large numbers of test papers by copy machine. Since it is easy to create test papers by drawing from on-line item banks, teachers tend to give tests whenever they identify weak points in students' learning progress, aiming at better student performance on high-stakes examinations. Hence, tests play a crucial role in students' learning.

Examinations for Accreditation

It was not until 1983, several years after the college entrance examination was reintroduced in China, that an exam to confirm the skills learned in primary and secondary education was considered. At that time, China's education system began to produce large numbers of high school graduates who failed the college entrance exam and left school frustrated. The *huikao* examination was thus designed and introduced to acknowledge and accredit the skills acquired during the final 3 years of upper-secondary education. Students who pass the *huikao* and who attain certain specified standards in moral education, social practices, and physical education earn a high school diploma designed to help them enter the labor market. The tests are developed and administered by provinces, municipalities, and autonomous regions. Thus, these assessments are not comparable across regions (Fang, Li, Bi, Song, & Wang, 2002). In some provinces, the results of the *huikao* are linked with the *gaokao* (college entrance examination), either by setting the *huikao* as the qualifying examination for the *gaokao* or incorporating students' performance on the *huikao* into the total score of the *gaokao* (up to 10%).

Another example of an examination for accreditation practice was instituted in 1981. According to this policy all citizens, regardless of their age, sex, race, prior educational attainment, and occupation are allowed to apply to take an examination administered by provincial-level agencies. Those who pass this test acquire either a degree or a certificate. It is mandated that holders of this degree or certificate be entitled to the same fringe benefits as those in the workplace with regular higher education degrees. Through such examinations, many people, such as the elderly, the disabled, and the disadvantaged, have obtained tertiary qualifications, credentials they would not have been able to obtain otherwise (*Gaige kaifang yilai de jiaoyu fazhan lishixing chengjiu he jiben jingyan yanjiu ketizu*, 2008a).

Examinations for Selection

In China, students' progress through education—from primary to lower-secondary school, from lower-secondary school to upper-secondary school, and from upper-secondary school to higher education—is to a great extent determined by examinations.

Examinations for School Choice

The importance of examinations relates to the distribution of the country's educational resources. In China, public schools used to be labeled "key schools" or "non-key schools," based on the performance of their students.[1] To enhance equity, key schools have formally been unlabeled in many regions. At the lower-secondary level, high-performing schools are still in many cases recognized as "quality education resource schools," while at the upper-secondary level, an array of "demonstration schools" has been certified upon reaching certain benchmarks. These schools boast more resources, better facilities, and better teachers. Students in these schools tend to perform better in the high-stakes entrance examinations that lead to higher levels of education. Admission into a quality education resource school or demonstration school is perceived as the first step toward university or college enrollment, which, in turn, implies better job and income prospects in the future. A mere 1-point difference in examination scores could mean success or failure for the rest of one's life.

During examinations, students' knowledge and ability to apply this knowledge are tested through single- or multiple-choice questions, as well as a limited number of open-ended questions that require writing essays in Chinese. Most of the time, students prepare for these assessments by rote repetition and drills. In the mid-1980s, some educators and policymakers grew concerned that such teaching and learning to the test would undermine students' creative abilities and the development of their socio-emotional skills, leading to negative effects on their health. Hence, the ethos of quality-oriented education and students' holistic development arose (*Gaige kaifang yilai de jiaoyu fazhan lishixing chengjiu he jiben jingyan yanjiu ketizu*, 2008b).

Since then, as part of efforts to reorient education away from examination performance to a more holistic approach of learning, the entrance examination to lower-secondary schools has been replaced by a policy of mandatory enrollment based on area of residence. Students are required to go to the school in the neighborhood where they registered their *hukou* or residence identity, regardless of their performance in school (Fang et al., 2002). Once primary schools and secondary schools were allowed to recruit a proportion of students of their choice; however, this was reduced to a minimum after the adoption of the mandatory neighborhood enrollment policy (Ministry of Education, 2014).[2] Lower-secondary schools tend to combine "special talent + recommendation + lottery." Specifically, schools can recruit students with special talents (e.g., in the arts, sports, or technology certified by district education authorities) and top-performing students recommended by primary schools (according to students' scores in the examinations in the final 2 years). They also use a lottery system to select specific proportions of students in the mandatory residential areas (Ministry of Education, 2014). Nonetheless, the performance gap between advantaged schools and disadvantaged schools, though narrowing, remains substantial. Examinations are still the most direct, if not the only, path toward upward social mobility. As a result, competition for a place in one of the quality education resource schools or demonstration schools remains strong.

Conversely, students' performance, particularly in the all-important examinations, was strongly associated with the amount of resources that a school was able to secure. For example, in Beijing, high-performing schools were once allowed to charge contribution fees from students of their choice and use up to a maximum of 70% of these fees for school development, infrastructure, and facilities, but not for teacher salaries. Moreover, the resources that local education authorities allocate to schools tend to be related to student performance and resources already available at the school.[3] Thus, all schools try to attract the best students. Some do so by partnering with private tutoring companies. However, after equity-oriented reform was instituted in 2014, such contribution fees were forbidden, and the resources allocated to schools are currently on an equitable basis. Better-performing schools no longer receive additional resources.

Examinations for College Entrance

Reinstituted in 1978, the college entrance examination stands as the most significant event in the education arena in China. Every June,[4] approximately 8 million students take 2- or 3-day tests for which they have prepared for 12 years. To a great extent, these test results determine the opportunities students will have in the future.

This examination began with testing a range of subjects, such as Chinese, mathematics, foreign language, politics, and an additional two subjects (history and geography) for students of arts, combined with three more subjects (biology, physics, and chemistry) for students of science. Originally, test papers were developed centrally and administered provincially. However, since 1985, as part of education reform, the national examination has been decentralized, and 16 provinces and municipalities have been granted the autonomy to develop their own tests. In the pursuit of "quality-oriented education," various schemes that test three traditional core subjects, specifically Chinese, mathematics, and foreign language—"3" in Table 1—plus locally designed additional assessment and evaluation elements ("x," "1," etc.) have been piloted.

Table 9.1. Various Schemes for College Entrance Examination.

Scheme	Core Subjects	Additional Subjects		Starting Year	Provinces
3+ x	Chinese, Mathematics, & Foreign Language	Integrated Arts	Integrated Science	1999	Majority
3+ Integrated Arts/Integrated Science + optional subject	Chinese, Mathematics, & Foreign Language	Integrated Arts + 1 Subject	Integrated Science + 1 Subject	2009	Zhejiang
3+1	Chinese, Mathematics, & Foreign Language	1 Subject from Politics, History, Geography, Chemistry, Physics, or Biology		2012	Shanghai
3+ learning performance assessment + comprehensive quality evaluation	Chinese, Mathematics, & Foreign Language	History + 1 Subject from Chemistry, Biology, Politics, & Geography	Physics + 1 Subject from Chemistry, Biology, Politics, & Geography	2008	Jiangsu
3+3	Chinese, Mathematics, & Foreign Language	Politics, History, & Geography	Physics, Chemistry, & Biology	2007	Hainan

Source: Cheng (2002); News Office of the Ministry of Education & China National Institute for Educational Research (2010)

In the case of "3+ learning performance assessment + comprehensive quality evaluation" for the province of Jiangsu, students have to attain the C level (out of four ranks: A, B, C, and D) in five out of seven subjects for learning performance assessment in order to qualify for the college entrance examination. Comprehensive quality evaluation is used only as a reference for university admission. The maximum score for each scheme varies from province to province, ranging from 600 in "3+3" and 750 in "3+x" to 800 in "3+ Integrated Arts/Integrated Science + optional subject."

Students' achievement scores in the *gaokao* are ranked within each province. The Ministry of Education proposes the admission quota for universities to the different provinces and sends them to the universities for confirmation before making a final decision. Most of the time, the universities simply agree with what is proposed by the Ministry of Education, which includes quotas for three groups of universities and colleges (prestigious universities, regular universities, and colleges, which have courses that are shorter in duration). It is up to the provinces to set their own cut-off scores for each type of institution. Generally, parents want their children to attend the best universities. This desire has intensified the competitive aspect of test preparation. The month for college entrance examination in China is often called "Black June" to reflect the anxiety associated with this period (News Office of the Ministry of Education & China National Institute for Educational Research, 2010).

EXAMINATIONS AND MANAGEMENT OF THE EDUCATION SYSTEM

How are these examinations developed? How do they relate to the management of the education system in China?

Curriculum, Textbooks, and Examination

Examinations for primary and secondary education are underpinned by textbooks and teaching guides. Likewise, the *gaokao* is underpinned by examination specifications developed on the basis of textbooks and teaching guides. Textbooks are therefore more central to student learning in China than in many Western countries. In China, the textbook is essentially the curriculum; teaching is based on one textbook from the beginning to the end of a semester. The lower the level, the more teachers rely on textbooks for teaching and testing (H. Fu, personal communication, December 31, 2014; R. Cao, personal communication, January 26, 2015).

Beginning in 1949, all schools throughout the country used the same textbooks for such core subjects as mathematics, physics, chemistry, and biology. In the early 1980s, education policy shifted from relying on a single set of textbooks to using more diverse sets tailored to the needs of the country's different regions. As a result of the 1987 *Regulation for the National Textbook Review Board*, government agencies, schools, teachers, and experts were all allowed to write textbooks that could be used after they were endorsed by the National Textbook Review Board and recommended by the Ministry of Education.

Since 2001, curriculum for primary and secondary schools in China has undergone a profound change with the creation of a new national curriculum framework and standards. During this time, the principle of "one curriculum framework, multiple textbooks" for primary and secondary education was institutionalized. Under the three-level curriculum structure, including national, local, and school-based curriculum, provincial governments were given the discretion to accredit textbooks for the local curriculum, and the choice of textbooks was delegated to district-county governments (Zhong, 2009).

By September 2001, 49 sets of textbooks covering 20 subjects (7 for primary school subjects and 13 for secondary school subjects) were endorsed and put into use in 38 pilot areas across the country. By the spring of 2009, the Ministry of Education had endorsed 115 primary school textbooks covering 10 subjects, 20 lower-secondary school textbooks covering 11 subjects, and 72 upper-secondary school textbooks covering 18 subjects (Shi, 2014). The content of the textbooks, teaching outline, and examinations vary from province to province. Diversity of textbooks led to diversity of approaches and methods of both teaching and assessment.

Pedagogical Research, Teaching, and Tests

Two types of professional organizations in China support both teaching and learning: educational research institutions and pedagogical research organizations. The former focus on policies and theory, while the latter concentrate on teaching in the classroom. Educational research institutions operate at national, provincial, and municipal levels. Many of them are part of the education administration agency. Pedagogical research institutions operate at provincial, prefecture (municipality), and county levels and consist mostly of veteran teachers. These institutions coordinate school-based research projects, distill best practices for replication, advise teachers on their practices, and develop and administer module-based tests and end-of-term tests (X. Shen, personal communication, December 26, 2014; H. Fu, personal communication, December 31, 2014).

Accordingly, the staffs of these institutions dedicate much of their effort to tracking teachers' teaching performance through class visits and through feedback provided to teachers on their teaching content and methodology. In doing so, the pedagogical researchers acquire thorough understanding of the students' levels (depth and intensity) of knowledge and skill, which then become benchmarks for test development.

Such pedagogical research is intertwined closely with teachers' professional development. In general, teachers usually devote half a day per week to district-level pedagogical research activity, and another half a day to school-level pedagogical activities. On these occasions, pedagogical researchers introduce textbooks and make recommendations on how to teach content in them. Pedagogical researchers or invited experts lecture about teaching philosophy and teaching strategies, and master teachers or new teachers demonstrate a lesson to an audience of teachers from the district (H. Fu, personal communication, December 31, 2014).

In addition, the pedagogical research institutions organize teacher training eight times per year for all teachers and provide an additional eight sessions per year for master teachers. In the early 2000s, many teaching research institutions were combined with teacher training colleges to integrate pedagogical research into teacher professional development activities (X. Shen, personal communication, January 25, 2015).

Examination, teaching, learning, and teachers' professional development are aligned with each other by means of pedagogical research. Thus, pedagogical research institutions manage the nation's basic education system.

RECENT REFORM AND FUTURE DIRECTION

The recent reform in learning assessments and the overall education reform were designed to promote quality and equity. In September 2014, a long-awaited new scheme of the *gaokao* examination and admission for primary, secondary, and postgraduate levels was issued. The new *gaokao* scheme is currently being piloted in Shanghai and Zhejiang before its scheduled nationwide extension in 2017 (Ministry of Education, 2015). The scheme included new approaches and strategies but also created new challenges.

Diversity vs. Reliability

The first step to reforming the college entrance examination was to steer the high-stakes examination toward multiple pathways to higher education institutions and to allow more choice among examinations. The examination for tertiary vocational institutions is separate from that for regular universities and colleges. Applicants for tertiary vocational institutions need to pass a separate examination of "Literacy + Occupational Skills." Apart from traditionally mandatory subjects (Chinese, mathematics, and foreign language), students can choose three subjects that fit their interests and abilities from a range of subjects in learning performance assessments at the upper-secondary level of education, rather than take tests on a pre-established set of subjects. Two tests of foreign language are held each year (Ministry of Education, 2015).

The challenge is to balance the presence of such diversification with the need to ensure reliability and comparability. The test papers applied in the various provinces, especially in those provinces using their own test papers, vary in spite of the national curriculum framework, as they are based on different examination specifications written by provincial examination authorities and the national examination authority.[5] As a result, students admitted into the same university in the same year from different provinces may perform at different levels. To address this problem, the Ministry of Education plans to increase the number of provinces using national unified tests.

Furthermore, the content of the test papers is made public right after the examination for the purpose of transparency and thus cannot be used in subsequent years. As a result, the items on test papers of the same subjects vary from year to year, making reliable comparisons over time impossible.

Quality vs. Validity

To moderate the high stakes attached to the examination and to strengthen "quality"[6]-based assessment, the "comprehensive quality evaluation" (*zonghe sushi pingjia*) was mandated as part of the college entrance examination in the new scheme. It was originally introduced by the Ministry of Education in 2002 and articulated in two more ensuing policy notes in 2005 and 2008. The evaluation attempts to capture qualities that cannot be easily assessed through written examination. It covers a number of dimensions such as moral values,[7] citizenship, learning abilities, communication and collaboration abilities, sports and health, aesthetics, and behavior recorded in students' portfolios in the form of teacher marks and scores (e.g., ABCD) (News Office of the Ministry of Education & China National Institute for Educational Research, 2010).

Such evaluation results are expected to be used as a form of reference for university admission, together with the scores from the university entrance examination. So far, they have been included in very few areas. Universities did not admit some students as a result of poor content in their quality-assessment portfolios (News Office of the Ministry of Education & China National Institute for Educational Research, 2010). Nonetheless, it takes time to substantiate the validity of such an evaluation and to develop adequate accountability mechanisms to avoid potential malpractice in the processes of implementation.

Strategy for Equity

The most recent reform scheme of the *gaokao* highlights a strategy of equity by prioritizing disadvantaged areas and disadvantaged students. For years, the government has tried to maintain fairness in competition by assigning higher quotas for university admission to underdeveloped areas. The new scheme further increases university intake from the underdeveloped inland and the western regions. The goal is to narrow the enrollment rate gap from the current rate of 6% to less than 4%.

CONCLUSION

Examinations are a cornerstone of the Chinese education system. They help secure a high degree of fairness in the allocation of educational opportunities, provide transparency for the social and economic merit of qualifications, and contribute to the high value that individuals and institutions place on education. Similarly, formative assessments are a central tool to the learning progress of students and the professional development of teachers. The high value placed on examinations by students, parents, and teachers indicates that their stakes are very high. These exams influence student learning and teacher instruction. The strong emphasis on exams means that the quality of Chinese examinations and assessments has a strong impact on the quality of Chinese education.

Policymakers will therefore need to carefully consider the trade-offs that are involved. To provide useful guidance to teaching and learning, examinations need to offer a high degree of validity in terms of measuring what is important for students to learn and for teachers to teach. This typically calls for complex and authentic assessment tasks that look beyond what students know and what students can do with what they know, and may involve human judgment in assessing student responses. At the same time, to maximize objectivity and ensure fairness, the examination tasks need to offer a high degree of reliability, which typically calls for simple task structures that can be scored without human judgment. Finding the right balance between those competing demands is difficult because there is always a risk in sacrificing validity for reliability, or authenticity for efficiency.

NOTES

1. In the late 1970s, the Ministry of Education issued a policy to establish a group of key schools aiming at a pyramid structure of primary and secondary schools, prioritizing resources for financing, infrastructure, and teacher and student intake for key schools (Zhang, 2011).
2. The policy has been implemented de facto since early 2015 at the provincial level.
3. Synthesis of three interviews (one with a researcher, one with a vice principal, and one with a deputy director of a district education commission); the interviewees requested anonymity.
4. Before 2003, the test was held in July.
5. Synthesis of two interviews (one from a national examination center and one from the Beijing municipal education examination institute); both interviewees prefer to remain anonymous.
6. Quality implies an integration of values, knowledge, competencies, etc.

7. Such as love toward motherland, people, labor, science, and socialism; also included are observing disciplines, obeying laws, being honest and credible, showing concern for the collective, maintaining social morality, and preserving the environment.

REFERENCES

Cheng F.P. (2002). *Zhongguo jiaoyu wenti baogao: Rushi Beijing xia zhongguo jiaoyu de xianshi wenti he jiben duice* [China education issues report: Realistic issues and fundamental countermeasures of education in China in the context of entry into WTO]. Beijing: China Social Science Publishing House.

Cheng, K.M. (2013). Shanghai: How a big city in a developing country leaped to the head of the class. In M.S. Tucker (Ed.), *Surpassing Shanghai: An agenda for American education built on the world's learning systems* (pp. 21–50). Cambridge, MA: Harvard Education Press.

Fang, X.D., Li, Y.F., Bi, C., Song, J.G., & Wang, H.Y. (2002). *Zhonghua renmin gongheguo jiaoyu shigang* [History of education of the People's Republic of China]. Haikou, China: Hainan Publishing House.

Gaige kaifang yilai de jiaoyu fazhan lishixing chengjiu he jiben jingyan yanjiu ketizu [Research team for historical achievement and essential development of education since reform and opening up]. (2008a). *Gaige kaifang 30nian zhongguo jiaoyu zhongda lishi shijian* [China's historical milestone education events within 30 years since reform and opening up]. Beijing: Educational Science Publishing House.

Gaige kaifang yilai de jiaoyu fazhan lishixing chengjiu he jiben jingyan yanjiu ketizu [Research team for historical achievement and essential development of education since reform and opening up]. (2008b). *Gaige kaifang 30nian zhongguo jiaoyu zhongda lilun chengguo* [China's significant theoretical education achievements within 30 years since reform and opening up]. Beijing: Educational Science Publishing House.

Liu, H.F. (2010). *Zhongguo keju wenhua* [China's keju culture]. Shenyang, China: Liaoning Education Press.

Ministry of Education. (2014). *Guanyu jinyibu zuohao xiaoxue shengru chuzhong mianshi jiujin ruxue gongzuo de shishi yijian* [Opinion on mandatory neighborhood enrollment for progression from primary school into secondary school]. Retrieved March 6, 2015, from http://www.moe.edu.cn/publicfiles/business/htmlfiles/moe/s3321/201401/163246.html

Ministry of Education. (2015). *Cujin gongping, kexue xuancai* [Promoting equity, scientifically selecting talents]. Retrieved from http://www.moe.edu.cn/publicfiles/business/htmlfiles/moe/s271/201409/174581.html

News Office of the Ministry of Education & China National Institute for Educational Research. (2010). *Duihua jiaoyu redian* [Dialogue on educational issues]. Beijing: Educational Science Publishing House.

Shi, O. (2014, June 26). *Jiaokeshu bainian* [Textbook for 100 years]. Seminar at the National Institute of Education Sciences.

Zhang X.L. (2011). (Ed.). *China's education development and policy: 1978–2008*. Beijing: Social Sciences Academic Press.

Zhong, Q. (2009). Yigang duoben: Jiaoyu minzhu de suqiu-woguo jiaokeshu zhengce shuping ["One standard, multiple versions of textbook": Pursuit of education democracy: A review of textbook policy in China]. *Research in Educational Development, 4*, 1–6.

CHAPTER TEN

Conclusion

What We Can Learn from High-Ranking Nations in Education

HANI MORGAN

Some world-class nations in education use many more appealing practices and experience fewer drawbacks than others. Problems exist, though, and may include students who endure high levels of stress and anxiety related to their academic work and a style of learning based on rote methods of study. High student scores on international tests do not equate to high levels of student happiness and healthy emotional development. Although international tests yield crucial information on the education of students, they usually provide little, if any, feedback on these critical components.

Additionally, these tests do not assess students on their artistic, moral, physical, and civic skills, aspects of education that many scholars from around the world consider important for youth. Consequently, educators have criticized their use, arguing that they narrow our concept of what education ought to be (*Guardian*, 2014). However, the PISA has recently attempted to gather data on the link between students' happiness and academic performance.

HEALTHY DEVELOPMENT OF YOUTH

As discussed in the chapter on South Korea, students in that nation outperform most other countries on international tests, resulting in its reputation as world-class in education. But youth there tend to endure more pressure, leading them to be less happy than those in other regions. Amanda Ripley's (2013) book contains a description of an American student who goes to South Korea to explore that country's culture. Although he loves the country, the warmth of its people, and their high expectations for what their children can do, he develops unfavorable attitudes about its school system when he interacts with students exhausted from their seemingly endless hours of study.

The great pressure on students to succeed academically contributes to Korea's youth suicide rate, the highest among OECD countries (Ahn & Baek, 2013). Students need to experience happiness during their years of formal schooling for healthy emotional development, but stress resulting from academic pressure precludes the conditions necessary for this to occur. In 2012, for the first time, PISA included a survey designed to measure student happiness. The survey showed that the Republic of Korea had the lowest percentage of students (60%) reporting to be happy (Nyamkhuu, 2014).

The findings of the survey were somewhat surprising, because some top-performing nations such as Korea scored poorly on the happiness scale, but lower-achieving countries, including Indonesia, Peru, and Thailand, were at the top of the list. These results should not lead educators to conclude that it is impossible for a country to have high-achieving, happy students, because the survey also showed that many East Asian countries experienced a sizeable number of students exhibiting those two qualities. Although these countries did not have as high a percentage of happy students as those from the nations topping the list, they managed to have a higher percentage than the OECD average (Nyamkhuu, 2014).

Nonetheless, in addition to South Korea, other high-performing nations in international testing suffer from problems that impede the emotional and psychological development of their youth—problems that stem from stress originating in school. Japan, for instance, has a suicide rate that is about 60% above the global average (Mckenna, 2015), and young people in Japan between the ages of 15 and 24 are one of the most vulnerable groups for suicide fatalities and attempts (Hidaka et al., 2008). As the chapter on Japan mentions, one of the problems this nation faces is bullying. From 2011 to 2012, school bullying reports in Japan increased more than 20%, and a survey spanning 10 months beginning in April 2012 showed that there were more than twice as many cases of teachers using corporal punishment on students during that period than in the previous 12 months (McCurry, 2013).

The school bullying problem in Japan contributes to its suicide rate and also to a state of reclusiveness known as *hikikomori*. Although school bullying is not the only factor linked to this condition, it does play a role. A sizeable number of students experiencing attacks from bullies in Japan isolate themselves from the outside world, staying indoors for periods of time that can stretch over months or, in some cases, even years (Adams, 2013). Most individuals experiencing *hikikomori* refrain from all social contact, including with their own family members, but continue to live in their parents' homes, holed up in their bedrooms (Norasakkunkit & Uchida, 2014).

Bullying in Japan differs from that in the United States in several ways. Unlike the United States, Japan has a homogeneous population and embraces values based on conformity. Thus, students who deviate from the norm increase their risk of being bullied more than in countries with greater diversity. Sometimes even teachers bully students. Recent statistics indicated that more than 80% of students had either been bullied or participated in bullying, and one survey found that 55% of Japanese youths had experienced *hikikomori* (Adams, 2013). In order to discipline students, teachers sometimes act in ways that would not be tolerated in other countries such as the United States. For example, they call students names like "imbecile," hit them, and even make sexual comments (Adams, 2013).

In addition to the bullying problem, stress on Japanese students comes from a rigorous academic lifestyle, somewhat similar to that in other high-performing Asian countries. They report fatigue, tension, and anxiety, and one survey found that 44.5% of elementary school students indicated that they frequently feel like "freaking out" (Treml, 2001). Since students in Japan go to school more days than in many other countries, attend cram schools, and regularly participate in club activities, they spend very little time talking to a parent. Moreover, some scholars criticize high-performing Asian nations, including Japan, for their lack of creativity.

CREATIVITY

According to Zhao (2012a), some world-class nations in education, such as China, will not produce people like Steve Jobs unless they reform their education systems. Although students in Shanghai, China, shocked the world in 2010 when they scored highest among all nations on the PISA in math, reading, and science, Zhao says the country did not celebrate, partly because the results were viewed with caution. Some skeptics have even questioned China's recent number-one PISA rankings because, unlike other countries, China was not judged according to students across the entire country, but only on the basis of two regions containing its most educated students: Shanghai and Hong Kong (Stout, 2013). Comparing these two regions with the results of other entire nations, as the media does, seems unfair. What is also misleading is the absence of mention of the way the Chinese view their recent PISA results and the major concerns they have about their educational system.

When the PISA results were announced in 2010, many Americans expressed concern over the poor quality of education in America, because countries such as China were making progress as the United States continued to stagnate. The results caught Secretary of Education Arne Duncan's attention, leading him to call these scores "a wake-up call," and even President Barack Obama voiced concern when he compared this problem to the Sputnik crisis (Zhao, 2012b). However, in China, rather than celebrate, parents and educators feared the outstanding results meant that China had failed to solve a problem it has been aware of for decades: overstressed students who devote too much effort to gaining book knowledge. The Chinese knew that high performance on the PISA resulted from the long hours students spent on academic tasks, but they also worried that these outcomes overburdened students and caused other detrimental effects.

In addition to high achievement on tests, other factors such as creativity and interpersonal skills contribute to school success (Niu & Sternberg, 2003). Although China increased its focus on innovation and creativity, these topics were usually neglected in its official strategic documents from 1978 until the mid-1990s, contributing to the view often advanced in the Chinese media and academic journals that China lacks these qualities (Pang & Plucker, 2013). While China's economic growth has soared in the past 20 years, in 2008 it produced only 473 innovations recognized by patent offices outside of China, compared with 14,399 from the United States (Zhao, 2012a). Liu Daoyu, a former president of one of China's top universities, said that one of the reasons Chinese students lack imagination is the constraining effect of the examination system in the country (Wu & Albanese, 2013). China's current economy is labor based, not knowledge based, and because it is rooted in cheap labor, it is volatile in a world where this type of labor is easy to find (Zhao, 2012a).

Researchers also criticize other world-class Asian nations in education for their inability to promote creativity. Critics sometimes say that although American students may not achieve high test scores as often as Asian students, they are more creative. They believe that American educators promote creativity by encouraging students to ask questions, whereas Asian cultures emphasize conformity and silence (Bracey, 2002). In East Asian societies, students respect their teachers greatly, expect the teacher to ask the questions, and speak only when the teacher addresses them (Kim, 2005).

Steve Wozniak, one of the co-founders of Apple with Steve Jobs, believes that very structured, formal societies such as Singapore discourage creativity and fail to produce people responsible for great inventions (BBC, 2011). Although some Singaporeans disagree with Wozniak, some of them concur that the country's rote methods of study, regimented curriculum, and pressure to conform do, in fact, make it highly unlikely that this nation will produce someone like Mark Zuckerberg (Zhao, 2012a). Wozniak refers to structured societies like Singapore to point out that they lack great artists, musicians, singers, and writers.

Japan and Korea are not exempt from this type of criticism. Like China and Singapore, these two countries produce some of the highest scores on international testing but sometimes generate unfavorable perceptions regarding their creative potential. One report, for example, by the 2010 Global Entrepreneurship Monitor

(GEM), ranked Korea and Japan 19th and 21st respectively on a list of 22 innovation-oriented, developed nations regarding their early-stage entrepreneurial activities (Zhao, 2012a).

CHEATING

The pressures of the exam-focused educational system in many Asian nations have led to cheating problems. In China, the use of proxies to take tests for students is a big business operated by organizations that sometimes advertise on the Internet, ask for photos from clients, and then attempt to find a proxy similar in appearance to the test taker (Bracey, 2005). Students also take advantage of today's high-tech resources to cheat. For example, 2,440 students taking a national exam to become licensed pharmacists in the city of Xian, China, used wireless earpieces to receive the answers to a test (Hunt, 2014). They were caught when abnormal radio waves were detected. A Chinese educational consultant mentioned that the high-stakes exam system promotes a widespread culture of cheating, but that most cases are less shocking than this one.

In another case, also in China, 54 external invigilators investigated a small area's high scores on the *gaokao* exam, because students in the city of Zhongxiang were disproportionately gaining the limited number of places at the country's elite universities (Moore, 2013). When high school students arrived at one of the schools to take the exam, investigators confiscated secret transmitters that looked like pencil erasers. Another group of officials caught people from a nearby hotel transmitting answers to the students. The investigation triggered a riot when parents came to pick up their children and discovered what had happened. The angry mob that instigated the riot felt that since cheating is endemic in China, not allowing their children the same advantage as others was unjust (Moore, 2013).

When a cheating scandal was discovered in South Korea, the SAT exam many students were hoping to take to study abroad was canceled in May 2013 at all centers in the country. Educators in South Korea believe that cheating has been a problem in that country for years. Unregulated cramming schools and tutors pay thousands of dollars for SAT test papers to enhance their results and attract new customers. The news of the scandal did not surprise one principal, who mentioned that Korea's extremely competitive school system promotes such cheating (Rivers, 2013). In an earlier case, police in Seoul investigated 27 students and, by analyzing photos on social security cards that did not match those used for admission to the test, determined that they had used proxies to take a test for them (Bracey, 2005).

Another case in Kwangju, South Korea, involved more than 140 high school students implicated in a cheating scandal. Students reportedly used cell phones to send and receive answers to the national exam, a test with great bearing on the university admission process. They paid between $285 and $850 to use this scheme, a plan designed to provide low-achieving students with answers they would get from high-achieving students in the exam rooms through cell phone messages (Brender, 2004). Similar events occurred in China when students used cell phones to send digital photos of exam questions to accomplices, who then sent the answers back to the test takers through text messages (Mooney, 2004).

Unlike universities in other countries that may evaluate students based on interpersonal skills and academic potential by using an interview or narrative format in addition to standardized tests, Asian universities emphasize standardized testing and rote learning, resulting in a do-or-die attitude toward exams that exacerbates the cheating problem (Montlake, 2006). The penalties of cheating include jail time and disqualification from taking exams again. One year in China, 1,700 students caught cheating on an exam were not permitted to take the test again. On another occasion in South Korea, criminal gang members using cell phones to send the answers of the national college entrance test to those taking it were jailed (Montlake, 2006).

High-achieving Asian nations endure some types of problems not often experienced in other countries. They may have more overstressed students who lack creativity and work long hours in a highly competitive environment that drives many youth to cheat. These issues do not mean that low-achieving nations cannot learn from high-performing Asian nations. It means that there are limitations to modeling the practices of world-class nations. It also means that we can borrow many more ideas from the high-performing countries with the fewest problems. But which of these has the most success and the least trouble?

LEARNING FROM FINLAND

Of countries in that particular set, Finland seems to be the one most thoroughly researched. The introductory chapter in this volume discussed limitations when borrowing Asian cultural attitudes in the service of education. Because high-ranking Asian countries have different values regarding work and education than many other countries, some aspects of their systems do not translate well in nations without similar ideals. These nations also experience the concerns just discussed.

A much more practical approach is to use a nation with consistently favorable results, fewer problems, and a value system that would likely be appealing to a wide variety of countries throughout the world. The nation that best fits this description is Finland. The research and descriptions of Finland's education system indicate that it receives much less criticism directed toward a lack of creativity and the stress placed on its students than the high-performing Asian countries. Finland's educational system is designed to prevent these problems in several ways.

First, schools in Finland, unlike their counterparts in Asian nations, do not rely on standardized tests to evaluate students' learning. Instead they judge students on their individual development and abilities by providing feedback in narrative form to describe learning progress and areas for growth (Darling-Hammond, 2011/12). Second, the teachers themselves determine students' academic performance, not external assessors (Sahlberg, 2011a). As a result of the near-complete absence of standardized tests and the increased freedom teachers have to teach the way they feel will most benefit students, Finnish students experience less stress than those in many other countries. The focus on learning rather than exams thwarts a style of teaching based on rote memorization and teaching to the test, and instead helps teachers to instruct students in a manner that allows them to discover knowledge. Finland's education system therefore usually receives less criticism about a lack of creativity than the Asian nations. Its education policy involves a high commitment to personalized learning and creativity (Sahlberg, 2011a), and one of the goals of the school system is to encourage student happiness (Olmstead, 2014).

Students in Finland attend school for far fewer hours and do less homework than those in many nations (Sahlberg, 2011b). Elementary students endure less stress than their counterparts around the world, in part because schools provide them with 75 minutes of recess per day—much more than the 27-minute average in the United States—and rather than constantly focusing on getting correct answers for tests, they participate more in arts and crafts (Abrams, 2011). Moreover, the intense competition among schools and teachers that places added stress on students, parents, and teachers in other nations, including the United States, is practically nonexistent. Finland's education policy focuses on cooperation and equity, with the result being a society where teachers and schools are not ranked and where parents are not worried about whether their children will be admitted to a good school (Partanen, 2011). The strong academic support available at each school enables Finland to thrive with virtually no private tutoring market (Libermann, 2011), a much more favorable condition than in many Asian nations, where families spend much of their earnings on tutoring.

Additionally, Finland averages fewer students per class than the OECD average at both the primary and lower-secondary level (OECD, 2011). Although some educators contend that class size has no effect on academic achievement, Schanzenbach (2014) argues that common sense and research show that students make more academic gains in smaller classes.

A culture of cheating on exams is unknown in Finland. Indeed, in addition to the description in the introductory chapter of this book suggesting that Finland has a utopian system, other authors have implied that this nation implements ideal practices that can be used to improve other systems in the world. Amanda Ripley's (2013) book, for instance, contains a chapter entitled "An American in Utopia," about a student from the United States who experiences Finland's educational system. Ripley suggests that countries achieving less than optimum results on international tests, like the United States, would benefit greatly if they were to implement an educational system analogous to Finland's. She emphasizes the advantages that students in Finland's system are afforded that the United States lacks. For example, in contrast to the mandatory master's degree required of teachers in Finland for basic and general education, the United States requires only a bachelor's. This is just one of many factors that make it much easier to become a teacher in the United States than in Finland.

Other factors include extremely selective teacher-education programs. In contrast to the United States, where only about 5% of teacher-education programs are highly competitive, with some having very few admissions standards, all of Finland's teacher-training programs are about as selective as MIT. Ripley contends that in the United States, students perceive education as an easy major, with programs requiring less difficult work, making it easier for them to receive high grades. Ironically, like the United States, Finland had a system of many mediocre teaching colleges before it underwent reforms. At one time it did not enjoy the reputation that it was to earn in the twenty-first century as a leading country in education. However, when it reformed, it restructured its teacher training colleges so as to become highly selective. Today these programs contribute strongly to Finland's success in international testing.

Ripley provides other examples to highlight Finland's superior system, including one involving teachers who coach sports teams. Whereas in the United States this is common practice, in Finland, educators would consider it to be ludicrous. More examples include a comparison between Finland's high standards for becoming a teacher and the lower standards used in the United States and other nations that show lackluster results on international tests. Ripley explains that if a teacher in the United States were compared to one in Finland in 2000, the American teacher could have taught a subject without majoring in it and graduated from a program with many fewer hours of hands-on training than the usual one year of residency required in Finland.

Some educators argue that it is not practical for countries with a culturally diverse population like the United States to look for ideas on reform from Finland, a nation with little ethnic diversity. Although the United States certainly is highly diverse, Finland's cultural and ethnic diversity has increased faster than that of any other European Union nation; the number of foreign-born residents in Finland has tripled in the new millennium (Sahlberg, 2011b). Another encouraging factor in borrowing Finland's methods is that Finland itself used ideas from abroad to achieve its success. For example, it relied heavily on the United States for its philosophy of education based on John Dewey's ideas, advocating for a way of teaching in which all students are offered proper opportunities and support in harmony with their diverse backgrounds, a type of model requiring the school to function as a small democratic system (Sahlberg, 2012). Other ideas it implemented from abroad are curriculum models, portfolio assessments, cooperative learning, and peer-assisted leadership, all innovations Finland imported from various nations including England, Canada, Australia, Israel, and the United States. Thus, Finland's success shows that using strategies that originate abroad is a feasible approach that other nations can and should experiment with.

Also important is the relatively short time it took Finland to transform its system and the cost-effective methods it used. In roughly 3 decades, from the implementation of its new education system in the 1970s to the new millennium, Finland went from merely mediocre (as seen on its international testing results in the 1990s) to leading-nation status in education (Sahlberg, 2012). The short time it took Finland to transform itself from mediocrity to excellence should create hope for the many countries enduring average or poor performance. Equally important is that Finland, compared to other countries, spent little in order to achieve its impressive results. In fact, from 1995 to 2004, Finland spent less than the average of what each OECD country spent on education, and significantly less than what the United States spent (Sahlberg, 2011b). It was able to achieve these impressive results through its efficient system, using methods such as effective intervention for students with learning difficulties to reduce grade repetition. Grade repetition not only costs a school more, it also embarrasses students and contributes to a less stimulating environment.

Although exploring Finland's remarkable education system can help reformers gain ideas about how they can transform a poor system, educational leaders need to realize that Finland is not perfect.

PROBLEMS IN FINLAND

One of the main concerns Finland is currently dealing with is its declining scores on a recent PISA test. Although overall its PISA scores were still impressive in 2012, they were not as high as in previous years, especially in mathematics, as its students dropped to 12th place. Pasi Sahlberg, one of Finland's leading authorities on its school system, expressed his thoughts on Finland's decline in *The Washington Post* in 2013.

Sahlberg believes the attention Finland received in the recent past on its desirable educational outcomes may have sidetracked its previous commitment to improvement. Another explanation Sahlberg offers for its decline involves the possibility that other nations are modifying their curriculum and are coaching students to take tests similar to the PISA. He believes that Finland should avoid what many other countries have done when attempting to improve their poorly performing systems, such as increase competition, accountability, or privatization of public schools, and instead concentrate on the holistic methods the nation successfully used in previous years (Sahlberg, 2013).

CLOSING THOUGHTS

Skeptics of evaluating different nations' education systems through international testing contend that this method is misleading and controversial. Although these comparisons yield important data related to a country's educational performance and potential for future prosperity, such critics argue that this method fails to consider crucial factors such as students' level of creativity and happiness. Although the strong emphasis on education in the high-performing East Asian nations is generally viewed favorably, it is associated with a wide variety of negative factors, including health issues related to high levels of stress, anxiety, depression, and even suicide (Kim, Lee, Chae, Anderson, & Laurence, 2011).

Furthermore, scholars sometimes criticize Asian teachers for teaching to the test in a manner that impedes the thinking skills that pupils will later need for successful careers (Lim, 2010). East Asian cultures are based on Confucianism, which stresses correct knowledge—measured today through a rigid standardized examination system encouraging rote learning and memorization (Kim et al., 2011). The intensive competition in Asian nations also leads to cheating problems, especially in China and South Korea.

Additionally, juxtaposing the results of one or two parts of China, as has been done recently through international tests, to those of other entire nations seems unjustifiable. Some scholars have found other seemingly biased methods of making these international comparisons. For example, Bracey (2008) pointed out that on one occasion, the PISA sample was biased against the United States because it consisted of Japanese students, all of whom were in the 10th grade, being compared to American students, over one-third of whom were in the 9th grade or lower. Bracey (2002) also questioned the strong link between high scores on standardized tests and a nation's economic position in the world, referring to the words of notable historian Lawrence Cremin in arguing that global competitiveness depends on actions taken by Congress, the president, and several federal departments, not by the school system.

Although critics of international testing make valid arguments, supporters of using tests such as the PISA for assessing different educational systems also make good points. First, as was noted in the introductory chapter, tests such as the PISA do not just measure what students can memorize or recall. Ever since the PISA test was first administered in 2000, it has focused on how students apply knowledge to solve real-world problems, rather than merely what they have memorized

(OECD, 2001). Students performing well on the PISA do, in fact, possess valuable skills that improve their chances of success in the real world.

Second, the "book knowledge" emphasized in Asian cultures is not worthless. In order to apply information well, a student first needs to know it. In order for students to think critically to solve problems, they need correct information to think about. In order to be creative, they need accurate facts and knowledge to put together in new ways. It is only when teachers overstress knowledge and neglect creativity and other components of education such as art, music, civics, moral development, and interpersonal skills that problems occur. This is a real dilemma that puts pressure on students and takes the joy out of education. Although many East Asian countries appear to be victims of such a detrimental practice, many of them also implement methods that would benefit other systems of education, such as the high standards they set for teachers and the commitment they have to disadvantaged students.

Although Bracey (2002) questioned the link between schooling and a nation's level of global competiveness and correctly pointed out that other factors have considerable influence on its economic prosperity, the studies mentioned in this book—especially in the chapter on the United States—show that there is in fact a connection between these two variables. Bracey used the words of historian Lawrence Cremin to discuss the impact of schooling on the economy, but the economy Cremin referred to was not the interconnected global economy we have today. Thus, Cremin's ideas may not be as valid today as when he conceived them.

By borrowing the methods known to work in the world-class nations in education with few problems, mediocre- and poor-performing systems can improve their own. Nations taking these steps will likely create an abundance of new opportunities for their residents, while those continuing to implement policies known to impede progress will undoubtedly continue to experience inequality and fewer opportunities for economic growth. It is only when we consider students' happiness, creativity, interpersonal skills, moral development, and appreciation for the arts, in addition to their academic performance in reading, math, and science that we can make evaluations about the future progress of today's students. Using all these factors together with high standards in teacher education programs and equal opportunities for all students will create an enhanced educational system for those countries experiencing mediocrity today.

REFERENCES

Abrams, S.E. (2011). *The children must play*. Retrieved from http://www.newrepublic.com/article/politics/82329/education-reform-Finland-US

Adams, K.A. (2013). The poison system in Japan. *Journal of Psychohistory, 40*(3), 174–186.

Ahn, S.Y., & Baek, S.J. (2013). Academic achievement-oriented society and its relationship to the psychological well-being of Koreans. In C.C. Yi (Ed.), *The psychological well-being of East Asian youth* (pp. 265–280). New York: Springer.

BBC. (2011, December 14). Steve Wozniak: "Think for yourself." Retrieved from http://news.bbc.co.uk/today/hi/today/newsid_9661000/9661755.stm

Bracey, G.W. (2002). Test scores, creativity, and global competitiveness. *Phi Delta Kappan, 83*(10), 738–739.

Bracey, G.W. (2005). Cheating update. *Phi Delta Kappan, 86*(8), 637–638.

Bracey, G.W. (2008). On the shortage of scientists and engineers. *Phi Delta Kappan, 89*(7), 536–538.

Brender, A. (2004, December 3). Cheating scam hits key test in South Korea. *Chronicle of Higher Education, 51*(15), A41.

Darling-Hammond, L. (2011/12). Soaring systems. *Education Review, 24*(1), 24–33.

The Guardian. (2014, May 6). *OECD and PISA tests are damaging education worldwide—academics*. Retrieved from http://www.theguardian.com/education/2014/may/06/oecd-pisa-tests-damaging-education-academics

Hidaka, Y., Operario, D., Takenaka, M., Omori, S., Ichikawa, S., & Shirasaka, T. (2008). Attempted suicide and associated risk factors among youth in urban Japan. *Social Psychiatry & Psychiatric Epidemiology, 43*(9), 752–757.

Hunt, K. (2014, October 28). *China catches 2,440 cheating students in high-tech scam*. Retrieved from http://www.cnn.com/2014/10/28/world/asia/china-exam-cheats/

Kim, K.H. (2005). Learning from each other: Creativity in East Asian and American education. *Creativity Research Journal, 17*(4), 337–347.

Kim, K.H., Lee, H.E., Chae, K., Anderson, L., & Laurence, C. (2011). Creativity and Confucianism among American and Korean educators. *Creativity Research Journal, 23*(4), 357–371.

Libermann, R. (2011, March 21). *The secret of Finnish schools*. Retrieved from http://finland.fi/Public/default.aspx?contentid=160066&nodeid=41807&culture=en-US

Lim, W.K. (2010, March 26). Asian test-score culture thwarts creativity. *Science, 327*, 1576–1577.

McCurry, J.J. (2013, May 9). Long troubled by school bullying, Japan now eyes zero tolerance. *Christian Science Monitor*. Retrieved from http://www.csmonitor.com/World/Asia-Pacific/2013/0509/Long-troubled-by-school-bullying-Japan-now-eyes-zero-tolerance

Mckenna, T. (2015). The suicide forest: A Marxist analysis of the high suicide rate in Japan. *Rethinking Marxism, 27*(2), 293–302.

Montlake, S. (2006, June 9). High-tech cheating in Asia's high-stakes exams. *Christian Science Monitor, 98*, pp. 1–2.

Mooney, P. (2004, December 3). Dogging cheaters in China. *Chronicle of Higher Education, 51*(15), A7.

Moore, M. (2013, June 20). *Riot after Chinese teachers try to stop pupils cheating*. Retrieved from http://www.telegraph.co.uk/news/worldnews/asia/china/10132391/Riot-after-Chinese-teachers-try-to-stop-pupils-cheating.html

Niu, W., & Sternberg, R.J. (2003). Societal and school influences on student creativity: The case of China. *Psychology in the Schools, 40*(1), 103–114.

Norasakkunkit, V., & Uchida, Y. (2014). To conform or to maintain self-consistency? Hikikomori risk in Japan and the deviation from seeking harmony. *Journal of Social & Clinical Psychology, 33*(10), 918–935.

Nyamkhuu, T. (2014). *PISA 2012: Happiness or performance?* Retrieved from http://www.unescobkk.org/education/news/article/pisa2012-happiness-or-performance/

OECD. (2001). *Knowledge and skills for life: First results from the OECD Programme for International Student Assessment (PISA) 2000*. Paris: Organisation of Economic Co-operation and Development.

OECD. (2011). *Education at a glance 2011: OECD indicators*. Paris: Organisation of Economic Co-operation and Development.

Olmstead, G. (2014, March 18). Why Finland's educational model is more conservative than ours. *The American Conservative*. Retrieved from http://www.theamericanconservative.com/why-finlands-educational-model-is-more-conservative-than-ours/

Pang, W., & Plucker, J.A. (2013). Recent transformations in China's economic, social, and education policies for promoting innovation and creativity. *Journal of Creative Behavior, 46*(4), 247–273.

Partanen, A. (2011, December 29). *What Americans keep ignoring about Finland's school success*. Retrieved from http://www.theatlantic.com/national/archive/2011/12/what-americans-keep-ignoring-about-finlands-school-success/250564/

Ripley, A. (2013). *The smartest kids in the world: And how they got that way*. New York: Simon & Schuster.

Rivers, D. (2013, May 10). *South Korea cheating scandal hits university bids*. Retrieved from http://www.cnn.com/2013/05/09/world/asia/south-korea-exam-scandal/

Sahlberg, P. (2011a). Lessons from Finland. *American Educator, 35*(2), 34–38.

Sahlberg, P. (2011b). *Finnish lessons: What can the world learn from educational change in Finland?* New York: Teachers College Press.

Sahlberg, P. (2012). A model lesson: Finland shows us what equal opportunity looks like. *American Educator, 36*(1), 20–27.

Sahlberg, P. (2013, December 3). Are Finland's vaunted schools slipping? *The Washington Post*. Retrieved from http://www.washingtonpost.com/blogs/answer-sheet/wp/2013/12/03/are-finlands-vaunted-schools-slipping/

Schanzenbach, D.W. (2014). *Does class size matter?* National Education Policy Center. Boulder: School of Education, University of Colorado Boulder.

Stout, D. (2013, December 4). *China is cheating the world student rankings system*. Retrieved from http://world.time.com/2013/12/04/china-is-cheating-the-world-student-rankings-system/

Treml, J.N. (2001). Bullying as a social malady in contemporary Japan. *International Social Work, 44*(1), 107–117.

Wu, J.J., & Albanese, D.L. (2013). Imagination and creativity: Wellsprings and streams of education—The Taiwan experience. *Educational Psychology, 33*(5), 561–581.

Zhao, Y. (2012a). Flunking innovation and creativity. *Phi Delta Kappan, 94*(1), 56–61.

Zhao, Y. (2012b). *World class learners: Educating creative and entrepreneurial students*. Thousand Oaks, CA: Corwin.

About the Contributors

Lawrence Baines, associate dean of research and graduate studies at the University of Oklahoma, has written 10 books and more than 100 articles on literacy, teaching, and public education. He has worked in hundreds of schools in the United States and around the world.

Christopher Barry is a faculty member in the Department of Psychology at Washington State University. His research areas include the role of youth self-perception in behavioral and emotional adjustment, evidence-based assessment of youth academic and psychological functioning, and outcomes tied to out-of-school learning experiences. His collaborative work on the impact of out-of-school STEM learning has received funding from the National Science Foundation.

William G. Brozo, professor in the Graduate School of Education at George Mason University, is the author of numerous articles and books on literacy development for children and youth, including *Wham! Teaching with Graphic Novels Across the Curriculum* and *To Be a Boy, To Be a Reader*. As a consultant, he has worked in educational reform throughout the United States and from the Balkans to the Persian Gulf.

Sarah Crain, coordinator for K–12 literacy for Stafford County Public Schools in Virginia, has a master's degree in literacy and is currently a doctoral student at George Mason University. Her research interests include adolescent literacy and authentic literacy in the content areas.

Jason D. Edgerton is assistant professor of sociology at the University of Manitoba. He has published numerous journal articles and book chapters on the sociology of education and is co-author of the textbook *Understanding Social Statistics* (Oxford University Press).

Veronika Eliasova is a graduate student in the Department of Sociology at the University of Manitoba. Her current research focuses on educational inequality and the empirical viability of Pierre Bourdieu's cultural reproduction theory.

Mike Forret is a senior lecturer in the Mathematics, Science, and Technology Education Department of the Faculty of Education at the University of Waikato. His background is in science and physics education, and he has a PhD from the University of Waikato. Mike teaches at the undergraduate and postgraduate levels and covers topics in science and technology education. He also supervises research students in these areas.

Vivien Geneser is associate professor of early childhood in the College of Education and Human Development at Texas A&M University–San Antonio. She writes about a variety of educational topics and is a co-editor of the journal *Early Years*. She was recently honored by Texas A&M University–San Antonio with the Faculty Teaching Excellence and Research Award.

Riitta Jyrhämä, PhD, is a faculty member and vice chair in the Department of Teacher Education at the University of Helsinki. Her research interests include teacher education, teachers' pedagogical thinking, and teaching practice supervision. She is a fellow of the Teachers' Academy and an active visiting lecturer in the educational field. She is developing a peer group mentoring program for new teachers during their induction phase.

Katriina Maaranen, PhD, is a university lecturer at the University of Helsinki in the Department of Teacher Education. Her current research interests include teachers' personal practical theories, the development of teacher-identity, and other topics involving teacher education.

Hani Morgan is an associate professor in the Department of Curriculum, Instruction, and Special Education at the University of Southern Mississippi. He is the author of over 30 published articles on various topics involving the education of K–12 students. He received a master's degree in international education from Teachers College, Columbia University, and graduated from Rutgers University with a doctoral degree in foundations of educations.

Logan Moss is a member of the School of Educational Leadership and Policy at the University of Waikato. He has taught educational policy and the history of education at the university since 1982 and is a past president of the New Zealand Association for Research in Education.

Lance W. Roberts, professor of sociology at the University of Manitoba and senior fellow at St. John's College, is the author of nine books covering issues in education, ethnicity, and comparative social change. His research on educational topics has appeared in leading sociology and education journals in Canada, the United States, and Europe.

Andreas Schleicher is director for education and skills, and special advisor on education policy to the secretary-general at the Organisation for Economic Cooperation and Development (OECD) in Paris. As a key member of the OECD Senior Management team, Mr. Schleicher supports the secretary-general's strategy to produce analysis and policy advice that advances economic growth and social progress.

Michael J. Seth is professor of history at James Madison University. He earned his PhD at the University of Hawaii and has worked with educational organizations in several countries. Seth is the author of four books, including *Education Fever: Society, Politics and the Pursuit of Schooling in South Korea* (2002) and *A History of Korea: From Antiquity to the Present* (2011).

Yan Wang is senior specialist and director of the Department for International Exchange at the National Institute of Education Sciences of China. Her research focuses on education policy, education reform, social studies of education, and international studies. She has authored, co-authored, and edited numerous articles, reports, journals, and books on various educational topics. She holds a PhD in education policy, administration, and social studies from the University of Hong Kong.

Hsiao-ping Wu is assistant professor at Texas A&M University–San Antonio. Her teaching specializations are applied linguistics, second language acquisition, and research methods in English as a second language (ESL). Previously, Dr. Wu taught English as a foreign language (EFL) in the elementary classroom in Taiwan. She is a recipient of the Texas A&M University–San Antonio Faculty Teaching Excellence Award. She is currently a TexTESOL board member.

Mano Yasuda is an instructor of Japanese language in the Department of Modern Languages, Literatures, and Linguistics at the University of Oklahoma. Her research interests include multicultural education and moral education. She has more than a decade of teaching service in various colleges and universities.

Index

A

Aboriginal Canadians, 80, 85-87
Abraham, C., 84
Abrams, S.E., 187
Adams, D., 130
Adams, K.A., 182, 183
Agency for Science, Technology, and Research (A*Star), 142
Ahn, J., 111, 182
Aikens, N.L., 46, 49
Albanese, D.L., 184
Amano, I., 75
American Federation of Teachers, 139
Anderson, J., 52
Anderson, L., 190
Andrews, P., 40
Ang, L., 140
Arani, M., 71
Arffman, I., 27
Armstrong, P.I., 46
Arora, A., 61
Arsenault, J., 87
Aso, M., 75

B

Baek, S.J., 182
Baines, L., 10, 75
Baird, J.A., 40
Barbarin, O., 46, 49
Basic Education Act (Finland), 24, 27, 29
BBC, 184
Benner, A.D., 48
Benson, J., 46
Berliner, D.C., 11, 38, 50
Best, R., 52
Bi, C., 171
Biesanz, J.C., 48
Blomberg, S., 22
Bobis, J., 52
Borman, G., 46
Bowles, S., 49
"boy crisis," 84
Bracey, G.W., 9, 184, 185, 190, 191
Brender, A., 186
Brochu, P., 89, 92
Brozo, W.G., 43, 44, 45, 50, 51, 52, 54
Buchmann, C., 43

bullying (Japan), 75, 182, 183
Butchers, A.G., 147, 152
By the Hand Charter School, 73
Byun, S., 116, 117, 122

C

Caccamise, D., 52
Cambridge International Examinations, 165
Canada and schools, 79–80
    Aboriginal Canadians and, 80, 85–87
    assessment of, 100
    "boy crisis" in, 84
    Canadian Association of University Teachers (CAUT), 84
    Canadian attitudes toward education, 99–101
    Canadian Council on Learning (CCL), 99, 101
    Canadian Education Association (CEA), 95, 99
    Canadian Education Statistics Centre (CESC) and, 88, 89
    Canadian Teachers' Federation (CTF), 85, 90
    "Canadian Way," 95, 98, 102
    challenges to excellence and equity in, 81–87
    Council of Ministers of Education, Canada (CMEC), 83, 89, 91, 92, 93, 94, 95
    educational expenditures in, 90–91
    educational policy in, 94–99
    gender and, 84–85
    homework and, 100
    homogenizing effect of large-scale assessment (LSA), 97–99
    immigrants and, 83
    lack of formal tracking or streaming in, 82
    Learn Canada 2020, 92
    male reading deficit in, 85
    National Longitudinal Survey of Children and Youth, 94
    organization and delivery of educational programs in, 79
    Pan-Canadian Assessment Program (PCAP), 97, 102
    PISA scores and, 79, 80–81, 101, 102
    private schools and, 83
    promoting inclusiveness and equity in, 92–94
        funding and, 93
        pre-elementary education as early intervention, 93–94
    public attitudes towards teachers in, 88–89
    seven factors for high performance of educational systems in, 96–97
    similarities among provincial jurisdictions, 95–97
    social inclusion and, 82
    socioeconomic status and, 81
    Statistics Canada and, 90, 91
    STEM fields and, 84–85, 101
    system structure and governance of education in, 91–92
    teacher salaries in, 87–88
    teacher status in, 87
    teachers and teaching in, 87–90
    teachers' work in, 89–90
    Truth and Reconciliation Commission of Canada, 87
    tutoring and, 101
    Youth in Transition survey, 84
Canadian Association of University Teachers (CAUT), 84
Canadian Council on Learning (CCL), 99
Canadian Education Association (CEA), 95, 99
Canadian Education Statistics Centre (CESC) and, 88, 89
Canadian Teachers' Federation (CTF), 85, 90
"Canadian Way," 95, 98, 102
Cao, R., 175
Caprano, M.M., 53
Caprano, R.M., 53
CareerCast.com, 138
Carnoy, M., 38
Cartwright, F., 89
Center for Education Benchmarking, 61
Center on Education Policy, 44

Centers for Early Childhood Education and
  Care (ECEC) (Japan), 65
Chae, K., 190
Chan, P.C.W., 83
Chandler, M., 117
Chang, H.J., 38
Chang, K.M., 170
charter schools, 73, 74
cheating, 185–86
Chenoweth, K., 11
Chien, N., 48
China and examination system, 169
  assessment for diagnosis in, 170–71
  "Black June" in, 175
  cheating on tests in, 185, 186
  curriculum in, 175–76
  demonstration schools, 172
  diversity versus reliability in education,
    177–78
  examinations for accreditation, 171–72
  examinations for college entrance, 173–75,
    177
  examinations and management of the
    education system in, 175–77
  examinations for school choice,
    172–73
  examinations for selection, 172
  future direction of education in, 177–79
  high-stakes college entrance examinations
    in, 169–70
  key schools and, 172
  lack of student creativity in, 184
  lottery system in, 173
  non-key schools and, 172
  number of patents in, 184
  origins of student assessments in, 169–70
  pedagogical research, teaching, and texts,
    176–77
  quality education resource schools and, 172
  quality versus validity in education, 178
  recent educational reforms, 177–79
  role of examinations in education system,
    170–75
  strategy for equity in education, 178–79
  student stress in, 184
  teacher training in, 177
  textbooks in, 175–76
China National Institute for Educational
  Research, 178
Choi, J., 121
Chosŏn Dynasty, 114
Chuy, M., 85
Clark, J., 164
Clark, N., 107
College Scholastic Ability Test
  (CSAT), 110
Common Core State Standards and, 8
Consultative Committee on the Post-Primary
  Curriculum, 150
Cook, J., 146
Cornell University, 62
Council of Ministers of Education,
  Canada (CMEC), 83, 89, 91, 92, 93,
  94, 95
Cragg, L., 53
cram schools, 118, 120, 121
creative economy, 121
creativity, 183–85
Cremin, L., 190, 191
Curriculum Planning and Development
  Institute, 131, 135–36

D

Dakin, J., 149, 152
Darling-Hammond, L., 2, 11, 99, 187
Dawson, W., 62
Davies, S., 83, 101
Dehaas, J., 85
Detroit Free Press, 74
Dewey, J., 4, 188
Dika, S., 52
Dimmock, C., 134, 136
DiPrete, T.A., 43
Dolton, P., 122
Duke, D., 2
Duncan, A., 183
Dunleavy, J., 89, 99

E

The Economist, 72
Economist Intelligence Unit, 108
education
 Asian cultures and, 10
 classes six days a week, 9
 effects of poverty on, 10–11
Education and Science Select Committee, 152
Education Law of 1949–1951, 113
Education Matters, 74
Educational Policy in Finland, 15
Ellington, L., 63
Emes, J., 90
engagement for learning, 50–53
Eurypedia, 30
Eveland, J., 128
Ewing, 147, 148, 149

F

Fang, X.D., 171, 173
Farkas, G., 49
Farrant, B., 46
Finnish National Board of Education (FNBE), 16, 23, 31, 32
The Finnish News Magazine, 27
Finland and schools
 absence of standardized tests in, 187
 amount of homework in, 26
 arts and crafts in, 187
 attitudes toward education in, 26–27
 average class size in, 25
 Basic Education Act and, 24, 27, 29
 basic principles of, 15
 class size in, 187
 comprehensive schools, 16
 creativity and, 187
 decentralization of education in, 31–32
 distribution of educational resources, 7
 doctoral education for teachers in, 21–22
 educational climate and practices in, 26–29
 educational lessons to be learned from, 186–89
 educational policies versus U.S., 188
 equal access to education in, 16
 expenditure on education in, 23–24
 Finnish National Board of Education (FNBE), 16, 23, 31, 32
 flexible education in, 30
 general education, 16
 inquiry-oriented teachers in, 19
 Ministry of Education and Culture, 15, 16, 26, 28, 44
 morning and afternoon care for 1st and 2nd graders in, 28–29
 National Core Curriculum, 16–17, 29, 31–32
 Opetusalan Ammattijärjestö, 30
 peer-group mentoring in, 22
 PISA Science data and, 28
 polytechnic institutions in, 17
 population statistics, 18
 private schools in, 17
 problems with educational system, 189–90
 professional development for teachers in, 22–23
 ratio of students to teaching staff in, 25
 research-based teacher education in, 18–22
 respect for teachers in, 26–27
 role of teachers' union in, 30–31
 school life in, 24–26
 statistics about, 15–16
 student happiness and, 187
 student welfare in, 29
 students with learning difficulties and, 8, 29–30
 teacher credentials in, 17
 teacher education in, 17, 20
 teacher freedom in, 187
 teachers' working days in, 24–25
 time spent in school, 10
 tutoring during and after school in, 27–28
 universities in, 17
 upper secondary schools in, 16
 vocational institutions in, 16
 welfare programs and, 11
Fleischman, H.L., 44

flexible education (Finland), 30
Fong, F., 86
Foy, P., 61
Frennette, M., 83
Frideres, J., 87
Fu, H., 171, 175, 176, 177
Fujita, H., 62
Fukaya, K., 71

G

Gadacz, R., 87
Garces-Bacsal, R., 139
Gates, B., 38
Geary, D.C., 45, 46
gender, 43–44
Gersten, R., 53
Gifted Education Law (South Korea), 121
Gilliard, J., 65
Gilmore, C., 53
Gintis, H., 49
Global Entrepreneurship Monitor (GEN), 184
global workforce, 6
Gluszynski, T., 89
Goh, K., 131
Goldstein, H., 40
Gordon, C.E., 86, 87
Granville, M., 52
Guardian, 181
Gulati, S., 86
Guppy, N., 83

H

Haight, W., 70
Halinen, I., 26, 31, 32
Hango, D., 84, 85
Hanushek, E.A., 9, 46
Hargreaves, A., 94, 95, 96, 97, 102
Harte, A.H.W., 151
Hartig, J., 40
Hautamäki, J., 16
Heckman, J., 50

Heikkinen, H.L.T., 22
Helin, M., 23
Hernandez, D.J., 48
Hidaka, Y., 182
High School Equalization Act, 113
Hilden, K., 52
Hillemeier, M.M., 49
Hodkinson, H., 21
Hodkinson, L., 21
Hogan, D., 127, 129, 132, 140
homeschooling, 63
Hong, B., 140
Hopstock, P.J., 44, 45
Howes, C., 48
Huff, W., 130
Hunt, K., 185
Hurmerinta, E., 31
Hytönen, J., 18

I

Iftin Charter School, 73
Ikuo, A., 70
International Association for the Evaluation of Educational Achievement (IEA), 5, 107
Institute of Technical Education, 141
International Baccalaureate, 165

J

Jaafar, S.B., 97, 98
Jakku-Sihvonen, R., 19
Japan and schools, 61–62
    attitudes toward education in, 62–63
    attrition among teachers in, 71
    bullying and, 75, 182, 183
    Centers for Early Childhood Education and Care (ECEC) and, 65
    changes in curriculum, 75
    charter schools and, 73
    critics of, 62
    curriculum of, 67–69
    early childhood education in, 63–65

expectation of teachers in, 74
hikikomori, 182
homeschooling in, 63
juku, 72, 73, 75
lack of discrimination against poor children, 73
life of a teacher in, 70–71
male teachers in, 70
mentorship of teachers in, 71
Ministry of Education, Culture, Sports, Science, and Technology (MEXT) and, 62, 64, 65, 66, 67, 72, 74
Ministry of Health, Labor, and Welfare (MHLW) and, 64, 65
National Center on Education and the Economy and, 67, 70, 74
National Entrance Exams, 70, 71–73
National Institute for Educational Policy Research, 68
options for older students in, 72
PISA scores and, 61
"pressure-free education" and, 66, 69
private schools in, 65–66
Report of the United States Education Mission to Japan and, 75
shokuin shitsu, 71
special education in, 69
structure of schools in, 66–67
student suicide rates, 182
teacher salaries in, 70
Tokubetsu-Shien-gakko, 69
Trends in International Mathematics and Science Study (TIMSS) and, 61
tutoring of students in, 72
World Economic Forum and, 62
Yutori Kyoiku, 66, 69
Jerald, C., 4
Jez, S.J., 75
Jobs, S., 184
Jokinen, H., 22
Jones, R., 65
Jordan, S., 69
juku, 72, 73, 75
Jyrhämä, R., 21, 27

K

Kairosity, 71
Kansanen, P., 18, 19
Karjalainen, T., 16
Kautz, T., 50
Kayama, M., 70
Keat, H.S., 133
Kim, K., 121, 122
Kim, K.H., 184, 190
Kim, S., 114, 119, 121
Kim, Y., 116
Kim-Renaud, Y., 107
Klecker, B.M., 45
Knowles, A., 85
Komazawa University, 63
Koo, S., 120
Korean Advanced Institute of Science and Technology (KAIST), 110, 118
Korean Educational Development Institute, 116, 117, 119
Korean Federation of Teachers' Association, 110
Korean Teachers Union (KFTA), 110
Korean University, 110
Kosunen, T., 18
Krokfors, L., 17, 20 31
Kupari, P., 27
Kupiainen, S., 16, 33

L

Ladd, H.F., 46, 471
Lassegard, J., 71
Lastra-Anadón, C.X., 9
Laukkanen, R., 26
Laurence, C., 190
Learn Canada 2020, 92
Learning Metrics Task Force, 39
Lee, H.E., 190
Lee, J., 127, 129

Lee, Y., 116
Li, Y.F., 171
Lim, W.K., 190
Linnakylä, P., 27
Liu, D., 184
Liu, H.F., 170
Looker, D., 84
Loveless, T., 43
Lotem, E., 46
Lowell, L., 2, 3, 9
Lynch, R.G., 43
Lyons, P., 165

M

Maaranen, K., 17, 18, 27
Maczuga, S., 49
Māori, 146, 152
Marcenaro-Gutierrez, O., 122
Marmot, M., 46
Martin, M., 61
Mason, H.G.R., 148
math literacy, 39, 41–42, 45, 48–49, 51, 54
McCurry, J., 75, 182
Mckenna, T., 182
McLaren, I.A., 147, 149
Meister School program, 109
Mercredi, O., 86
Meyer, D.K., 52
Mijs, J.J.B., 49
Mikkola, A., 18
Milanovic, B., 50
Milne, A., 50
Ministry of Education (China), 173, 175, 176, 177, 178
Ministry of Education (New Zealand), 152, 157, 158, 159, 160, 161
Ministry of Education (South Korea), 108, 109, 111
Ministry of Education and Culture (Finland), 15, 16, 26, 28, 44
Ministry of Education, Culture, Sports, Science, and Technology (MEXT) (Japan), 62, 64, 65, 67, 72, 74
Ministry of Education Singapore (MOE), 129, 130, 131, 132, 134, 136, 137, 139, 141, 142
Ministry of Health, Labor, and Welfare (MHLW) (Japan), 64, 65
Ministry of Manpower, 142
Martin, A.J., 52
McKinsey Global Institute, 116
McNamara, D., 52
Mistry, R.S., 48
Montlake, S., 186
Mooney, P., 186
Moore, M., 185
Morgan, P.L., 49
Moss, L., 152
Mullis, I., 61, 62
Murdoch, J.H., 150
Murray, S., 43

N

Nagayama, M., 65
Nanyang Technological University, 135, 137, 142
National Assessment of Educational Progress (NAEP), 45
National Center for Educational Statistics, 42, 61
National Center on Education and the Economy, 67, 70, 74
National Certificate of Educational Achievement (NCEA), 161, 165
National Commission for UNESCO, 152
National Core Curriculum (Finland), 16–17, 29, 31–32
National Institute for Educational Policy Research, 68
National Institute of Education (Singapore), 134–35, 136, 137, 138, 139, 141, 142
National Longitudinal Survey of Children and Youth (Canada), 94
National Textbook Review Board, 176
National University of Singapore, 142
Nazareth, L., 90
New Teaching Center, 22

New Zealand, 145
   achievement and unit standards, 162
   administrative structure of education system, 146–48
   bilingual and Kura Kaupapa Māori schools in, 164
   class sizes in, 160
   consolidation of small schools, 152
   curriculum of schools in, 148–49, 160–61
   disadvantaged students and, 152
   early childhood education, 153
   Education Act and, 146–47, 148, 157, 159
   Education Amendment Act, 151
   education of Māori and Polynesian children, 152
   education assessment and, 161–62
   educational reforms of the 1990s, 153
   educational system today, 153–63
   fees and donations for education in, 159–60
   general organization of education system, 153–54
   history and development of education system in, 146–53
   history of, 146
   impact of neoliberal policies on education in, 153
   management of schools in, 157–58
   national education standards and, 164
   official language of, 146
   PISA test scores and, 147
   population statistics, 146
   primary/intermediate schools in, 153
   scholarships in, 162
   school attendance in, 159
   school decile ratings in, 158
   school terms and, 158
   secondary education in, 149–50, 154
   significant changes to education system, 163–64
   students with special needs, 151–52
   system of standards examinations, 148–49
   teacher preparation in, 162–63
   teacher training in, 151
   tertiary education and, 154
   Trends in International Mathematics and Science Study (TIMSS), 152
   types of schools in, 154–56
   typical school day in, 160
New Zealand Correspondence School, 152
New Zealand Department of Education, 149, 153
New Zealand Parliamentary Counsel Office, 157, 159
New Zealand Qualifications Authority, 162, 165
New Zealand Teachers Council, 162, 163
New Zealand Wars, 146
Niemi, H., 18, 22, 23, 30
Nitulescu, R., 85
Niu, W., 184
No Child Left Behind, 43, 45, 102
Norasakkunkit, V., 182
Nyam, khuu, T., 182

O

Oakford, P., 43
Obama, B., 38, 184
Oh, J., 121
Olmstead, G., 187
Opetusalan Ammattijärjestö, 30
Organisation for Economic Cooperation and Development (OECD), 2, 4, 15, 38, 39, 41, 43, 48, 49, 51, 52, 54, 61, 63, 64, 65, 71, 81, 82, 88, 107, 112, 120, 127, 128, 141, 145, 187, 191
Organisation for European Economic Cooperation (OEEC), 5,
Osaava Verme, 22
Ozuru, Y., 52

P

Paine, S.L., 4, 6, 7, 11
Pan-Canadian Assessment Program (PCAP), 97, 102
Pang, W., 184

Park, H., 107, 121, 122
Park, J., 117
Park, S., 120
Parsons, J., 52
Partanen, A., 187
Pasion, A., 63
Pearson, 108
Pelczar, M.P., 44, 45
Peterson, P.E., 9
Pintrich, P.R., 50, 52
PISA (Program for International Student Assessment), 4
   critics of, 40, 190
   description of, 5
   Economic, Social, and Cultural Status index, 49
   history of, 39
   link between happiness and academic performance, 181, 182
   low-achieving Finnish students and, 28
   math literacy and, 39, 40
   reading literacy and, 39
   scientific literacy and, 39
   study effectiveness, 120
   what it measures, 39–40
Plourde, L.A., 50
Plucker, J.A., 5, 184
Pohang University of Science and Technology (POSTECH), 110, 118
Podmore, V.M., 160
Post Primary Teachers Association, 160
poverty, 10–11
Powell, M., 73
Pressley, M., 52
Program for International Assessment of Adult Competencies (PIAAC), 38
Program for International Student Assessment (PISA). *See* PISA
Progress in International Reading Literacy Study (PIRLS), 5, 102

R

race, 40, 41
Race to the Top, 102

Rappleye, J., 62
Rather, D., 138
Raugn, D.P., 40
Ravitch, D., 38
reading literacy, 39, 41, 44–45, 47–48, 50–51, 53
Regulation for the National Textbook Review Board, 175
Reich, R., 38
Reinikainen, P., 27
Report of the United States Education Mission to Japan, 75
Resmovits, J., 38
Ripley, A., 119, 120, 127, 181, 187, 188
Rivers, D., 185
Rosli, R., 53
Rothstein, R., 38
Rounds, J., 46
Rowe, M., 52
Rueben, K., 43
Rutkowski, D., 5
Rutkowski, L., 5

S

Sahlberg, P., 4, 7, 8, 11, 27, 28, 32, 187, 188, 189
Salzman, H., 2, 3, 9
Sarjala, J., 11
Saxe, J.G., 37
Scanlon, L.A., 21
Schanzenbach, D.W., 187
Schiff, R., 46
Schleicher, A., 4, 5, 6, 7, 11
Schunk, D.H., 50, 52
scientific literacy, 39, 40
Secondary Schools Act, 150
Sengupta, U., 86
Seth, M.J., 111, 112, 113, 114, 115
Seoul National University, 110, 118
Seventh Curriculum, 109
Shanghai, proficiency rates in math, 9
Sharpe, A., 87
Shelley, B.E., 44
Shen, X., 171, 176, 177

Shi, O., 176
Shimbun, M., 67
Shirley, D., 94, 95, 96, 97, 102
shokuin shitsu, 71
Siljander, A.M., 22, 23
Silver, R.E., 136
Simola, H., 32, 33
Simpson, M.L., 54
Sinclair, K., 146
Sinclair, R., 87
Singapore and schools, 127
    ability-based, aspiration-driven phase of national development, 132–33
    Agency for Science, Technology, and Research (A*Star), 142
    assignment of best teachers, 7–8
    attitudes toward teachers, 129, 138
    bilingualism in, 131, 136
    collaborating for effectiveness, 136–37
    community groups and, 8
    crime rate in, 142
    cultural perspective about, 129
    Curriculum Planning and Development Institute, 131, 135–36
    development of skilled workers in, 132
    dropout rates for students, 142
    efficiency-driven phase of national development, 131–32
    English as shared language, 131
    Finnish education policies versus, 188
    general certificate of education and, 141
    gifted education and, 141–42
    higher education in, 142
    historical perspective of education, 129–30
    Institute of Technical Education, 141
    location and demographics, 127–28
    Ministry of Education Singapore (MOE), 129, 130, 131, 132, 134, 136, 137, 139, 141, 142
    mother tongue languages (MTL) policy and, 136
    multiculturalism in, 136
    Nanyang Technological University, 135, 137, 142
    National Institute of Education, 134–35, 136, 137, 138, 139, 141, 142
    National University of Singapore, 142
    parental expectation of schools, 139–40
    PISA scores and, 127, 128–29
    scholastic achievement data, 128–29
    stress among students, 140
    structure of educational system, 134–42
    student-centric, values-driven phase education development, 133–43
    student achievement in, 139–40
    survival-driven phase of national development, 130–31
    Teach Less, Learn More, 133
    teacher dispositions, 139–40
    teacher preparation in, 137–38
    teacher professional development in, 138–39
    teacher recruitment in, 137
    teaching as a profession in, 138
    Thinking Schools, Learning Nation, 132–33
    Trends in International Mathematics and Science Study (TIMSS) and, 132
    unemployment in, 142
    Values in Action Program, 133
Singh, K., 52
Snyder, L., 52
socioeconomic status (SES), 46
soft skills, 50
Song, J.G., 171
South Korea and schools, 107–8
    attitude toward teachers, 122
    cheating on tests in, 185–86
    College Scholastic Ability Test (CSAT), 110
    cram schools, 118, 120, 121
    creative economy in, 121
    cultural attitude toward education, 114
    early childhood education in, 140
    "education fever" in, 114, 115
    Education Law of 1949–1951, 113
    equalization of education, 113
    evolution of the school system in, 112–14
    financial burden on families, 116–18
    Gifted Education Law, 121
    High School Equalization Act, 113

higher education in, 118
historical background of, 111
hours of classroom attendance, 108
impact of Japanese rule on, 114–16
inequality and creativity in, 120–22
international rankings of universities in, 118
Korean Educational Development Institute, 116, 117, 119
Korean Federation of Teachers' Association, 110
Korean Teachers Union (KFTA), 110
literacy rate of, 107
Meister School program, 109
Ministry of Education, 108, 109, 111
multicultural approach to education in, 121
PISA scores and, 107
pressure on students in, 119–20
primary and secondary education in, 108–9140–41
private spending on education, 117
private tutoring, 117, 121
problems and challenges today, 116
rapid progress in educational development, 112
rote memorization and repetitive drills, 122
Seventh Curriculum, 109
"SKY," 110
student stress and, 181
student suicide rates, 120, 182
study effectiveness, 120
teacher preparation in, 109–10
teacher salaries in, 109
Uniformity of Education, 112
university students studying abroad, 119
Sperring, A., 21
Spring, J., 37, 49
Statistics Canada, 90, 91
Sternberg, R.J., 184
Stevenson, H.W., 10
Stewart, V., 4, 8, 138
Stigler, J.W., 10
Stixrud, J., 50
Stoet, G., 45, 46
Stout, D., 183
The Straits Times, 127

student skills and strategies (United States), 52–53
study effectiveness, 120
Su, R., 46
Suh-young, Y., 120
Suomen Kuvalehti, 27
Surpassing Shanghai, 4
Sutherland, L.M., 21
Syrjäläinen, E., 21

T

Tan, C., 134, 136
Tasman, A., 146
Taylor, L., 52
Teach Less, Learn More, 133
Thiessen, V., 84
Thinking Schools, Learning Nation, 132–33
Thrupp, M., 153, 165
Times Higher Education, 118
Tirri, K., 16
Tokubetsu-Shien-gakko, 69
Tong, G.C., 132
top-performing school systems
    borrowing educational practices of, 6–7
    critics of borrowing educational practices, 8–10
    determination of, 4–6
    high-quality curriculum based on standards and, 8
    lessons from, 181
    similarities of world-class nations, 7–8
    United States placement among, 38–39
Treaty of Waitangi, 146
Treml, J.N., 183
Trends in International Mathematics and Science Study (TIMSS), 5, 61, 102, 107, 132, 152
Truth and Reconciliation Commission of Canada, 87
Tsuneyoshi, R., 71
Tucker, M., 3, 4, 9
Turner, J.C., 52
Turpel, M., 86
Tynjälä, P., 22

U

Uchida, Y., 183
Uniformity of Education, 112
United States and education, 2–3
  achievement gap and, 43
  alternative teacher certification and, 74
  charter schools and, 73
  Common Core State Standards and, 8
  creativity and, 184
  disadvantaged districts and, 2
  gender, students and, 43–44
  history of, 3–4
  implications of PISA scores for, 43, 45–46, 49–50, 52, 54–55
  math literacy PISA scores and, 41–42, 54
  media and, 2
  No Child Left Behind, 102
  PISA scores and, 2, 37
  impact on US economy, 6–7
  placement among top-performing educational systems, 38–39
  race, students and, 40–43
  Race to the Top and, 102
  reading literacy PISA scores and, 41, 44–45, 47–48, 50–51, 53
  serving the disadvantaged, 11
University of California, 22
University of Helsinki, 17, 18, 19, 20–21
University of Waikato, 151
Urzua, S., 50
U.S. Bureau of Labor Statistics, 38
U.S. Department of Education, 44, 45
U.S. Department of State, 75

V

Välijärvi, J., 27
Values in Action Program, 133
Van de Werfhorst, H.G., 49
Van Pelt, D., 90
Vasquez Heilig, J., 75
Veller, R., 52
Vergari, S., 92, 94, 95, 96, 99

Vitikka, E., 31
Volante, L., 97, 98

W

Wang, H.Y., 171
The Washington Post, 189
Way, J., 52
White, J.P., 86, 87
Willis, D., 62
Willms, J.D., 81
Woessmann, L., 9, 46
World Economic Forum, 62
Wozniak, S., 184
Wu, J.J., 184

Y

Yamamura, S., 62
Yasuda, M., 65
Yew, L.K., 130, 131
Yonsei University, 110
Yoshida, R., 75
Youth in Transition survey (Canada), 84
Yutori Kyoiku, 66, 69

Z

Zhao, Y., 183
Zhong, Q., 176
Zubrick, S., 46
Zuckerberg, M., 184

www.ingramcontent.com/pod-product-compliance
Ingram Content Group UK Ltd.
Pitfield, Milton Keynes, MK11 3LW, UK
UKHW022239230426
12048UKWH00018BA/1346